George P Burnham

A Hundred Thousand Dollars in Gold

How to make it

George P Burnham

A Hundred Thousand Dollars in Gold
How to make it

ISBN/EAN: 9783743313224

Manufactured in Europe, USA, Canada, Australia, Japa

Cover: Foto ©ninafisch / pixelio.de

Manufactured and distributed by brebook publishing software (www.brebook.com)

George P Burnham

A Hundred Thousand Dollars in Gold

PREFACE.

The introduction to this volume will be brief, inasmuch as those who may honor me by perusing the work will no doubt incline to get at the contents of this peculiar nut, at once; preferring the kernel to the shell.

I will therefore simply say, by way of preface, that the generous patronage bestowed by the reading public upon my previous work issued by the publisher of this book, prompted me to prepare the succeeding pages, now submitted in this narrative form.

The recommendations and advice herein contained result from a forty years' experience and acquaintance with the business world. I am aware that carpers may incline to criticise a literary production bearing such a title as that which I have chosen for this book; but it is *original* — to say the least of it. And I add that this volume is written for the public, not for the critics.

It is very true that "A HUNDRED THOUSAND DOLLARS IN GOLD" is not considered a very large sum to be accumulated by a single person, within a decade or two of years steadily devoted to active prosperous trade, at the present time, in our enterprising, money-making country. Yet this is enough, for most of us, individually; and more than many of us acquire and *save*, in a life-time.

Within the writer's business experience, he has twice gained and earned — and nearly lost — just such a fortune! If the hints and suggestions contained in the rehearsal of the modes in which such a competency was acquired by veritable parties, and the indicated warnings against the course through which it may be lost, are studied — as set down in these pages — a goodly measure of sterling benefit will inure to the reader; who, while he may be entertained with the narrative, may thus learn "how to make it" for himself, how to save it, how to use, and how enjoy it — when once it is secured.

The several examples we have cited are literal illustrations, and many more of a similarly interesting character, where prime success has attended honest and duteous effort in the right direction, might have been presented in confirmation of the theory we have aimed to elucidate.

It is believed, however, that the presentation of the numerous facts and suggestions embodied in this volume will offer real encouragement to the poor young man who may have the disposition to emulate these exemplars, and who resolves in earnest seasonably to win his way against "the odds that wait on fortune," however forbidding and unpromising may be the circumstances and surroundings of his early years; since every man, however humble, is in a great measure the carver of his own pecuniary destiny, and all history bears testimony to the fact that "men may second Fortune, but they cannot thwart her — they may weave her web, but they cannot break it."

GEO. P. BURNHAM.

MELROSE, October, 1875.

CONTENTS.

CHAPTER I.

A FEW NOTABLE AMERICAN MILLIONNAIRES.

Do-nothings and Do-somethings. Our men of wealth. A. T. Stewart, Stephen Girard, John Jacob Astor, Cornelius Vanderbilt, Wm. B. Dinsmore, Robert Bonner, Alvin Adams, P. T. Barnum, Chas. Knox, Elias Howe, Nicholas Longworth, James Gordon Bennett, Sen'r., the Lorillards, the Williams', the Schencks, the Jaynes, *et als.* How they made their fortunes. Typical cases, and representative workers. What man has done, man may do. The road to wealth is ever open. 17

CHAPTER II.

THE BEGINNING. TOUCHING HARD PAN.

The 'Great Fire' in New York. The panic of 1837. Broken Banks. No money, no work, no prospect. Poor artisans, clerks, and mechanics. What could they do? Adversity and distress. Our characters at the bottom of the ladder. The dry-goods salesman, the broker's clerk, the poor printer, the toiling inventor, the impoverished bookkeeper, the up-country drover, the well-to-do farmer, the rustic beauty, and the faithful wife. A triple board-bill settled. The watch pawned. The young wife's jewelry sacrificed. The jew and the sufferers. Only "three per cent a month" 38

CHAPTER III.

WHAT A DAY MAY BRING FORTH.

One hundred dollars in hand. Two dollars left. A good action rewarded. What next? "We'll go to work." The young men hunt in couples. Nothing to do — and everybody to help do it. The muscular clergyman's advice. "Forward — march!" A hopeful attempt. No! "We don't want any clerks." Hard times, in earnest. A liberal offer. The young wife's encouraging words. Sanguine youths. We'll make a hundred thousand dollars, yet! — "*I can't.*" Well — "I will try." Our lads are as good as their promise 56

CHAPTER IV.

HOW TO BEGIN TO MAKE MONEY.

Our heroes pass the crisis. How they began to "make it." The true and the false way. Diligence, earnestness, wit, and skill. The route to wealth a plain one. Spend *less* than you earn. The broker's clerk meets with a genial farmer. Old Blount offers the city lad employment. He goes from State Street Boston, to the Connecticut River. What the "nice young man" finds there — who he meets — what he is good for — and how he manages to get on, in his new vocation. "The difference between patent leather and cowhide boots, is mostly in the *shine*, lad!" 67

CHAPTER V.

MORRIS DEANS IMPROVES HIS PROSPECTS.

The State Street boy is introduced to the "Sunnyside" household. Miss Eunice Blount — the farmer's buxom daughter. Young Morris shows the old hands how to milk a fractious heifer. He doffs the broadcloth, and dons the homespun. "Owe no man a dollar. Pay as you go — or go without." Stick a pin there, lad! Morris takes charge of the fancy stock cattle on Blount's farm. "He's smart — this boy. I reck'n we'll make a man of him, after a spell" . . 85

CHAPTER VI.

HOW MORRIS DEANS MADE, AND SAVED IT.

Good Farmer Blount, and the little ones. Haying-time and rare sport for the children. Aunt Chloé, the darkie attendant. Homeward bound. "Look out, Mass'r! Don't yer obertip us!" The new hand goes forward — every time. Blount values, and advises him. "It's easier to make, than to save it, lad." How much is *enough?* Who is contented? A trite illustration, in answer. Money in the Savings Bank, is a handy thing. An advance in pay. How "Sunnyside" farm was earned. A small fortune for the late city broker's clerk. Old Uncle Philip demonstrates the power of music . . 95

CHAPTER VII.

A "BIG THING" FOR POOR ELY HAWES.

Our dry-goods salesman locates in New York. Frank Meyers could say 'Yes,' but never 'No.' He obtains a new position. The cotton-goods' buyer. New York is not Boston! Why Meyers made money — and lent it. How his gains increased. He finds his old chum, the machinist. Six thousand against six hundred a year. Ely Hawes shows his new invention. Frank Meyers is pleased, but puzzled. "It's a big thing, Ely!" His friend urges the inventor to try New York with it. What he concludes on 113

CHAPTER VIII.

HOW FRANK MEYERS MADE, AND LENT IT.

How much does it cost for a Patent? A pleasant letter for Ely Hawes. The machinist thinks he will visit Washington. Meyers lacks a 'balance-wheel.' He makes new loans. The Wall Street sharpers catch him. $6,000 out, in three days. Castles in the air. Who wins at the Stock Exchange? Query — who! A colossal fortune for a born fool. Seven millions made in eight months. Eight millions lost in four months afterwards! A veritable case. Our friend Frank Meyers 'sees the elephant' — and learns a useful lesson. "No more for me, gentlemen!". 127

CHAPTER IX.

FRANK LEARNS HOW NOT TO LOSE IT.

A GOOD way not to lose your money, when you get it. The philosopher's stone. Buy a hundred, not a thousand shares, "for the rise." What "a corner" will do for the small fry. Brokers' commissions bigger than speculators' "margins." How *not* to do it. Frank Meyers visits the Wall Street menagerie, and gets acquainted with the 'bulls and bears,' at only three thousand dollars cost. Cheap enough! A luckier hit. A good investment. Now — keep cool . . . 137

CHAPTER X.

HOW BRAVE ELY HAWES FLOURISHED.

ELY Hawes invents a curious Bank Safe Lock. He goes to Washington, to patent it. What he thought the capitol was. What he found it to be. A full purse, and a light heart. Getting into the wrong shop. A pot-bellied native. "I want to get a Patent." How Ely didn't "get" it. Too late! "God bless us, sir — it is past two, P.M." Hard-working government clerks. Poor fellows! "Is the building on fire?" Who are you? "I'se Mass'r Greene's boy, sah." The model lock. Prospects ahead. Slower than a turtle with a slow fever 145

CONTENTS.

CHAPTER XI.

MR. GREENE AND MR. POMPUS: EXAMINERS.

"Mr. Zintsing Pompus, Examiner, sir." **How hard they** toil — at reading the newspapers! "Mr. Greene, **one word, if you** please?" A polite man. Which **Greene?** There's **six** of 'em. Ely's "Impenetrable lock." The invention of "Mr. Orze" is duly **filed, as a** *Safe*. No hurrying in this Department, sir. A little technicality. **What a** man must do 'to begin right,' to obtain a patent. **Is this all?** "Call in four weeks, and we will tell you when to — call again, sir." **Mr.** Zintsing Pompus enlightens Mr. Hawes — not much! 164

CHAPTER XII.

OUR YOUNG MECHANIC MAKES A POINT.

LAWYER Shrood helps the anxious inventor out. A moderate charge! He 'knows the ropes' — he does. Ely gives his **work** into Shrood's hands. The turtle and his burthen. A precious 'slow coach.' **Patent** Agent Shrood gets on. An unfortunate accident. **Ely goes under.** The runaway team. "He is dead, sir!" Not quite. A long **season** in doors for Ely. Convalescence. Recovery. A triumph, at **last.** Hawes secures his Letters Patent, and bids adieu to Washington, **its** shams, and its miseries. "Say, Frank! I've got the documents!" . 180

CHAPTER XIII.

HOW REUBEN DOWNER MADE, AND SAVED IT.

THE mode adopted by the poor printer **to** 'make **it.**' **A** tight fit to get **on, and pay his way.** "I will one day be **rich.**" His duty at the case, as foreman, as editor, as proprietor. **What one man can do.** The N.Y. weekly *Leader*. A sharp dodge. Something **new.** "Buy the N.Y. **Leader!**" What for? "Fannie Firm writes for the N.Y. Leader." Who **is** she? A right smart paper. A live editor. A grand project. A big circulation. Brains, pluck, and perseverance did it. A decided success. Who is Reuben Downer? 194

CHAPTER XIV.

HOW DAVID, THE DROVER, MADE HIS PILE.

DAVID Morehead, the New Hampshire Drover, strikes out for himself. Deacon Rounds does not aid him, over much. He takes to horse-flesh, nat'rally. Old Rounds flourishes, and David tries it on. "You know

CONTENTS. xi

how it is, **yourself**, deacon." Grimes' played-out **New** Hampshire farm. David buys it, stocks it, and progresses on **it**. **Polly** White, and how she married. The Morgan colts. What **David did** with them. A lively trade. Old Winkham's trotter. What became of him. "He's a good 'un, sure's you're alive!" **A** winner 204

CHAPTER XV.

THE STORY OF "SPOT," FARMER BLOUNT'S FAMOUS DOG.

THE Newfoundland at Sunnyside. He makes himself friendly. Where he came from. Miss Eunice tells his romantic story. **The** visit **of** Blount **to Cape** Ann Lighthouse. He falls in **love** with "Spot" there. The poor Lightkeeper, and the generous offer. The sale and delivery. What "Spot" was good for. The wreck — the prowess of the big dog. The rescued child. The grateful Captain. A noble beast. His value on the farm. Spot's portrait, from life . . . 216

CHAPTER XVI.

MORRIS AND DAVID MAKE A MUTUAL GOOD TRADE.

MORRIS Deans sees the trotting gelding. David makes another good trade. Morris is pleased! He goes to New York with his fancy colt. Reuben Downer examines this fast 'un. A ride with the wind. The old friends meet in a sit-down at Delmonico's. The Morgan horse, again. "What is his time?" Away down in the twenties. "Good enough!" Ely Hawes getting ready for the Institute Fair. The trial of speed. "Let him wait, Morris. Three months hence, we'll see." The promised turn around the mile-course 228

CHAPTER XVII.

HOW MR. TWEEDLE MADE, AND LOST IT.

A CONTRAST **in the** modes of making money. The fate of a man who began wrong. Mr. Tweedle **a** natural living mistake. What true genius is, and what is false Tweedle's choice. The Tammany ring. Tweedle a Sachem. **He asks no** questions. "Worth a million?" "Yes — and five times more." **How** he made it. How he didn't keep it. The community good critics. Where did he get it? Out of the public till! The arrest — the defiance — the trial — the sentence. Mr. Tweedle drops. The Penitentiary receives him. He is indignant — but beaten — and his Tammany friends **are** astounded 245

CHAPTER XVIII.

"TWO-TWENTY-TWO" FOR THE MORRIS DEANS COLT!

"A **nice** 'un to look **at**," **and** "a good 'un to go!" Reuben Downer shows what he knows about a horse-shoe. A drive over the Bloomingdale Road, behind Downer's flyer. Morris Deans puts his new pony around the track in 2.31. "He's a good colt." **He is** placed in training. Morris returns to Sunnyside. A later trial with the new trotter. A big price for an imported bull. "2.22, marked time," for the **Morris Deans colt.** "He is yours, sir, at your offer — $25,000!" **Morris** begins to 'make his hundred thousand,' sure 262

CHAPTER XIX.

HOW A SECRET "INFORMER" MADE IT.

Mose Topley, the informer. His early history. A 'mysterious man.' **He** travels on his cheek, carries no luggage, and pays no bills of *his* contracting! The Expressman's account of Moses. He gets a fat office, in the secret service. **What** he does about it. The Congressman's opinion of Moses. Who knows him? Nobody! He bags his pile. A Committee sit upon Mose. He is called as a first class witness. "*He* can tell us all about it." Only $390,000 for Moses! The Committee learn a heap from *him*. — Exit Moses, with his plunder . 274

CHAPTER XX.

TWO CLEAR HEADS SOMETIMES BETTER THAN ONE.

Fred. Fordham, **the** bookkeeper, **improves his chances.** His wife Fannie looks after **the savings.** A genuine 'helpmeet.' Fred. is **surprised.** What a true woman **can do. How Fannie did it. "Two heads better than one."** Frank Meyers' salary increased. Downer's weekly "Leader" proves a "big bonanza." **Morris Deans** on the high road to fortune. Old Blount better off than ever. David Morehead and Polly, his wife. Ely Hawes finds competitors. The telling advertisement. Ely's new lock — and what he did with it . . . 290

CHAPTER XXI.

EVERY MAN THE ARCHITECT OF HIS OWN FORTUNE.

What "invention" is. A description of Ely Hawes' new Patent. What he thought of it, and what others found it. "The children cry for 'em!" How do you open it? That is the question. The approaching Institute Exhibition. Ely is around, with his Safes. Who will win the Society's Grand Gold Medal? $5,000 deposited in the closed rival Safes. The proposition, and the contest. Twelve hours allowed. Ely's new Lock to be first picked, or burst. All right, so far. 308

CHAPTER XXII.

WHAT HAPPENED AT THE GREAT INSTITUTE FAIR.

The rivals in earnest. A laudable ambition. Ely Hawes thinks **he** has conceived a good thing. What the public thought. A manly challenge. The contestants draw lots for the first trial. Ely loses. Morris Deans and Eunice come down to the Fair. The old inventor is puzzled. Another advertisement. Ely shows the toiler how to do it. But he doesn't learn! The secret of the lock. Eight hours — ten — twelve — and "time!" is **called**. But Ely Hawes' new lock stands the test. **"It is a good one, sir.** *I* say so — and I know" . . . 318

CHAPTER XXIII.

FIVE THOUSAND DOLLARS, AND THE GOLD MEDAL

Another day's work upon the rivals' locks. Ely Hawes tries his hand at it, in turn. A big crowd witness the experiment. Where is the key? A curious conception. Ely toils nine hours, but does not succeed. Three hours' time, yet. Once more. $5,000 in gold inside the safe, the reward. An hour before eight, P.M., he wins! The triumph. The Society's Gold Medal. Ely is happy. *His* Safe lock pronounced the best in the world 328

CHAPTER XXIV.

FRANK MEYERS GETS STRANGELY **BEFOGGED.**

Morris Deans and Eunice Blount at the Fair. Morris puts his lady friend in charge of Frank Meyers. They go through the Exhibition. Frank is smitten. He asks questions. "Is Eunice engaged to Morris?" Of course she is — only it proves otherwise! Frank is inquisitive. Eunice explains. Meyers is astonished, but gratified. Here is *his* opportunity. Eunice invites him up to Sunnyside. He accepts the invitation, and will win her — if he can 337

CHAPTER XXV.

THE TRAMP'S STORY, AND BLOUNT'S OPINIONS.

A useless class. How the tramps live. A story by the leader. Eunice Blount's early history. The "orfiin." How she came into Blount's hands. Her prospects. The new-comer from Boston. **The** lovers. Will they wed? "That's what's the matter, up at Sunnyside farm, lads." Old Blount's opinions. Raising mushrooms. "A cure for the potato-bug." The farmer makes his points, and the Brandville postmaster notes them down. Simon Slow gathers a new wrinkle, while Morris is pleased with his employer's triumph 345

CHAPTER XXVI.

THE FRIENDS TOGETHER AT SUNNYSIDE.

A JOLLY meeting at Sunnyside Farm. Frank Meyers, Reuben Downer, Ely Hawes, Fred. Fordham, Fannie, and David Morehead visit Morris Deans, at old Blount's estate. What they see, and what they do there. "Old times — when we were poor!" The prospects of our heroes. *All* on the right road, at last. How they made it — how they saved it — how they kept it — and what they did with their fortunes. Frank Meyers proposes to Eunice. How she replies. The departure, and a "coming event" 362

CHAPTER XXVII.

WHY SHOULD WE NOT HAVE "PANICS"?

ANOTHER side of the picture. The panics of '57 and '73. What caused them, mainly. A painful record. Facts for considerate men. Corruption and defalcation. The crimes of peculators, speculators, and public robbers. A huge "black list"! Why we experience 'hard times' in 1875. Millions stolen, squandered, and filched from the poor and middling classes. Counterfeiters, treasury robbers, bank defaulters, money thieves, and their victims. Why not look for chaos, amidst such recklessness? 376

CHAPTER XXVIII.

A HUNDRED THOUSAND DOLLARS IN GOLD.

MORE than a hundred thousand dollars, each, for our heroes. How it was earned — and how it was saved. The true principle, and the right method. Who are these men? "Go, thou — and do likewise." — The wedding at the farm. Who wins the rustic beauty, at last? A happy time at Sunnyside. All hands present. The beautiful bride and her gallant husband. The fate of Morris, Eunice, Frank, Ely, Reuben, David, Fannie, Fred., Farmer Blount, and Deacon Rounds. The bridal tour, Niagara and the White Mountains. Little "Daisie Deans." Four years afterwards. "Spot," and the boy baby. — Finale 393

DOLLARS IN GOLD.

HOW TO MAKE IT.

EUNICE BLOUNT — THE BELLE OF BRANDVILLE.

A HUNDRED THOUSAND DOLLARS IN GOLD.

HOW TO MAKE IT.

CHAPTER I.

A FEW NOTABLE AMERICAN MILLIONNAIRES.

"Gold, gold — hard and cold! heavy to get, and light to hold —
Hoarded, bartered, bought and sold; stolen, borrowed, wasted, doled!"
But, best of all is well-*earned* gold, to soothe the years as we grow old.
Then, save the shining yellow gold — ever so grateful to behold —
So "handy in the house" we're told. For now, I ween, 'mongst young or old.
There's none about so dull and cold, to scorn a hundred thousand, gold.

THE male portion of the population of the United States is made up largely of two distinct classes of people — to wit, the inert do-nothings, and the ambitious do-somethings; the latter sort among us fortunately being very considerably in the majority.

"*I can't do it*," never yet accomplished any thing, in this busy driving world of ours; "I WILL TRY," has performed wonders — as history and experience has fully attested, in the past as well as in more recent American annals.

The reader's attention is invited to a few patent facts, at the outset of this work, covering what is not universally known of even these notable instances of colossal wealth, to-day possessed by some of our "merchant princes," who began their business lives with but little or very moderate pecuniary means.

The millionnaire Alexander T. Stewart of New York, whose individual property is now reckoned at a valuation of sixty to eighty millions, commenced life in a small retail dry goods store on lower Broadway, less than half a century ago, with scarcely a hundred dollars to his name.

He was a diligent, sedulous worker, however. A man of brains, courage, ardor, and determination to win his way. An honorable, upright, industrious, frugal man, as well — who, when he had been a dozen years in trade, had accumulated more than a hundred thousand dollars, which he saved and husbanded, and increased, through persistent care and earnest devotion to his calling, until at last he has come to be beyond comparison the richest merchant in the United States.

As a rule, it is certainly encouraging to contemplate the reality of the fact asserted by Emerson, that "man is born to be rich, or that he inevitably grows rich by the rightful use of his best faculties." Yet a too eager pursuit of fortune, ordinarily, is inconsistent with a severe devotion to truth; while the Bible tells us how "he that maketh haste to be rich, shall not be innocent."

And, although Providence has decreed that the common

acquisitions we aim to become possessed of — to wit, money, grand houses, and dominion — are not infrequently bestowed on the inert or indolent, still all those things which go to make up *true* riches, must be attained through our own labor, and the skilful application of our own talents to the proper improvement and advancement of our condition in life.

In the case just now quoted, the subject spoken of was a young Irishman, who arrived in America without friends upon this side of the Atlantic, without money, without business experience, and possessing no iota of advantage over thousands of the young men of that time, or those of to-day, in this country.

But he had laudably resolved to "make his fortune;" and what he lacked in commercial knowledge, or ready means, he brought with him in soundness of head and heart. He was industriously inclined, and honest in purpose, and these good qualities gave him a fortunate send-off.

Mr. Stewart gathered a little stock of goods, from time to time, and devoted himself at first two-thirds of every twenty-four hours, for years, to his store duties. He was the first man in New York who announced the nowadays common newspaper notice we meet with, daily, "Every thing marked down to cost, for cash!" And the result of this original plan to turn his cheap stock into gold surprised him, agreeably. His shop was directly crowded with eager cash customers, his shelves and counters were emptied, at a profit, his money-drawers were filled, and from that time he commenced the steady ascent toward the acquisition of the splendid fortune he is **now** master of — and which places him, as we have said, pecuniarily **at** the head of the list of American merchant princes.

The late Stephen Girard, of Philadelphia, was another instance of like **sort.** He commenced his remarkably successful career a poor laboring man, and after an active business life, the years of which were devoted to earnest steady work, Girard died worth millions; **and** he left a creditable fame behind him, as one who had " begun from very small beginnings," but who prospered wondrously through his own continuous well directed efforts to conquer fortune — from the outset.

John Jacob Astor's history is more familiarly known **to** most Americans. This man was "**a** poor Dutchman in Manhattan," who began with a few dollars, and after years of hard toil, sturdy application, and honest dealing in **a** small way, **he went** forward **with rapid** strides, until he could count his thousands by **hundreds;** and eventually bequeathed to his sons **many** millions — since swelled through the skilful management of his successors to the largest solid real estate fortune, unquestionably, in this country.

Cornelius Vanderbilt, whose estate is variously estimated to be worth up to half a hundred millions or more, in round numbers, was forty years ago possessed of but indifferent means. **He has** been a continuous worker —

hand and brain — from the beginning. And his present enormous wealth affords another instance of the result to be attained by genius, pluck, hard work, good management, and a straightforward course of honorable dealing towards one's fellow-men.

Mr. Vanderbilt has **had** his 'ups and downs.' In his peculiar sphere of business, he has assumed large risks, and oftentimes his fortune has 'vacillated in the balance,' through his daring mode of operations. But he has won — in the end. And to-day he may look back upon a busy changeful career, indeed, but his reputation as a shrewd, sound, thorough, far-sighted business-man from the beginning, can never be gain-said.

Some thirty years **ago,** William B. Dinsmore, of **New** York — now at the head of the Adams Express Company — came from northern New England a poor young man, in search of an opportunity to begin the world, advantageously. Uniting with Alvin Adams of Boston (after whom this great Company is named,) he entered upon duty in Mr. A.'s employ, at board-wages, in the then novel business of running a " parcel express " from Boston to New York. Neither Mr. Dinsmore nor Mr. Adams was **at** that period overburdened with ready money. But both **were** young men of **courage,** stamina, determination, and good business capacity.

Alvin Adams was a pioneer in the Express business, following at an early day the work commenced by W. F. Harnden — who died in January, 1845. Mr. Adams came from Vermont a young man, and embarked in the produce trade in Boston, in which pursuit he lost his entire means; when he turned his attention vigorously to this new vocation (then quite in its infancy) which for three or four years he managed almost alone, amidst the fluctuations of a trying and difficult period.

But his naturally steadfast and determined character carried him forward to eminent success, at last — although the first few years of his experience as an Express-man were attended with most disheartening surroundings.

But he had faith in his purpose. And though the novel undertaking he became engaged in was neither encouraged by paying patronage for a while nor looked upon by other men at that time as probably productive, in a pecuniary view, Mr. A. plodded on in his work dutifully and earnestly from the start, and had the satisfaction of seeing his enterprise finally an exceptionally promising and flourishing business.

After the death of Mr. Harnden, the Adams Express became an "institution." He subsequently branched out, and uniting with W. B. Dinsmore, these two active workers made their new mode of parcel-transportation a positive need among the mercantile men, bankers, brokers and jewellers of New England and New York.

The routes were extended to Philadelphia and South — at last to California, and across the Atlantic. And to-day the originators of this now indispensable enterprise are among the wealthiest and best esteemed business-men in this country — who have *earned* their fortunes and their honors through persistent, straightforward devotion to their calling, to the successful end.

Their proposed enterprise was at first deemed a problematical undertaking, by outsiders. Neither admitted " I cannot do it," in their vocabulary, but both said " *I will try*." Within a dozen years, they each had upwards of a hundred thousand dollars in gold to their credit in the banks of New York and Boston (as we can avouch,) and to-day, the honorably earned fortune of either of these gentlemen is counted up among the millions. They began at the bottom of the ladder, and steadily step by step they have ascended to the topmost round, as successful business-men.

A little more than twenty-five years ago, we happen to know that Robert Bonner (of the New York Ledger) was as poor in purse as most of us would care to be. But he was as shrewd as ever was Scotch-Irishman, (for this was his nativity), and as sharp as the veriest Yankee that ever dwelt in or quitted old Connecticut. Withal, Mr. Bonner was a man of untiring energy, carried a level business head on his shoulders, was indomitably persevering, and possessed the courage and manliness to conceive and follow the right — every time.

He went to New York a poor but industrious and capable printer. After a few years of toil, he bought out the " Merchants' Ledger " (then a sickly commercial sheet) and went to work with a will to make his paper a leading literary weekly. In less than ten years, he "owed no man a dollar," and was the rightful possessor of twice "a hundred thousand dollars in gold," honorably earned through steady application of brains, and the exercise of earnest sound judgment, in an enterprise that was his own — literally, from the start.

Besides making the fortunes of several of those who have served him for years as contributors to his "New York Ledger," Mr. Bonner has paid hundreds of thousands of dollars in those years to other parties, for advertising. He is to-day the owner of a stud of horses that alone cost him two hundred thousand dollars more, and is a millionnaire besides — in solid property, over all. Another remarkable result of capacity, vim, self-reliance, and honorable well-directed business tact.

Is there anybody who has never heard of or seen Phineas T. Barnum, Esq., the showman — now Mayor of Bridgeport, Conn.? We should say there is *not* — at least in this country! Well. He is another Connecticut Yankee — in the grain. About thirty years ago, with a purse so light that he could count the number of *shillings* it contained, in a single breath, Mr. Barnum concluded to purchase the American Museum, in New York — which was then offered for sale, (at Scudder's death) for $15,000. And when some friend who knew the impoverished condition of Mr. B., asked him what he intended to buy this establishment with, he answered good-naturedly, " With brass. For gold or silver have I none." And so he did!

He bought it "on time," went about the fostering of his enterprise with skill and good judgment, worked like a beaver for seven years, paid for his Museum, and another bigger one, and continued on with giant strides toward a generous fortune.

Then came Tom Thumb, Joice Heth, and Jenny Lind — at last. And now — at the head of his colossal Hippodrome — the once "poor Barnum" is a millionnaire, among the rest. And he owes this triumph and his ample fortune to his own tact, his industry, his perseverance, and his ready wit.

John Listar, an Englishman, adopted an original mode to make a fortune, from a very trivial beginning. Mr. Listar took it into his head that there were "millions in it," more or less, and many years ago he concluded to attempt to utilize common silk rags, which he purchased vast quantities of, and experimented with.

At the outset, he bought all the silks rags he could find, at a cent a pound, and up to about 1865 he actually expended over a million of dollars, first and last, and spent years of study and toil over his project — but without success. He had sought to turn these rags into *velvet*, and believed in his scheme, though he was not rewarded for a long period, in his pursuit.

Never daunted however with the difficulties he encountered, he persevered in his chosen work, and eventually hit upon a successful process; and within the last ten years he discovered and put into practice a method of converting this silk refuse into velvet of the choicest quality. This patient untiring application to his one idea has resulted in making him very wealthy, while he now manufactures profitably, from silk rags, the finest velvet produced in England.

Mr. Charles Knox (who has not heard of "Knox, *the* New York hatter"?) commenced his career without a shilling, in 1845, thirty years since, in a small shop in Fulton Street. He served his apprenticeship with Leary, at the trade. For ten years, after '45, he went on slowly but surely, and then "branched out," with rare success.

In 1855, he employed six hundred hands in his establishment. He worked himself as ardently as did the others, and he kept everybody about him busy. In fifteen years he had amassed over "a hundred thousand dollars in gold," and is the wealthiest man — in his line of trade — to-day, in America. He had brains, too, naturally; and he possessed the talents to push his way up to success, honorably, dutifully, and always genially and temperately — with a devotedness to business rarely equalled, and never excelled.

"But all these millionnaires were *lucky*," I hear it perhaps suggested, by the superficial reader. Now this I deem mere fallacy.

Who ever heard of or knew a diligent worker, an early riser, a prudent young man, who was careful of his earnings or his gains — and honest, withal — who had cause to prate about "luck," good or ill?

There is no such thing in real life as "mere luck." Only the shallow-brains believe in luck — or circumstances. Good men, strong men, stout hearts, clear heads, brave souls believe in cause and effect; for there are *no* chances so unlucky from which really clever people may not be able to reap some advantage. And none are so 'lucky' that there will not be found plenty of indolent or brainless fools who may turn them to their own disadvantage.

"Luck" waits, like Micawber, for something to turn up. Labor, genius, tact turns something up. Luck whines and croaks. Genius sings and whistles. Luck waits on chance, or 'providence;' labor on character. Luck halts, and craves Heaven's aid — when Heaven never helps those who neglect to help themselves.

We might point to scores of other instances of well-known self-made men, who have come up through their own energies, unaided in the beginning by money, or capital, to the possession of splendid fortunes.

To say nothing in detail of other millionnaires — the Lorillards, the Brandreths, the Schencks, the Jaynes, the Wanamakers, the Simmonses, the Holloways, the Childs', the Petersons, the Lawrences, the Longworths, the Shaws, the Grovers, the Singers, the Hoes, the Wilsons, the Bennetts, the Potters, the Beaches, the Greeleys, the Scrantons, the Vicks, the Judds, the Demorests, and a thousand others — to some of whom we shall find occasion to refer, hereafter, in this volume, more at length — we conclude this opening chapter with the record of one more instance of "luck through pluck;" with the subject of which we were personally well acquainted, for many years.

We well remember meeting Elias Howe, the original sewing-machine man, one day, in the store of a fashionable tailor on Tremont Row, Boston, about twenty-five years ago, where the famous originator of "the needle with the eye near the point" happened to be present, with his *first* machine in his hands — which he was exhibiting in this establishment, at the time.

Mr. Howe went out of the store, in a melancholy mood.

"What has he got?" we inquired.

"A new-fangled machine," said our friend.

"For what?"

"A sewing-machine, he calls it."

"To *sew* with?"

"Yes — so Elias fancies. But it is not worth a fourpence. One of his gimcracks, that he is crazy over. It will never come to any thing."

"And Howe is very poor, too?"

"Poorer than a church-mouse! He can't pay his bread-bill, to the baker, to-day."

"But he is in earnest, determined, ingenious, and an honest man."

"That is so. I really hope he may succeed in life. He never can do any thing with *that* thing, however," concluded our friend, wisely, as he then fancied.

Well. This identical sewing-machine, which Elias

Howe was at that time toting about under his arm, and boring his friends with a description of, which has since been exhibited all over the world, may be seen to-day at the Howe Sewing-machine Co.'s office, on Broadway, New York; and shortly after the above occurrence took place, Mr. Howe had a dozen machines built in a shop in Gold Street, in that city.

These were sold to a bootmaker in Massachusetts. They were a success. And he went on slowly — toiling, working, studying, experimenting, and perfecting — while he fought infringers, and for seven years almost starving — when his receipts began to reach a few hundreds of dollars, net, annually, and then some thousands. And within twelve years thereafter, his income was over two hundred thousand dollars in gold, per year!

The factory run by the Howe Company (Elias's successors) at last accounts employed nearly a thousand operatives, the sales reach two millions and a half a year, twenty thousand of these machines are sold in foreign countries — and the profits are enormous. So much for Elias Howe — another man of brains and zeal and courage.

These instances we open with. All these are millionnaires. A hundred thousand dollars to any one of these mentioned parties, in the height of the eventual success which attended their vigorous and determined efforts, would be a mere 'drop in the bucket' of their wealth. And yet not one of them *began* the world with scarcely a dollar in ready money.

Erastus Fairbanks, of "Platform Scale" notoriety, died wealthy and honored — but his early life was a succession of hard struggles and privations. His brothers Thaddeus and Joseph P. who succeeded him, had their up-hill course, too, for years. Horace and Franklin Fairbanks, now at the head of this vast enterprise, have latterly become among the wealthiest and most prosperous inventors in America. John F. Henry, a leading American druggist, began twenty years ago with a few dollars, and to-day is counted among the "heavy men" of capital in New York. Forty-odd years since, James Gordon Bennett — previously in association with Major Noah, Jas. Watson Webb, and Horace Greeley — was at the foot of the stairs, pecuniarily. He inaugurated the "N. Y. Herald" amidst most inauspicious times, and under the most unpromising circumstances. But he went onward and upward to the grandest pecuniary success, from a very trivial beginning, and died worth millions.

Geo. W. Childs of the Philadelphia "Public Ledger," is another instance of similar rare success, through individual effort. Mr. Childs went to Philadelphia thirty years ago, a friendless lad, and began life as a shop-boy with a bookseller. He became a partner in this house, subsequently, then purchased the "Ledger" newspaper, and has honorably risen in less than twenty years to be a millionnaire. Chas. A. Shaw of Biddeford, Me., from early boyhood has been a toiler, and inventor. He has seen the rough side of life — but he has gone up from poverty to wealth with steady strides, through earnest application, and energies constantly devoted to attaining an honorable competency and merited position. Dr. Joseph H. Schenck, who commenced life upon a tailor's board, and afterwards established himself in Philadelphia, and introduced the famous "Seaweed Tonic" and other medical preparations bearing his name as discoverer — started with nothing. After thirty years of hard work and careful management, he is now immensely rich, and stands at the head of his profession, in Philadelphia, near where he now resides in splendor and ease. Thirty-five years ago, T. B. Peterson, the great Philadelphia publisher, was a journeyman printer, at the case. Now he is at the head of a flourishing book-house known the world over, and is in the enjoyment of a splendid income, from property accumulated by his own honest, vigorous, skilful efforts, in the legitimate business he has made himself master of.

An interesting leading article recently in the New York Weekly, on the subject of "self-made men," pointedly observes that "when we glance over the long list of characters (in the Old as well as the New world) who have raised themselves through their own efforts to eminence, it would seem as though there are certain ennobling qualities, to produce which, a soil of privation and poverty is requisite."

A large number of these poverty-stricken men in early life is mentioned, who subsequently rose to wealth and standing through their own latent talents, unaided by fortune or influence outside of the humble sphere they severally occupied for many of the first years of their existence; but who struck out for themselves and found their opportunity, which they diligently improved and followed out — at last — to pre-eminent success.

Of these we may refer to Hans Christian Andersen, the popular Danish poet, recently deceased, who was the son of a poor shoemaker, and who came near starving to death, in his youth. Raphael Carrera, the opulent President of the Republic of Guatemala, commenced his career in life as a drummer-boy. Dumas, the rich novelist and play-writer, was an illegitimate son of a West Indian planter and negress, and was in a starving condition in Paris, until, through his own exertions he worked his way up to success. Herring, the wealthy animal painter, began his "art life" as a painter of signs. Sir Richard Arkwright, the noted English inventor, was at first a barber's apprentice. Charles Dickens, in his young years, was a strolling actor and news-reporter. Stansfield, the famous landscapist, was a common foremast hand on shipboard, many years.

John Bunyan, the illustrious author of "Pilgrim's Progress," was a tinker. M. Thiers, the well known scholastic French Minister, was a charity-boy, and afterwards a printer's "devil." Johannes Rouge, the great leader in the German Catholic movement, was a poor shepherd-boy. De Foe, the popular author of "Robinson Crusoe," was a butcher's boy. Marshal Ney, Duke of

Elchingen — whom Napoleon I. named "bravest of the brave," was by trade a cooper. Christopher Columbus, a poor Italian sailor-lad, was the discoverer of a continent. Mons. Daguerre — of original "daguerrotype" process fame, was early in life a poor scene painter. Captain Cook, the renowned navigator, was but a common sailor, at first. Tom Hood, the famous English humorist and poet, was brought up to the engraver's trade.

Among distinguished Americans, may be mentioned Elihu Burritt, the blacksmith's apprentice, known to-day the world over as the foremost linguist of the age. Andrew Jackson, the successful General and President of the United States, came of Irish emigrant parentage. Henry Clay of Kentucky was in his early years an humble clerk in a local Court in Virginia. Abraham Lincoln, President, was born amidst poverty and want. Henry Wilson, Vice president of the United States, was a poor shoemaker, but a few years ago. Daniel Webster, the renowned American statesman, was a poor farmer's son. Andy Johnson, Vice-president and President, commenced his career upon a tailor's bench. Horace Mann, the eminent educationist, was reared in poverty. Benjamin Franklin, the philosopher, was a soap-boiler and tallow-chandler, in his early experience. Horace Greeley was a printer's apprentice, but rose to the highest rank in journalism. Robert Owen, the brilliant philanthropist, was a poor shop-boy in a grocer's establishment. N. P. Banks, the distinguished statesman, was a toiling machinist, during his minority — afterwards **Governor, Congressman, and Speaker of** the House, **at Washington.** Phil. Sheridan, **Lieut. General of the U. S. Army, was** formerly a street news-boy. Nath'l Greene, the great American general, **was in** early life **a journeyman** blacksmith. **Gen. U. S. Grant, President, was a few** years since engaged **as a leather-tanner, in the western** country. **Wm. Lloyd Garrison** served his apprenticeship to the trade of a cabinet-maker. John C. Calhoun, the great Southern statesman, was the son of an Irish emigrant.

All these eminent men in after life — though some of them did not acquire great pecuniary riches — began their several careers at the foot of the ladder without means, and all went up to proud eminence, or wealth, or high position, through their own exertions. And we might go on multiplying interesting examples of a similar character.

Is there **not** encouragement in **these** facts? encouragement for **the poor and down-hearted, and also a rebuke for those who constantly harp upon the wrongs** of the humble, **and the impassable barriers between high and low?** Each man is the architect of his own fortune, and success is ever conquered by the brave and persevering. Though "fortune brings in some boats that are not steered," still, as a rule, the mould of a man's fortune is in his own hands.

There are in the community many young men who fail to see, or are slow to believe, that the success we have thus noted can come, to other young men, in these later times, as it came to the representative individuals we have alluded to, in former days.

To such doubters we can only say " of course it won't, if you do not try it on." Myriads of opportunities that have millions in them, are yet to be discovered. But they must be sought for. These " chances " do not turn up of themselves. They must be turned up, by the earnest, determined, willing, active workers among us — or they remain to be discovered by future Girards, or Astors, or Vanderbilts, *et als.*

A remarkable instance in point is reported in the public journals of to-day. A marvellous new motive power is said to have been discovered by a Mr. Keeley, which the world is promised the benefit of — now that it is asserted to be practically perfected.

This invention, after long years of study and experiment, is described as a mysterious force which exerts from three to twelve thousand pounds to the square inch in propulsion, and is under perfect control of the operator.

The new motive power referred to is created in a secret way, in a small machine three feet by two — without steam or electricity — and it is claimed that it will propel a train of a dozen cars a hundred miles without replenishing.

The force is generated from common air and common water, only; and the discovery promises to do away largely with the use of steam locomotives and coal upon railways, as well as steam power upon ocean and river boats! If this power is ever practically established, what are the inventions of the telegraph, the steam-engine, the sewing-machine in comparison to *this* — for a money-making project?

Now the discoverer did not bring his invention to this state of perfection by sitting on a log with folded hands and declaring "I can't do it." He said "I will *try*." And after many experiments upon a limited scale, he proposed in the summer of 1875 to put a machine before twelve Pullman cars, freighted with passengers, and at a cost of a few dollars only to run such a train from Philadelphia to New York at full average railway speed, without halting, en route.

If it can be accomplished — as the inventor confidently claims — this is another wondrous achievement in the current march of improvement; and demonstrates our assertion that there are ample chances yet for brains and courage among us. But we must turn them up.

"There are few Stewarts, Astors, Vanderbilts, or Girards, to-day," we fancy we hear another reader exclaim, as he peruses these lines.

This may be true. Yet we have among us scores and hundreds like the others herein named; and there are tens of thousands who possess their "hundred thousand dollars in gold," who have earned and saved it, as these very men gained and saved their millions — through earnest work, and tact, and genius, and sound resolution.

To this latter class we shall turn our attention, in the

succeeding chapters of the present volume, in detail; since to carry out the points in our chosen title, we shall aim herein to show the industriously inclined ambitious poor young man "how he may make" his hundred thousand dollars, at the least, through profiting by the truthful examples adduced in the pages that follow.

These cases are typical. What man has done, man may do again. In the progress of the age in which we live, to-day, there occur as many golden opportunities, and far better chances for the coming youth to build a fortune on, than could have existed in the far-away years when the successful men we have now briefly spoken of, began their career.

And surely among the American people, nowadays, we have hosts of young men as shrewd, as keen, as sound, and as able to conquer fortune, as were the early men we have described, with their meagre opportunity — as we shall see.

CHAPTER II.

THE BEGINNING. TOUCHING HARD-PAN.

The "Great Fire" in New York city, which occurred about the middle of December 1835, preceded by a year or more the famous panic of '37; which last event carried disaster and ruin to so many merchants, manufacturers and traders in America.

This conflagration has never been equalled but twice in this country, in extent — those occurring at Chicago and Boston, (in more recent years) exceeding the New York losses, no doubt, very largely.

We were an eye-witness to both the New York and the Boston 'great fires;' and on the former occasion we chanced to be employed in a large house having its headquarters then in the Merchants' Exchange building, on Wall Street — in the rear of which magnificent edifice the memorable burning broke out, at about nine P.M., upon one of the coldest December nights ever known in New York.

There is no doubt that this terrible visitation, in midwinter — which destroyed the whole business section of lower New York city — had much to do with the "panic" that so soon succeeded this unfortunate event; for thousands of merchants, brokers, bankers and traders were ruined by that terrible fire.

The few years immediately preceding the commencement of the middle of the present century — culminating in the never-to-be-forgotten monetary panic of 1837 in this country — witnessed more failures among the mercantile men of the United States, and especially in New York and New England, than during any prior period in the existence of this people as a nation.

The banks in all directions suspended. Small merchants succumbed entirely, and larger houses went hopelessly under. Traders in all branches of commerce missed the faces of their customary patrons. The retail stores were comparatively deserted — and no business of any description was transacting, that compared with that in the "good times" which the commercial community had enjoyed for years preceding.

There was no money to be had. Specie was locked up in the bank-vaults, as a measure of self-protection on the part of those institutions. Accumulated stocks of foreign goods were a drug. Domestic fabrics were heaped up in the leading warehouses, in quantities far beyond the present or immediately prospective needs of the market. Factories shut down, in whole or in part. Operatives were thrown out of work. Clerks were discharged, and workmen were idle — by thousands. And universal chaos in ordinary traffic seemed to have come again.

Importations halted, and exportations came to a stand still, comparatively. The productions of our Western fields — the cereals of the fertile States beyond the Ohio — ceased to move, in consequence; and from the hitherto thriving prosperous and busy merchant or retailer down to the farmer, the mechanic, the factory-worker, the salesman and clerk, the field-hand and day-laborer, the 'long shoreman, the shipper or sailor — landmen or seamen — *all* shared in the generally disastrous final break-down in American trade.

Everybody was at his wits' end, and no two persons could seem to account for this adversity, upon the same theory. Notes went to protest, the wary curtailed their business ramifications, and prudent men reduced their family and store expenses. Credit was completely destroyed.

The few who had means quickly locked up their money, in alarm. The many who had only their hands or brains to work with, could find no remunerative occupation for either. And, imposing upon the necessities of their less fortunate fellows, the speculators and sharpers and soulless small brokers took every advantage of the common disaster, right fiercely — whenever and wherever the opportunity presented itself to avail themselves of this rare harvest in *their* experience.

As is customary, at such times, discharged factory hands of both sexes crowded their way into the cities and large towns, and these were supplemented by an influx of un-

THE YOUTH WHO BELIEVES IN "MERE LUCK."

"The anxious but unambitious lad sits by the wayside, and longingly looks into space for something that may turn up to his future advantage, perhaps." [CHAP. iii. page 66.

employed mechanics, in all trades. — While hundreds and thousands of "young men from the country" huddled down to the great centres of trade, in the hope of getting something to do to support life, since their occupation at home was gone, and they were unable to procure a living with the friends among whom they had been reared.

In the midst of this panic and universal adversity, we call to mind many a case of woe and want — from which large number we select the careers of half a dozen typical characters, to illustrate our present work; each one and all of whom we had the opportunity to become well acquainted with — first and last — the events in whose actual lives furnish us with ample material in the way of moral to adorn our present tale.

In a modest city boarding-house, there were at this period three young men of different ages, each of whom had begun life in separate establishments; but all of whom found themselves at about the same time out of employment, in consequence of this crash in the prospects of the business community.

They were a dry-goods salesman of twenty-four; a broker's clerk of nineteen; and a talented young mechanic and embryo inventor of twenty-one years of age. The first one — Frank Meyers, had been out of business, since his employers' failure, over three months. The second — Morris Deans, had but recently been discharged by the broker, for economy's sake. The third — Ely Hawes, had been struggling two or three years without success, as yet, in the attempt to perfect an invention he had conceived (but had not yet brought out, to his mind) upon which he intended one day or another to obtain a patent — and afterwards 'make his fortune' with.

All three of these young men were now "hard up," so far as the possession of the needful was concerned. They were completely out of funds. And the prospect before them offered to neither much encouragement, amidst the distress that surrounded them on every side. They were every-day friends — but, alack! neither of the hopeful trio had it in his power to assist the other, much, at this appalling hour.

Their accommodating landlady had waited upon them, patiently, but *she* had got to the point where the grocer, the butcher, the baker, and the candlestick-maker had been constrained to notify her that they must have money, or they should be compelled to "shut down on further supplies."

But, though the good woman carried this information to her guests, the three young men could not respond to her delicately expressed desire for payment of their over-due board bills. For, what could they do? They were out of work — they could get nothing to do, at the time, they had no money. And they could not pay.

This was the upshot of the conference, at present.

"And yet," said Meyers, feelingly to his companions, "it is rough on the Widow Bean!"

"That's a fact," responds the boy Deans. "But *I* can't help it, just now. Can you, Hawes?"

"Not as I knows of," replied Ely, coolly. "I haven't earned a sixpence in ten weeks. And I don't know when I shall — from the present outlook."

"How comes on your patent, old fellow?" queried Meyers.

"Only so-so," returned Hawes. "But it will *come* — at last. It's a question of time, o' course. I've got it all *here*," he continued, hopefully, touching his broad full forehead. "And one o' these fine days, it'll come out, all right."

"How much do you owe the widow for board, Ely?" asked Meyers, at this point.

"Eight weeks."

"Thirty-two dollars," said the clerk.

"Exactly, my boy — to a dot. And you?"

"Six weeks — thirty dollars."

"And Morris, what is Goody Bean's claim against you?"

"For nine weeks' feed, to-morrow."

"That is thirty-six dollars more."

"Precisely," returned the clerk.

"Ninety-eight dollars then, in all, we three stout healthy able-bodied young men owe this poor widow, for the bread and meat we have devoured at her hospitable table."

"Call it a round hundred," ventured the lad Morris, good humoredly.

"And she can't afford to be kept out of it, my dear fellows — sure's you're alive" — added Meyers.

"That's so, Frank," agreed the other two. "But what in the world can we do? I wish I had the money — or knew where to get it. But I don't, Frank — for my part," observed Hawes.

And at this juncture, the three young men ceased to talk upon this not altogether agreeable subject — each turning over in his brain the probabilities of the chances as to *when* the Widow Bean would be likely to be gratified with the color of that nearly one hundred dollars, honestly due her, up to that hour.

And while this by-scene was transpiring at the boarding-house, another similar event had come to pass — from the same prime cause — in a distant part of this same business-panic-stricken city, with other characters whom we will here introduce to the reader.

A young man and his wife, (with two sweet babes) were conversing earnestly that morning in their humble home.

The youthful husband had just come from the chamber to the keeping-room, with a little box the wife had sent him after. And he said tenderly, "it is precious hard, Fannie, I know; but these are mighty hard times, I can tell you."

"That is true, Fred. I see it, and realize it, as well as you do," returned the wife.

"What with one thing and another, I don't see that the prospect is likely to grow much more promising, either, for the present."

The young wife sighed, as her good-natured husband placed in her hand the small jewel-box containing her simple and not over costly wedding-set of jewelry.

Upon her lap lay her second infant. Behind her chair, their first-born, a happy mischievous merry girl of four years, was amusing herself with her kitten and toys, upon the carpet.

The youthful parents had just finished their frugal morning meal. And Fred had brought down the little jewel-casket, containing the Etruscan brooch, the ear-drops, and the bracelet which Fannie Selwin, (now Mrs. Fannie Fordham) had worn upon her marriage-day, the wedding gift of her kind but not over well-to-do mother — now four years previously dead and gone.

Fred Fordham had been out of business several months. It was away back, in the panic of '37. He was now entirely minus money. The rent was due, the grocer's bill was unpaid, the winter was cold, the fuel was gone, and the wedding-jewelry of Mrs. Fannie was about to be sacrificed, to raise a little ready cash to " tide them over " the pinch they encountered, in that adverse wintry season.

"It is hard to part with them, Fred" said the wife, holding the box in her hand, and taking her last lingering look at the pretty bawbles. " But you must take them, and get the most you can for them."

" It is for *you*, Fannie — and the babies," said Fred affectionately. "*I* could get on — somehow. But you and our little ones must not suffer."

"I comprehend it all, Fred," returned the wife "Take them. They will bring fifty dollars — at the least. And this sum will greatly help us, for the time being."

The impoverished husband received the box of jewelry from his gentle wife's hand, and left her to nurse the infant while he hurried away to dispose of the trinkets — since he could do nothing, now, without a little money; and he had been unable to earn any for a long time, indeed, in his experience.

Fred quickly found his way to the Square where were located side by side a dozen pawn-brokers' shops.

Over the door of the principal establishment, there hung three gilded balls — the sign of the Jew who advanced "ready money upon old gold and silver," (so his card read,) and who "paid the highest prices" for these genuine articles.

This was the kind of purchaser Fred desired to meet. It was his last resource, until the dreadful times changed. And he must get the most he could, this time. When these ornaments were gone, and when the money he obtained for them was expended — what next?

There were no more!

But Fred was sanguine, and hopeful. Before his fifty or sixty dollars now about to be realized should be used up, he would find employment.

At least he hoped so.

Mr. Isaacs, the Jew, carried a head on his high round shoulders not unlike that of a fat baboon. He was merciless in his plan of extortion, and as keen as a brier in a trade.

Ensconced in his antiquated wooden chair, behind the iron railing beside his strong box, he awaited his customers with a stupid expression upon his hairy face; but he was always ready to advance money upon good security, and knew no friendship towards Hebrew or Gentile, in his sharp transactions. He bought cheap, and sold dear. And this was the way Mr. Isaacs declared *he* contrived to " make an honest dollar," from time to time.

This man examined the jewelry-set. Then he scanned the face of the young stranger who offered them for sale. Then he said, in broken English —

" Vot you vant vor 'ems ? "

" How much are they worth ? " queried Fred, who did not know what their real value might be.

" Not moosh," said the pawn-broker, weighing the set.

" They are gold ? " suggested Fred. " And *good* gold, too — eh ? "

" Vell, t'ey may pe goot colt," continued the sharper. " I ton't shay nottin' apout 'ems. Vot you ax vor 'ems ? "

" I would like to get a hundred dollars for them," ventured Fred. " They cost more than that, a few years ago, no doubt."

The Jew grinned sarcastically in the young man's face, and pushed the jewelry towards him, with a dubious expression, as he replied —

" You ton't know moosh apout t'ese dings."

"No. I don't. You *do*, probably. What will you give for them?"

"Vell, t'ey arn't vort' *arf* a under'd tollers, mine fren."

"Not fifty!" exclaimed Fred.

"No. Nor vorty."

"Will you give me forty dollars cash for them?"

"I ton't vant 'ems."

"Not at forty?"

"No," said the broker.

"How much, then?"

"I vill giv' you dirty tollers vor 'ems."

"Thirty dollars, only!"

"Dat ish all. An' if you vants 'ems, any tay mitin von year, you can hav' 'ems ag'in, vor dirty-vife tollers," concluded the pawn-broker, after another careful scrutiny of the articles.

The sharper meant nothing serious in this assurance. He knew very well — or fancied he did — that the applicant was forced to this procedure, and that he probably would never return to reclaim the articles, at any price.

Fred took the set in his hand, left this shop, and essayed to trade at another establishment, near by.

After trying five of the stores in the neighborhood, at neither of which could he get an offer exceeding twenty-five dollars, he returned to the Jew; who received him as if they had never met before.

"Vot you vants, mine fren'?"

"You may have them."

"Vot pe t'ey?"

"At thirty dollars, sir."

"Vell — vot vor?"

"These jewels."

"Zhooels? Vot you call 'ems?"

"I showed them to you here this morning," said Fred. "You offered me thirty dollars for the set."

"Dish mornin'?"

"Yes. Don't you remember?"

"No," says the Jew. "I dinks you make mishtake."

"O, no! Yours is the only shop with three golden balls over the door. I was here about nine o'clock, to-day," replied Fred, wondering what this old shyster was driving at.

He handed him the jewelry. The broker weighed the articles again, and said, as if he had never seen them until that moment, "I dinks t'ey are vort dwendy-vore tollers."

"You offered me thirty dollars for them, two hours ago!" said Fred, not a little perplexed at this treatment.

"I ton't vant 'ems!" continued the Jew, turning away. "I cannot giv' you dirty tollers vor 'ems."

"What is the *most* you will give?" demanded Fred, afraid to leave him again; and supposing that if he tried any of the parties who had offered him twenty-five dollars for them, they would drop to twenty, perhaps, or less — upon a second application.

"I vill give you dwendy-vife tollers," said the Jew. "But not another shent."

"Take them," responded Fred exhausted, and out of patience.

And with **twenty-five** dollars in cash, he returned to his wife and babies, once more.

"Is that all, Fred?" asked Fannie, when he explained how he had succeeded.

"Yes, love. And this was the best I could do, after trying at half a dozen different places."

"It isn't much, Fred."

"No! It will last us two or three weeks, however."

"And then?"

"Meantime, I shall find something to do — I trust."

"I hope so," returned Fannie. "But — if not?"

"Then I will leave you and the little ones — and go away from this neighborhood, somewhere, and 'seek my fortune,' Fannie," said the good-natured young husband, in his customary sanguine tone.

The quiet wife, resigned to her fate, was thoughtful; but she did not "borrow trouble." There were those — as she well knew — worse conditioned than herself; though she also knew that Fred had already parted with all his own superfluities, before this, to keep the wolf from the door.

Now they had almost reached hard-pan — thought Fannie!

But "God is over all," she murmured, hopefully. "These hard times can't last forever. We are young, in the enjoyment of good health, and Fred has brains and capacity. The cloud is lowering at this hour, and dark —

as well. Who knows but it has its silver lining, nevertheless?"

And then she turned to the pretty infant boy upon her lap, and forgot the gloom that had momentarily passed over her prospects, as she tossed the chirping babe in her arms; who, amid his joyfulness, seemed to call back the sunshine in her heart, which this transient cloud had shadowed.

"Halloo, Fred!" exclaimed Fordham's old schoolmate, — Meyers — meeting the hard-pressed young husband as he left the broker's office, with his five-and-twenty dollars in his hand.

The youthful father had just come from the shop with what he had been able to obtain from the merciless jew, for the contents of his wife's jewel-box.

He didn't care to expose his poverty to his old associate, though he knew very well that they were both 'in the same boat' so far as their business prospects were involved.

"How are you, Frank?" responded Fordham, cheerfully.

"Where you been, Fred?"

"In, yonder."

"To see our 'uncle,' eh?"

"Uncle? No — he's no relation, that I know of."

"Isaacs, isn't it?"

"Yes. I believe that's the broker's name. He's a confounded old jew.

"Had a trade with him?"

"Yes, a small one."

"And he's got the best o' the bargain, I'll warrant."

"That's so, Frank!"

And then Fordham briefly told his former chum all about his little affair with the Israelite.

"Well — I'm sorry *you* are hard up, like the rest of us," observed Meyers, "for you have got a wife and two babies to look out for. I think there's two, eh — Fred?"

"Yes. And it's mighty hard sledding, just now, Frank."

"Well — keep up heart, old boy. It'll all come out right, at last. *These* times can't last long, that's a sure thing."

"No. I hope not. What are *you* doing down here?" asked Fred at this juncture.

"I'm going into Riley's."

"He's another jew!"

"No. — Not exactly — though he's a broker."

"Hard up, too — eh, Frank?"

"Yes. But I'll soon be better off, I trust."

"Well, good-by, Frank. Come round and see us. Fannie and the babies will be glad to meet you."

"Thank you. I will," returned Meyers, as the two friends separated; and Frank entered Riley's pawn-shop, a moment afterwards, where he intended to leave his Adams chronometer, that cost near two hundred dollars a year or two previously; upon which he hoped to be able to raise a hundred dollars in cash; with which he had determined to discharge the three board bills due the Widow Bean — without farther delay.

Mr. Riley was a Yankee. But he was as sharp as were his neighbors. The Adams watch was a good one.

He advanced a hundred on it, for six months — at three per cent per month.

And Meyers took his hundred dollars — and went his way back to his boarding-house, rejoicing.

CHAPTER III.

WHAT A DAY MAY BRING FORTH.

FRANK MEYERS naturally possessed a soul altogether above buttons.

"I'm as poor as Job's turkey, boys," he said to his mates, with a pleasant smile, when he encountered them two hours afterwards, with his five bright twenty-dollar notes in his hands. "But look a' here, lads!"

And he flaunted the clean bank-bills above his head, in great glee.

"What do you say to this, Ely?" he asked.

"Where'd you get it?"

"Borrowed it."

"I wish *I* could do that same sort of thing, then!"

"Where?" asked young Morris.

"Of 'my uncle.' Who else, pray, in times like these?" returned Frank, glibly.

"I have no uncle," observed the lad, with a dash of feigned melancholy.

"Nor I," joined Ely. "I wish I had. I'd go for him, now, sure!"

" This money, I borrowed of my uncle *Isaacs*, the pawn-broker," said Frank, explaining himself. " At three per cent a month — for six months. It will cost me eighteen dollars for the use of it, if paid at that time, promptly."

" And if not ? "

" My two-hundred-dollar watch goes up — if I am not then able to redeem it."

" Pledged your watch ! "

" Yes, boys. For myself, and for you. We three lads owe the Widow Bean ninety-eight dollars, to-morrow. I am going to pay up that old score, and I shall have two dollars left. I made it ' an even hundred,' as you suggested, Morris — exactly."

" Yes. Well " — continued the lad, " I am not the owner of a two-hundred-dollar watch, unluckily."

" Nor I, by Jupiter," exclaimed the poor inventor. " But I hope to be — one of these days."

" When you can do so, conveniently — repay me, boys. That's all," said Frank, indifferently.

And the widow's heart and eyes were gladdened wondrously, next morning, when Frank Meyers, for himself and his two companions, handed her the full amount of their three board-bills, due up to that day.

A good action, bestowed on no matter whom, carries with it its own reward. But it is the *motive* (not so much the act,) that enhances the value of such deed. And Frank Meyers had been entirely unselfish in this friendly act, for he had moved in this upon the golden rule — though the valuable watch was the gift of a dead relative — and he felt confidently assured that he was doing as he would have been done by. He knew that either Ely or Morris would have shared with him their last shilling — had they had any shilling left so to share.

But they hadn't!

And now Frank Meyers himself and his two friends were upon a par, in their financial condition.

"I have got just two dollars, boys," he began, in a jocular tone —

"And nary a watch," suggested the broker's clerk, in a good-natured way.

"While either of you two chaps have —"

"Nary a red," responded Ely, smiling.

"Well — what shall we do?" asked Frank.

"Go to work," replied Morris.

"A good idea, boy! Where?" inquired Frank, cheerily.

"There you have me," returned the youngster. "If I but only knew!"

"Or I," said Hawes.

"Or *I*," added Meyers.

"From to-day, fellows, let us remember that our board begins to run up, again."

"That's so," said Ely.

"We haven't any more money to meet the next bills with."

"Nor watches —"

"Nor any thing else!"

"Except brains"—ventured Frank.

"And pluck"—suggested Deans.

"And good will"—added Ely.

"Now, lads," continued Meyers, "I am the oldest—"

"And the smartest," hinted Morris, complimentarily.

"And I propose that we start out forthwith upon a hunt—"

"For snipe?" asked the boy.

"No! Listen—you young chatterer. We will go each in a different direction, and canvass the city thoroughly, for ourselves and for one another. The times are shocking, I know. I have been bred to service behind the counter in a fashionable dry-goods house, and I know my business; but my trade isn't worth much, to-day. Now I saw, not long ago, that a London preacher uttered in his pulpit sentiments something akin to these: 'if I were to fail in my present calling, brethren, he said, I would take to literature. If I failed in that, I would try commerce, perhaps. If I could not succeed in that, I would drive a cab for a living—or saw wood. And failing in this, I would take to blacking boots. But I would *not* sit down and wait on Providence for some lucky turn in fortune's wheel—while I had health and strength, and possessed the moral courage that the God of nature has implanted in my heart!'"

"Who preached that sermon, did you say?"

"A London clergyman."

"He was a brick, by Jove!" exclaimed Ely. "*He* would make a mighty good hand at inventing, sure's you're alive! You couldn't discourage *him*, easy — that's a fact."

"Well, didn't he talk it about on the level, Ely?"

"He did."

"Isn't it good advice?"

"Tip top."

"Let us profit by the suggestions, then."

"I don't care to saw wood," suggested young Deans.

"Nor do I wish to undertake to drive a cab," said Frank. "I should make but an indifferent whip, no doubt."

"And I don't propose to black anybody's boots, at present, if I know myself," continued Ely.

"No! There is no need of this. Yet the true principle underlies the hints embodied by the parson in this brief sermon, nevertheless, for the man who has to labor for his living. And so *we* will neither of us sit down and trust to luck, while we can get *any* thing to do that is respectable and decent for respectable and decent young men to perform."

"That's it!" exclaimed Ely.

"Now, then — let's move!"

"Forward," said the lad, promptly.

"Face front!" added Ely.

"March!" concluded Frank, as the three friends left the boarding-house together, in excellent spirits — agreeing to "report progress," at evening, and compare notes regarding their efforts during this eventful day in their experience.

"You're the seventh young man who has been in my store to-day, after a place," exclaimed a surly curmudgeon of a retailer, to Morris, who thought he would try this shop, for a chance — as the three friends wandered about the city, that day.

"I tell you I don't want anybody. I've got more clerks round me now than I can pay wages to," persisted the shop-keeper. "And the times are awful."

Ely looked through all the machine-shops, in at the patent-agents' offices, (for he was a clever young draughtsman,) among the inventors, and engine-builders. Everybody was discharging their help. They did not want to hire.

Frank Meyers went among the wholesale houses, and diligently sought for an opportunity where he could "make himself useful;" but no one had a use for him — and he found nothing available.

But he "had been there," before this! He was not seriously disappointed, and in no wise discouraged. He floated over to the humble lodgings of his former schoolmate, Fordham — where he met Fannie and the babies. Fred had "gone out to look for business," the young wife said. He had been idle over four months.

"It is a hard time for the young men about," said Fannie sympathizingly, when Frank had informed her of his own situation — not unlike that of her husband.

It was late in the afternoon when Fred returned to his own house, where he found Meyers awaiting him.

"What are you doing, Frank?" asked the latter, as he entered, in his usual good spirits.

"Nothing!"

"And you find plenty to help you do that same, just now, eh?"

"That is so, my boy. Fannie tells me you have been busy in this line, some weeks, Fred."

"Four months, and more. And I've spent about the last dollar I've got, Frank!"

"Why, bless you, my old friend — why didn't you say so, before?" exclaimed Frank, patronizingly. "Don't you want to borrow?"

"Have *you* got any thing over, Frank?" asked Fred hopefully.

"Yes, indeed."

"That is lucky, to be sure, my friend."

"And you are welcome to it, my dear fellow! I had a hundred clean bright dollars, this morning," continued Frank, dubiously, taking out his flattened wallet — that looked now as if an elephant had recently stepped upon it — "and if I had known you were short, I'd ha' helped you to the extent of my humble ability. Why didn't you mention it? Here!" he continued. "This is what I've got left, and it is quite at your service, my boy."

And with this pleasant little speech, he dug out the two dollars from his pocket-book, with a magnanimous expression — as if it had been two hundred, instead!

"Two dollars!" shouted Fred.

"That is all I've got left, Fred."

"Ninety-eight dollars gone, in one day, Frank?"

"Just so," responded Meyers.

"Well, keep it. You may want it, before night — at that rate," replied Fred.

And then his old schoolmate told him what he had done with his ninety-eight good dollars.

"All in the same box, I find," continued Fordham, with the merest tinge of an unconscious sigh at the prospect.

"Can you help it, Fred?"

"No, I can't, Frank."

"Nor I. *We* haven't brought about this adverse state of things, though we are among the sufferers by this wretched panic and prostration."

"When will the times be better?" asked Fred, with a trusting look in his candid friend's face. "That is the question, now."

"Yes, Fred. I have heard this conundrum propounded on several occasions latterly, by many another. But I am unable to guess it."

"I give it up," responded Fordham.

"No! Not yet, my boy. That won't do, in *your* case, mind you."

And his strong-hearted chum pointed to the silent wife — and babies.

"I see. Yes. You are correct. But, bless you, Frank — I am not discouraged at all. Only — at the same time — it is tough — this present prospect, 'eh?"

"Right. But we shall all weather the storm, be sure of it. Hawes, Deans, and myself are alike 'upon our oars.' But we can't starve, in this land. And the clouds will lift, after a while."

"I hope so," concluded the young husband.

"What luck, boys?" asked Frank that night, when the other three friends met at their boarding-house — after their first day's earnest search for business.

"With me," said Ely — "nix."

"And me," added the lad Morris, "ditto."

"And I," said Frank, "found nothing, to-day. But we will try it on again, to-morrow."

"And next day," rejoined Ely.

"Yes, and the next," persisted the boy, trustfully.

"And it will come — at last," concluded Frank. "Fortune may do her worst, lads, whatever she may compel us to lose, so long as she never makes us sink our manhood, or sacrifice our honesty and will to do the right, upon opportunity. We are poor enough to-day —"

"That's a fact!" interrupted Ely.

"But *I* intend one day to be rich, boys!"

"What do you call being rich, then, Meyers?" asked the broker's lad.

"When I possess a hundred thousand dollars that I can call my own, lads, I will be content," said Frank, modestly.

"A goodly sum," returned Ely. "That is my mark, too, sooner or later."

"Out of what?" asked Morris.

"My brains, boy. I've got it here — I tell you," he added, tapping his cranium. "And when my patent is secured, and my new invention is perfected, I will not only astonish the world, but I will make a hundred thousand dollars with it, if I live to see it matured."

"A hundred thousand dollars!" murmured the lad, "is a pile of money, gentlemen! If I ever have one fourth of this in *my* hands, that I know belongs of right to Morris Deans, I will not seek for more. I shall be satisfied with this. It is a competence."

"But four times this is a better competency, my boy."

"So it is. I wish you may get it, Frank."

"I will try," said Meyers.

"And I!" followed Ely, spunkily.

And so they did — all three.

The days and weeks went by, still, without much change. But the panic wore away, at last. The skies brightened. Everybody had touched hard pan. Then business opened up, at length — slowly, and surely. And the crisis passed.

At the end of two months, our four representative young men began to "see daylight," once more.

They resolved to make their hundred thousand dollars, each. And how they went about it — as well as the measure of their subsequent success in life — will be detailed truthfully in our subsequent chapters.

We present two illustrations, showing two sides of character applicable to the points under consideration.

Facing page 40, the anxious but unambitious lad sits by the way-side and longingly looks into space for something that may turn up to his future advantage, perhaps.

The other shows our manly type of worker — Ely Hawes; who is ardently busying himself at his bench.

There is the indolent, and here the industrious youth. Which of these is represented by the young man whose eye may fall upon these lines, to-day?

TURNING SOMETHING UP.

CHAPTER IV.

HOW TO BEGIN TO MAKE MONEY.

THIS country is unlike all older nationalities of the world, in respect of the opportunities current for amassing fortune, through one grand special feature — to wit, the cultivation of its widely extended and readily obtainable cheap territory.

No other country on earth to-day offers as this does a tithe of the solid inducements to the vigorous, industrious, enterprising youth who is blessed with health and strength and good intentions, to win a fortune by applying himself determinately to the tilling of our virgin soil — in a thousand prime localities that might be pointed out — east, west, and south.

We are all aware that there be other fields, and other channels of trade — in commerce, arts, mechanics, and professions, whereby a goodly fortune may be accumulated, under given circumstances; in some of these more rapidly, perhaps, than in others. But no means are surer, none safer, or more promising, in the long run, than this just mentioned; for it is literally as it is poetically true that " the *farmer* feeds us all."

The nabob may ride through his own palace-gate, the merchant may amass his millions, the lady may sweep along in gorgeous array, the sailor may plough the far-away seas, the artisan may toil, the lawyer may plead, the mechanic may build, and

> " Great work may be done, be it here or there,
> And men may work worthily, everywhere.
> But fall to each, whate'er may befall,
> The farmer must feed them — after all!"

In this connection, take a single well accredited example of the accumulation of solid wealth through very simple means associated with rural husbandry, in the instance of Samuel Long and brother, who were reared near Newmanstown, Penn.'a.

These two young men have proved enterprising as well as model farmers, in the Key-stone State. Less than twenty years ago, they went to New York city with scarcely one hundred dollars in cash between them, and to-day they control the wholesale market of that metropolis in the egg-business.

The success of these persons has been remarkable — but it is only a single instance showing what may be done through steady application towards a given project, rightfully attended to from the start, and persistently followed up, as these now well-to-do young men have pursued their chosen vocation.

These men have got rich on eggs, simply. They now own seven extensive farms, upon which they have erected magnificent buildings, in the latest style of improved modern architecture; and at this writing they are building a superb Mansard structure, hardly excelled in this country.

They have two large ice-houses, in which they " preserve eggs" in quantity, from time to time. One of these was recently put up along the Lebanon Valley Railroad, for convenience in transportation of their accumulating egg-freight. It has iron floors, and holds thousands of barrels of eggs.

These brothers have a large Western trade. They buy when eggs are plenty and low-priced, lay them down in bulk, and sell when the price is at the best. Thus they have made fortunes; and the world is still open to the industrious and shrewd American, in various ways — as simple in method as this appears to be — if the enterprising man will but look about him, in right down earnest, and take hold of his opportunity, seasonably.

Yet notwithstanding the indisputable fact that no enterprise or calling embarked in, in our land, is so certain in its average returns to the able-bodied young man who diligently pursues the life of the intelligent agriculturist, we may daily note the universality with which Americans are forsaking this kind of avocation — in all directions.

At the very time when manufactures, trade, clerking, and skilled mechanical labor are at their worst, and when thousands upon thousands in the over-crowded business-centres are left out of employment, in these hard times, it is a fact that farmers find it difficult to obtain good help to forward and gather their growing or matured crops, and this complaint has been general among this class of workers especially during the past two or three trying years.

There is no social error more glaring than that of indulgent fathers who raise boys to no occupation or calling save what they can gather in " clerking " it, nowadays.

A Philadelphia paper recently contained an advertisement for a young man in a railway office. In a single day, there were received nine hundred and eighty applications for this one place, for which only "moderate compensation " was promised.

This shows a large excess of young men lying about loose in our cities, who are disposed to avail themselves of the do-nothing process, whereby to earn a precarious subsistence; for, at the best, such 'situations' can offer permanency to but very few of those out of employment, and who are inclined to " do any thing " except work for a living.

But what is first and foremost of the greatest consequence in *any* undertaking, as a business-pursuit in life, is a decision or choice of the kind of vocation the young man will follow. When this is selected, the next important thing to be observed is, the following out of this pursuit, unflinchingly, to the end — holding steadily in view the truthful maxim that whatever is worth doing at all, is worth doing *well*. And thorough perseverance surely wins, at last. The greatest work is accomplished not by physical strength, but by application and persistence. The formidable granite palace is reared by single stones placed one upon another. And the man who walks three hours a day, may in seven years' time have passed over a space equal to the circumference of the globe!

Whatever is acquired with difficulty, is best retained. And he who *earns* a fortune, is the man who best appreciates it, and is the most careful to preserve it — be it small or great. "Show me a young man," said Charles Fox, " who has *not* at first succeeded, but who has nevertheless gone steadily on, in the face of vicissitude, and I will back him to do better in the end than he who is fortunate upon his first attempt."

Few things are impossible of accomplishment in life, to which are applied thorough diligence, wit, and skill. And nothing is so hard to find out, that persistent search will not discover it. "That policy," says Colton, "which is able to strike only while the iron is hot, will be overcome by that perseverance which, like Oliver Cromwell's, can make the iron hot by striking."

As the constant falling of a single drop of water upon one spot will wear away the hardest stone, so the nerve that never relaxes, the steady pursuit never once given up, the eye that never blenches, the heart that never faints, the brain that never ceases to devise, the thought once fixed that never wanders — these are the champions of victory!

Determined perseverance in the right direction, gives

power to weakness, and opens up to poverty the world's wide wealth. It spreads fertility over the barren landscape, it bids the choicest fruits and flowers spring up and flourish, where only thorns or briers grow before. And whoever *perseveres*, is bound to CONQUER.

Good old Ben Franklin declared that the road to wealth is as plain as the road to mill. And so it is. But the direct route is too frequently mistaken. And young men are apt to get in the by-ways, or off the highway that leads to fortune, through lack of discernment at the proper time, when entering upon the commencement of their journey.

The clerk, or salesman, or mechanic whose salary may be a thousand dollars per annum, but who carelessly expends twelve hundred, in a year — will *not* make haste to get rich. The young man whose income is five hundred dollars, annually, who expends but four hundred and a half in a twelvemonth, and who puts the remaining fifty only out at interest at six per cent for thirty years — say from the time he is twenty — may find a pretty fortune in gold at his bankers, when he reaches fifty years of age.

True economy is of itself a grand revenue. Not parsimony — not meanness — not penuriousness. The youth whose father has taught him to live upon a little, is indebted to that parent's wisdom far more than is the lad whose father's care has bequeathed him a competency. And the man was right who regarded nothing as cheap that was a superfluity — since what one does not need, is dear at any price.

This axiom may be set down as true: "no man is rich, whose expenditures exceed his means, and no one is poor, whose income exceeds his outgoes." It is frugality, sound economy, honesty, and industry that make the poor man rich. And if we manage to be an economist in prosperity, there is no fear about this matter in adversity.

"Poor Richard" uttered a meaty sentence when he penned these words: "Let honesty and industry be thy constant companions, and spend one penny less per day than thy clear gains. Thus, shall thy hide-bound pocket soon begin to thrive, and thenceforth never again cry with the empty belly-ache. Neither will creditors insult thee, nor want oppress, nor hunger bite, nor nakedness freeze thee."

Young Morris Deans, the former city broker's clerk, had handled millions of dollars in the three years he had been employed in State Street, Boston. But his master failed, during the panic, and Morris could obtain no new situation in the line of his late vocation. He was compelled to turn his thoughts in another direction, therefore, as we have seen.

When business revived, the married book-keeper, Fred Fordham, fortunately secured a position, (at a reduced salary,) and went to work again in the counting-house. Frank Meyers left Boston for New York, where he subsequently found employment in a wholesale domestic dry-goods house. Ely Hawes, the embryo inventor, stuck to his 'model-machine,' and slowly pursued the chosen object of his life.

All these characters we shall meet again, as we proceed. Now we have to do with the boy — Morris Deans; whose career we will follow first, for convenience, and learn how he succeeded, for the nonce, in his beginning to make money.

Young Deans had been a very good broker's clerk. For nearly three years he had gone forward steadily, but his salary had been (in those days) never more than six dollars a week. At first, but four. Then five — and during the last year six dollars.

Yet he had contrived to live upon this. He boarded at a modest house, and made his income pay his expenses, mostly. But he had very little 'over.' And when he lost his place, he was without means — to the last dollar.

He was an orphan, and he knew he must depend upon his own energy and talents for sustenance. But he was willing, smart, capable, stout of heart and strong in limb — and he was determined to make his way, if he could get hold of *any* kind of work that would support him, and open up a chance prospectively in his future.

He was now past nineteen years old. He had come to the city from the Cape, at sixteen, obtained the situation in the stock and money broker's office, and had acquired a goodly knowledge of securities, the keeping of accounts, and the true value of interest and commissions.

He was a bright, cheery, able-bodied, comely lad, and was not afraid of work — though, in his calling in the city, he had not been required to perform any sharp manual labor, latterly.

Before he came to Boston, however, he had been reared upon a worn-out farm in Barnstable County; where he remembered to have been "a son of toil," in his younger days, and where he had had a goodly experience, for his years, among hard workers, who were healthy, honest, and content.

The change from country to city life, had changed the quiet boy to an ambitious lad, for the time being. But when adversity overtook him, he thought over all the chances — looked his condition straight in the face — and said to himself and to his companions "I will do any thing I can perform, that is honest and honorable, to get a living." A wise resolve.

In the course of his service with the stock-broker in State Street, young Deans had come across a burly, portly man of about fifty years of age, who came to Boston twice a year to collect his interest-money upon some shares of stock he owned in the old solid Massachusetts Bank, where the lad's employer had been in the habit of depositing his funds.

This man was a well-to-do farmer, named Howard Blount — who had had occasion several times to do business, briefly, with the broker where Morris was a clerk. He took a fancy to the lad, and vouchsafed him frequently a pleasant remark — as he came and went, every six months — upon meeting the young man.

But nothing came of this until the broker failed. And then it chanced that old Blount came down to Boston t collect his income, one day — in the midst of the monetary troubles.

These adversities had occasioned *him* no inconvenience, however. His twenty thousand dollars, placed in the stock of the strong old institution he had chosen for the purpose of investing, were as safe as gold coin in the mint. And regularly, twice a year, he came to draw his three per centum dividends.

He dwelt at Brandville — in Western Massachusetts. His farm was a good one. It lay upon the margin of the Connecticut River, and comprised two hundred and thirty acres of splendidly tilled land, upon which he cultivated huge fields of grass and grain, and where he kept a large herd of superior cattle, and other live stock. His domain was taxed at two hundred dollars the acre. And Howard Blount was known to possess in real and personal estate more than a hundred thousand dollars — clear of the world.

Blount was eccentric, in some of his ways, but he was a good solid honest citizen, and loved his calling. He had been bred a farmer and cattle-raiser. He had one of the finest landed estates upon the Connecticut River, and he was esteemed a first-class good man, in the main.

He was a stout old fellow, himself, his cattle were fat and sleek, his pigs were as fat as the others, his poultry was fat, his dog was fat, his good wife was robust and portly, his sheep were fat; and every thing about this great stock farm at Brandville was in high health and thorough good keeping.

Old Blount came down to Boston to collect his dividends, and met young Morris Deans, recently the broker's clerk — who was then in search of a new situation, which he had not yet been able to find.

"Out o' business, eh?" inquired the farmer, pleasantly.

"Yes, sir. My employer has given up, and I am thus thrown out of work."

"Yes. Got any money saved up, boy?" asked Blount, kindly.

"No!" responded Morris. "I never had any money over, from week to week, unfortunately. I never earned more than my actual current expenses. And so it all went for board, and clothing and washing, you see."

"Yes. Well — what are you goin' to do, now?" queried the farmer.

"Any thing I can get to do," returned Morris, promptly.

"Yes. I see," said Mr. Blount, thoughtfully. And he eyed the lad scrutinizingly, a moment, as if he were doubtful about proceeding further with a thought that just then entered his head.

"No — you wouldn't do, I reck'n," concluded Blount.

"Wouldn't do what, sir?"

"You wouldn't answer, I'm afeard."

"For what, if you please?"

"You wouldn't like it."

"Like what? Business — do you mean, sir?"

"No. I was a thinkin', Morris — that, perhaps — but, no — it is no matter. You couldn't stand it," said Blount.

"Stand *what?*" persisted the boy, whose curiosity was now excited, and who fancied he saw a chance — of some kind. He didn't know what, and he had got to that point where he didn't care, if it were only to better his poor condition.

"Well," continued the pursy farmer, good-naturedly, "your hands are a heap too small to swing a flail, or grasp a scythe-snath. An' you couldn't cut six foot o' cord-wood in a week, that's a fact! No — *you* won't answer, boy."

"Do you want to hire a hand, Mr. Blount?" asked Morris, seriously.

"Well, I do, young man. An' I'd give you a chance, right willin'ly, if I thought you could stan' the work. That is to say, if you can't do better."

"What is the pay, sir?"

"Twenty dollars a month, and your livin', if you can do the work, lad."

"Will you give me a chance to try it, sir?"

"Do you think you'd like farmin', you city-bred youngster?"

"I was brought up on a farm, sir," responded Morris, proudly.

"*You!*" exclaimed Blount.

"Until I was sixteen."

"Is that so?"

"Mine whar yer g'wine, now, Mass'r Blount, an' don't obertip us!" cried Aunt Chloé, the darkey attendant — as the jolly party of little ones, nestled snugly in the top of the hay-load, were being driven down the steep hill, toward the spacious Sunnyside barns. (CHAP. vi. page 96.

"I have been 'city bred' only three years, sir."

"I didn't know it."

"And I am stronger to-day than I ever was, Mr Blount," urged the lad, "while I never was more needy.'

"And you'll try it, again?"

"I will, sir, gladly."

"At twenty dollars a month, an' found?"

"Yes, sir. That is twenty dollars a month more than I ever yet earned in my life!"

"When will you begin?"

"When do you want me?"

"Right away. Ploughin's begun already, and sowin' 'll come right along. I would like you to come at once."

"To-morrow?"

"To-day, if you like."

"When do you return home, sir?"

"To-night — in the stage."

"I will join you, then."

"It's a bargain," said Blount. "If you like me, an' I like you — and you like farmin' and stock-raisin', lad, I'll do well by you, hereafter."

"Thank you, sir. I will try," said young Deans, with a thankful heart.

And an hour afterwards, he found Frank Meyers and Ely Hawes, not a little elated.

"How do you make it, boys?"

"Nothing, as yet."

"Fred Fordham's gone to work again, I hear."

"Yes, I know it," said Frank. "And I am going on to New York, to look for a chance."

"Well, *I've* got a place, thank heaven!"

"Where?"

"With old Howard Blount, in Brandville."

"At what?"

"Farming."

"Farming?"

"Yes, and stock-raising."

The two friends smiled.

"You grin, boys. Well, I am to get more pay there than I ever did yet, and I can do the work like falling off a log, I can tell you."

"Glad of it."

"We all thought we'd try what we could get, since we couldn't have what we desired, exactly. Didn't we?"

"Yes. You are right. Go in, my dear fellow. You'll make your fortune, of course."

"That is how old Blount made his, at any rate," suggested Morris, cheerfully.

"It's a very respectable calling."

"And profitable," said Ely.

"Yes; and I will like it," continued Deans," if it's such a place as I hear it is."

"When do you begin?"

"To-morrow. I go over, to-night. In sixty days, Frank, I will send you your borrowed money — for the board-bill, you know."

"I congratulate you, my boy. No doubt you'll do well there."

And thus the three friends parted, while old farmer Blunt accompanied by his newly hired man Morris Deans took the mail-coach at evening, and arrived at the Brandville farm, at early noon next day — without previous announcement there of their coming.

Morris knew nothing about the household of his new employer. But during the journey up from Boston, the rather talkative old man gave him a brief description of the premises, of the stock he kept, and hinted at what duty he expected the ambitious lad to perform.

The young man was in excellent spirits, but had no idea who or what he was to encounter at the Blount estate. He only congratulated himself upon his brightening prospects. He had begun to make his fortune, at last, so he fancied!

"Let those laugh who lose," said Morris, mentally, as he entered upon this new experiment, "for those who win are sure to be pleased. Old Blount is a sterling man. He has made his fortune, legitimately, in tilling the soil. I will put forth my best efforts, and we shall see how we come out, in the end."

"It is a change, young man," ventured Blount, advisedly, as they journeyed along towards his beautiful home; "and you will find the employment and surroundings at Brandville quite different from those you have latterly been accustomed to."

"I shall apply myself to the new occupation with earnest good will, sir," returned the lad, promptly.

And he meant just what he said — for he believed that the farmer's proposal to him was really a god-send, and that he was now upon the road to prospective good fortune.

MORRIS DEANS — THE CITY LAD.   MORRIS DEANS, ON THE FARM.

CHAPTER V.

MORRIS DEANS IMPROVES HIS PROSPECTS.

The agricultural proprietor and his young assistant reached the Connecticut River farm at early dinner-time.

"We call the place Sunnyside," said Blount, when they alighted, and were entering the great old-fashioned square white mansion.

Then he pointed the lad to the broad fields sloping down westward, towards the shining Connecticut that flowed majestically past the wide-stretching acres of old Blount's estate — dotted here and there with cattle-herds, and sheep, and horses, in the bright green pastures.

It was early spring-time, but the grass had started abundantly in that region, and the trees were just being clothed with their first verdure.

The house stood upon the highest portion of the upland, and the prospect looking west and north and south was very agreeable to the eye — the broad landscape stretching out over wide plains, and rolling ground beyond, to the hills and woods of Berkshire.

"Come in, Morris," said Farmer Blount, kindly

"Here. Let me give you a hand with your trunk," he said, as the lad took up his box, that contained his scanty wardrobe, a few books, and all his worldly effects.

"It isn't heavy," returned Morris, pleasantly, declining the old man's aid, and shouldering the box.

Nor was it very bulky, to be sure! Yet it contained his little all.

"Come in. Set it down in the entry, just now. We'll see what'll be done with it, by and by," continued the farmer. "This way, now," he added, leading on to the keeping room, upon the southerly side of the house.

And as the new-comers entered, a matronly woman of five-and-forty rose to greet her husband, and saluted him with an affectionate kiss of welcome; as was her wont, upon 'father's' return from his occasional temporary absence from home.

"This is my wife," said Mr. Blount. "It is Morris Deans, my dear — from Boston. He has come up to live with us. I have hired him to work upon the farm, with the rest."

"You are very welcome, Morris," said the lady, kindly.

And Morris took her extended hand, and replied that he was happy to meet so pleasant a lady, in what might be his new home, in the future.

"Seems to me you don't look much like a farmer, nevertheless," observed Mrs. Blount graciously, when the first civilities of reception were over.

"He's a stout lad, mother, notwithstanding his genteel

looks," returned Blount. "In this holiday rig he has on, he *don't* look very formidable, that's a fact. But he's been living in the city three years, and the young lads have to dress differently there. You must get off these store clo'es, though, Morris, after dinner; and we'll see what we can do for you, to make you look more like one of us. You have other clo'es in your trunk, I s'pose?"

"Yes," said the lad.

But this was the only complete suit he had to his back!

They were soon called to dinner. And a right enjoyable repast it proved, too. Both men were hungry, and they ate with an appetite sharpened by their long stage-ride.

The other two hands who worked on the farm came in, and Morris was introduced, all round.

"This is my darter, Eunice — Morris," finally said the old man, as he presented a buxom young woman, who entered last.

And before they left the table, all hands felt reasonably acquainted.

There was no restraint, no balking, no undue reserve, at "Sunnyside." But a hearty welcome greeted the lad at his new location, and he felt quite at home, after two hours' acquaintance there.

Miss Eunice was a very nice girl; as fresh as a rose, healthy, hearty, happy, and comely. The coming of Morris was a surprise to her, as it was also to her mother, Mrs. Blount. Indeed, it was equally unexpected to old

Blount, himself — for he had no idea of making an engagement with *this* young man, though he was in want of additional help on the farm, and calculated to get a man directly upon his return from Boston, if he did not chance to meet with one there.

After dinner, Blount took Morris about over the estate, and showed him his fine live stock — his horses, colts, cattle, sheep, swine and poultry.

They interchanged a pleasant chat, and the old man was equally astonished at the lad's intelligence and ready appreciation of every thing he saw. Then he said —

"You can go over to the store, by and by, Morris, and get yourself an outfit. Your clothes are entirely unsuited to our work."

"Thank you. I will, sir. You must do me the favor to become responsible for what I shall need, though, for I am short of ready money. I will pay you out of my first earnings, of course."

"That will all take care of itself, Morris. I have no account, there. But they keep a great variety of every thing needful for the inner or outer man, at the store, which is also our Brandville Post office. I will go with you. I'm a cash man myself, and the postmaster is an old friend. But I owe no man a dollar — except the current wages for the month to my farm-men. I pay every thing, monthly — and have no " little bills " coming in, you see."

"That is a very good plan," said Morris, "when one is able to do it, conveniently."

"I always make it a point to buy nothing, contract for nothing, and have nothing that I can't pay down cash for, when I get it. Then it is my own, and nobody can dun me for it — eh?"

"An excellent system, sir."

"It is one of the first and most important lessons to learn in business life, Morris. If you haven't the money to pay for what you want, go without it. Wear your old coat, or hat, or boots, a little longer — if it be clothing. Wait till you can earn the money to pay with. Never run in debt. Don't give notes, or due-bills, or promises — for money."

"All of us can't manage thus, sir — though I admit it is an admirable theory."

"True — there are cases" —

"Mine, to-day, for instance?"

"Yes. But I speak of the *rule*. Buy for cash, and pay as you go — or go without — except in extremity. Stick a pin right there, my lad."

When Morris had selected his new working clothes, and fitted himself to a comfortable but heavy pair of stout brogans, the old man noticed the stylish city shoes which the lad had worn up from Boston, and smilingly remarked, as they left the country store — "The difference between patent leather and cow-hide boots, is mostly in the shine, lad — after all!"

Morris looked down at his genteel glistening gaiter-boots, and appreciated the force of his good friend's pleasant allusion.

"But you won't mind this change, I see. It need not be violent. Take hold of your new vocation leisurely. You may do well, if you can stan' it."

"Never fear me, sir. I have known what hard work is, ere this."

"Keep out of debt — do your best — and I will help you to get on, my lad," added his employer.

"Thank you, sir. I will bear your advice in remembrance. It isn't comfortable to be in debt, I know."

"In debt? It is to be in bedlam, boy! Never run into debt, while you can keep out of it, without starving."

"You never have occasion to purchase any thing, on time, I take it, sir."

"Never. My farm has no mortgage or lien on it. My live stock is my own, paid for, when delivered. I owe no man any thing, and never will. When I increase my possessions in any way, I buy for cash. I sleep the sounder, lad, and feel the freer to move about whither and as I will, in consequence. But here we are. Come in."

They had reached the country store, which they entered, and Morris selected a ready-made suit of stout satinet, a good pair of deming overalls, a thin jacket, a cheap straw summer hat, a heavy pair of working brogans, and old Blount paid the bill — fifteen dollars, for the lot.

The sack the lad had on cost him eighteen dollars, alone — in Boston. He smiled, remarked that this was an economical beginning, at any rate, and together proprietor and man returned to the farm.

Next morning, bright and early, Morris was up and out in the stables, seeing to the feeding of the cattle.

"Are you a good milker?" inquired the old man, coming into the great cow-barn, a moment after the lad made his appearance there.

"I used to be, sir. But I haven't touched a cow's udder for three years."

"Try this heifer, then. She's a little oneasy — an' frisky like. But it's a good chance to ascertain what you can do, in this line," said old Blount, who rather expected to see the young cit kicked across the barn floor, before he got through with his attempt upon this balky young animal, who threw her head up, and ears forward, as the cleanly-dressed stranger approached her, cautiously, milk-pail in hand.

"She's an Ayrshire," said Morris, looking in her bright clear handsome face. "And a good 'un, too."

"That's so," returned Blount. "Look out for her, now. She's quicker'n a colt; an' she'll give you her horn or heel, afore you can say 'Jack Robi'son,' my lad — if she don't take to you."

The young man went straight up in front of the spunky beast, placed his hand gently upon her muzzle, stroked her face, talked to her as he would have done with a coy cosset, and in five minutes' time had her as completely under his pleasant influence as if he had known the heifer all her life.

Then, smoothing back her silky coated sides, he stooped and commenced to draw her udder, carefully and gently — succeeding in clearing her milk-bag, and filling the pail, while the hitherto mischievous witch stood calmly submitting to the handy manipulation of the late broker's clerk, as if she rather enjoyed his skilful handling and kindly treatment; to the astonishment of old Blount, and the admiration of the other two men, both of whom had had a vast deal of trouble, previously, with what they called this " vicious young wench."

" Well done, my lad," exclaimed Blount. " You *can* milk a cow, that's a fact."

"No trouble with *her*, at all events," said Morris, triumphantly. " I'll soon get my hand in, again. I used to be clever among cattle, when I was a boy. I like 'em. But you can't abuse an Ayrshire, or an Alderney. They're high-strung, in the blood, sir. I know 'em."

From that morning, old Blount put Morris Deans in charge of his splendid herd of milkers; and with this little performance, commenced his new experience at Sunnyside farm.

" Morris Deans is the handsomest young man that ever came into this town, mother," said Eunice Blount, that forenoon, as the old lady and pretty daughter sat together in the great keeping-room.

" Handsome *is* that handsome *does*, my dear," returned the mother, looking up from her sewing, at her child's animated expression, as she uttered this compliment for the new-comer.

"Oh, I know that, mother. But isn't he a nice looking young fellow."

"He comes from the town — where he has been well bred, no doubt. And his appearance is greatly in his favor."

"Father would never have brought him here, if he hadn't known something about him, of course. But he don't look much like a farmer, as you say, that's a fact."

"I can remember when your father was as nice looking a young man as Morris is, Eunice."

"As genteel, mother?"

"Quite, my dear!"

"Ah, you think so, mother."

"I know so, deary."

"Then father Blount was a very handsome young man, to be sure."

"So he was. He is forty-eight years old, *now*, Eunice."

"*Then* he was twenty — eh, mother?"

"Yes. That is Morris's age, to-day, I hear."

"And I am twenty-one — mother."

"Yes, deary. Older than this young man is. What of it, Eunice?"

"Oh — nothing — nothing," returned the girl, softly, as she turned aside, and resumed her work upon the sampler she was busy in embroidering.

"You have dropped a stitch in your work, Eunice," observed Mrs. Blount, leaning forward towards her daughter. "Two! Two stitches — there. Do you see?"

"So I have, mother," returned Eunice, coloring up a little.

"Pick them up, and be more careful, then. You'll spoil your pattern. Here comes father."

The old farmer entered to take his early lunch, at this moment.

"That lad's a trump," he said, to his wife, as he laid his slouched hat upon the sideboard edge.

"Who, father?"

"Young Morris. Smart as a steel trap, and as vigorous as a two-year-old stag. We'll make a man of *him*, I can tell you," continued the old gentleman, briskly. "He don't look it, but he knows a heap more'n the average of young farmer-lads that I have ever encountered."

"He is city raised, though, you said?" queried Mrs. B.

"Only partially. Morris was brought up to farming on the Cape, until three or four years since, and he hasn't forgot his early training, I can tell you. He's got a little town-polish on, by being in a State Street broker's office, o' late. But this'll soon rub off, and he will turn out a right good hand for us, I've no doubt."

And so he did — to be sure.

CHAPTER VI.

HOW MORRIS MADE, AND SAVED IT.

The good-humored proprietor of Sunnyside was deservedly beloved by his neighbors, and he was considered among his acquaintances quite an oracle.

His opinions were respected, and he was relied upon by those who knew him best, for the plain reason that he was devoid of cant or pretension, and his honesty and thrift had both long been proverbial, in the region round about Brandville.

He was variously known among the people as, "good old Blount," "farmer Blount," or as "Uncle Blount," among the children of the neighborhood.

The little ones never 'teased' him, and he loved their merry society, though he had but a single child he called his own — Miss Eunice — now grown up to blooming womanhood.

Whenever "uncle Blount" returned from market, where he frequently went to the shire town of the County with his load of vegetables, lambs, calves, or what-not, (for he attended to this duty himself, personally, many years,) his wagon or hay-cart would be crowded with the lads and lasses of the village, whom he brought back from school, or picked up on the road. And he enjoyed their noisy rollicking pleasure and antics right earnestly, old as he was.

In haying-time, when the cart was heaped up with its two-horse load of new-made hay, on its way to the barn from the fields, old Uncle Blount had his bevy of boys and girls upon the top of it, snuggled down among the sweet odored Timothy and clover, as regularly as he went and came, during the early harvest-season.

"Look out, now, little ones!" he would cry, in cautionary tones, as the lively nags went down the long steep hill, towards the farm-houses, with the heavily heaped-up hay-load, upon the top of which were ensconced Tom, Dick, and Harry — with Jennie, Kate, and Posey.

"Look sharp now, babies! Don't tumble down and crack your crown. Steady! Whoa — there! Mind yer eye, ponies!" [See illustration, page 79.]

And away they rolled, homeward, with the boys yelling and clinging to his neck, and the girls shouting with laughter and fun, as Aunt *Chloé* the stalwart colored woman, in the centre of the group, hung on to the children, and screamed " Mine wot yer 'bout now, boys! Look out whar' yer g'wine — mass'r Bl'unt. Don't obertip us. Hi — yah! 'Ere we be — an' all right!" as the stalwart nags scrambled with their precious burthen in upon the shining clean barn-floor, at last, in safety.

Ah, those were jolly days at Sunnyside, indeed! Old Blount was never happier than when thus surrounded by the little folk, who loved him dearly; and for whom the steady old farmer had no cross words, no snarls, no churlishness, however madly they pranked, or rioted, in their innocent mirthfulness.

"They're seein' their best days," he would say. "Let 'em enjoy their brief happy childhood. I love 'em — and they love me. This last is much the best! They are the sweetest boon God gives us. Let 'em romp and scream. It does 'em good. Ah! what a poor world would this be indeed, without the smiling faces of these little men and women!" the kind old farmer would exclaim, as he encouraged the antics of his noisy tiny neighbors.

Morris Deans went straight along "upon an even keel," at Sunnyside. He was happy, contented, wellfed, had good pay, and really found that he was not called upon to work very hard — as he viewed it — after all.

He rose early, and applied himself assiduously to duty, all day long. This had been his habit from childhood. So this was therefore nothing new, or irksome.

Old Blount quickly ascertained that he could employ this young man to better account than by setting him to cut cord-wood! He was the best hand he had upon his place, among cattle and horses. He could accomplish more at any work he undertook to do, than any man employed by him. He was a splendid penman, and he could keep his accounts far neater and with better accuracy than he was able to do, himself.

Thus the lad came quickly to render himself very serviceable to Blount, who appreciated his talents, tact, and good disposition, deservedly.

By the time that the first fall harvesting came round, Morris had got to be quite at the head of affairs, out-of-doors, upon old Blount's farm.

He learned a little every day, too. He was a good student — for, he said to himself, shrewdly, " now is *my* opportunity, I fancy !" And so he studied, and read, and practised experiments upon the place, and among the stock.

All of which his employer smilingly approved, from time to time — for the lad was strangely successful in his little schemes and innovations, as he went along, and made them all turn in a goodly revenue for farmer Blount's benefit.

And meanwhile Morris had profited and was constantly improving his mind largely, through the timely advice and suggestions which the experienced farmer and stock-raiser made to his young friend, as they toiled, or rode, or walked, and chatted, in the fields or at their leisure at home.

"It isn't a difficult thing, Morris, to *make* money," said Blount, one day as they sat conversing upon business matters, practically.

"That is, I mean to say that it is not hard *merely* to "make money." Anybody can do this, who possesses ordinary common sense, and who is willing to work for it."

"But all of these people don't get rich, nevertheless, sir."

"No. And that was what I was just about to explain, my lad."

"It is easy to make it — but it is so difficult to *save* it, after it is acquired. I have somewhere read that the Baron Rothschild asserts, though it requires a deal of boldness and caution to make a fortune, when you've got it it requires ten times as much good wit to save, or keep it. I think the great banker is right, Morris."

"I hope I may one day have a competency," returned Morris, "of my own, to try the experiment with! I reckon I shall be able to keep it, if I ever chance to get it."

"A competency, eh? Well, Morris — what is that?"

"Enough. Sufficient."

"For what purpose?"

"For my needs, sir."

"Ah, yes. That would, in your view, be 'enough' — eh?"

"Enough is as good as a feast, sir. Nobody wants more than *enough*, I suppose?"

"Ah, you s'pose — eh? Now, tell me, lad. Did you ever happen to know any one who had 'enough'?"

"Well, sir. Speaking for myself, I never had any thing. So I can only speak of others."

"Exactly. That is my question."

"Well, sir — I don't call to mind any particular individual, at this moment —" continued Morris, thoughtfully, "upon whom I can place my finger — who — was absolutely satisfied —"

"Precisely, my boy. That is it. You don't find any such men, in this world. *Nobody* has really enough."

"I guess you are right, sir — from your stand-point."

"Guess I am? I know I am. Let me call to your notice a trite illustration, lad. And this is *true*, the whole world over. You have heard this story. It is not new, but it will bear retelling: —

"A man of wealth had grand possessions, and was measurably satisfied with his fortune. He saw around him many who envied him, who were well-to-do, but not so rich as he.

"'None are content with the lot which Fortune bestows upon them — be it great or small,' he said. 'There is no man who has *enough*, whatever may be his accumulations!'

"And at once he went to work to prove his assumed position, for his own gratification. He sent for a painter, and ordered him to put these words conspicuously upon a large sign-board: —

THIS FINE ESTATE, FREE FROM
ENCUMBRANCE, WILL BE GIVEN AWAY
BY THE OWNER, TO THE HAPPY MAN
CONTENTED WITH HIS LOT,
WHO POSSESSES ENOUGH. WHO TAKES IT?

"This sign was placed upon a pole, and displayed by the road-side, in front of the rich man's door.

"Everybody who passed, stopped to read this seemingly unselfish but eccentric proposition. The poor man growled, and went by. The well-to-do smiled, and said 'it is a good jest.' The rich, but grasping, noted it and exclaimed 'he is mad — he wouldn't do this foolish thing.'

"And then a canting avaricious neighbor came, and claimed the estate; for, he affirmed, "I am content with *my* fortune: I have enough, thank Heaven! So, give me the title-deed."

"Are you sincere?" demanded the rich man.

"Indeed I am."

"You are contented with your lot?"

"I am, sir."

"And you have *enough?*"

"Yes," said the pretender.

"In fortune's name, then, what do *you* want of my estate?" demanded the nabob. "Get away with you."

Morris smiled, and 'saw the point,' he said.

"No, my lad. We none of us have ever reached that happy condition where we think we have enough."

"I should call enough — say twenty thousand dollars that I could count my own," asserted Morris, confidently.

"This is the height, then, of your aspirations — eh, Morris?"

"It is, just *now*, sir."

"Then you have changed your mind, perhaps, upon this point?"

"Well, sir — I used to think that if I ever counted up *ten* thousand dollars, of my own, I should be content with it."

"Now you think twenty thousand?"

"Twenty — yes, sir."

"So you perceive even *you* are not content! Ten isn't enough.' So would not twenty be, my lad."

"I trust I may live to see the ten thousand," said Deans, cheerfully, "notwithstanding."

"Well, you are doing very well, lad. Go on. Earn — save — and KEEP. That is the secret. It isn't the acquiring simply. When you get it, *keep* it."

"Thank you, sir — I am listening," returned the young man, dutifully.

"What is your age, Morris?"

"Twenty, come Christmas, sir."

"You will then have been at Sunnyside, if we live, eight months."

"Exactly, sir."

"It isn't far away. The fall work is nigh concluded. You are out of debt, I hope?"

"O, yes sir — long ago."

"And you have some money in the Savings Bank, I know."

"Thanks to your generosity — yes sir. But not much."

"How much, then?"

"Less than a hundred dollars, sir. But, with the wages you have paid me, and the little opportunities you have allowed me to make a few dollars, otherwise, from the fancy poultry and cosset lambs I have raised, I shall be able to add another hundred to this, by New Year's."

"Good. From that time, I will increase your pay, Morris, to thirty dollars a month, in cash, for the coming year."

"Thank you, sir. I will endeavor to deserve your favor," returned the lad, gratefully.

"Next year you shall have all you can make from the sale of your fowls and lambs, too."

"Thanks, sir."

"And now, let me tell you another little story, upon the subject we sat down to talk about, my lad," continued Blount.

"I was raised a farmer, Morris. I served seven years — after I left school, at near fourteen — under a hard master, but an honest man.

"He paid me less than half the wages you are earning, now; but he instilled into my young mind, through constant urgent advice, what was ten times over of more value to me than the mere money he grudgingly allowed me. *He* taught me the "hidden art" that I have striven to impart to you, my lad: to wit, how to make and save money."

"I am listening, sir."

"When I was twenty-one years old, I struck out for myself. I had in bank eight hundred dollars. This I had saved — in seven long years of straight hard toil."

"A little fortune, sir!"

"A very little one. But I bought, with this — and paid for it, remember, cash on the nail — the piece of ground lying yonder, by the brook, some sixteen acres."

"This was long ago, sir?"

"Yes. Almost thirty years. I went to work in earnest, then, bought two or three head of cattle, half a dozen sheep, a flock of poultry, built the little shanty you see under the brow of the hill — which aunt Chloé occupies now — and paid for every thing, as I went along. I made a few hundred dollars, and *saved* it, in the next three years."

"A bachelor?"

"Yes. You shall see. Then I bought — and paid for — this piece of upland, on our right. This gave me twenty acres more. Land was then high, in this region, at five-and-twenty dollars the acre. Two years afterwards, I owned the thirty acres on our left. And all was paid for."

"You were making money, sir."

"So I was. But slowly, yet. Next year, I married the daughter of the builder of this house. The old man died. His farm was mortgaged. I bought it at the subsequent foreclosure sale, and paid for it, mind you. My wife proved a prudent careful frugal woman. We went on happily, together — and Eunice came to bless us.

"My live stock increased. I have raised hundreds of fine cattle, good horses, and sheep here. I still bought land, adjoining me on either side — and always paid for it, when I bought it. To-day I have got two hundred and thirty acres in as good a farm as stands out of doors, beneath the sun. And it's *mine*, lad. My own. I began with not a thousand dollars in cash, earned with my own hands, less than thirty years ago. You couldn't buy "Sunnyside" for one hundred thousand dollars in gold, to-day, lad — if I wanted to sell it — which I don't."

"It is a nice place, sir."

"I earned, it boy. No speculating, no dodges, no dwarf pear-tree or tulip-humbugs, no indolence, no rum, no cheatery — brought me up to where I stand, now."

"No doubt of that, sir."

"At twenty, Morris, you will have two hundred dollars, you say — in hand?"

"Yes, sir."

"You have heard my proposals, for next year?"

"I have, sir."

"You accept?"

"With gratitude."

"It is simply your due — this increase, Morris. At twenty-one years old, *you* may have at command fully eight hundred dollars, in cash, if you follow my suggestions. Get it, and save it."

"I appreciate this advice."

"You have begun aright, lad. And you will make your fortune, if you go on steadily, and persistently. Thus *only* can you make money — in reality."

"I value your good counsel, sir."

"Over and above all, Morris," added Blount, seriously, "we should bear in mind what is the true enjoyment of the good that God provides us with. It is easy to get, but not so easy to save and keep it. It is harder still to learn how to enjoy it, wisely and rationally.

"The greatest enemy in life is over-indulgence, in one form or another. The lowering of the true standard perils the length of the course. We should be industrious, enterprising, and ambitious; but withal, we should be prudent, sound in judgment, and always firm in our self-control. To the absolute command of one's appetites, he owes his average length of days, yet not this continuity alone. But that which gives our lives the power to enjoy, and which makes our increased and increasing existence worthy of being called "a lease of life," and not a simple dull drowsy stupor — my lad.

"In whatever we do, we should be zealous to "act *well* our part; there all the honor lies." A good German writer embodies a life's lesson in a few words, when he tells us that "art is long, life is short, good judgment difficult, and opportunity fleeting."

"To act is easy. To think well, is more difficult. To act according to our thoughts and promptings, always, is troublesome. All beginnings are agreeable, since the threshold is the place of expectation. The boy is astonished. His impressions guide him. He learns, as he plays. Earnestness comes upon him by surprise.

"The *spirit* in which we act, is the chief matter of

Uncle Philip would set the darkey child in his high chair, beneath the vines, and with his violin recall past hours. [Chap. vi. p. 110.

consequence. Action can only be understood and represented by the spirit. No one knows what he is doing, while he acts *rightly*. Of what is wrong, however, he will always be conscious. The true student learns from the known to unfold the unknown — and by degrees he gradually comes to be the master," concluded Blount, as they separated.

The hut across the fields, upon the first lot of land he purchased years previously, and to which Blount called the attention of Morris, was occupied by Aunt Chloé and her little negro family.

Her husband worked upon the farm when he was able, but he had been an invalid for a year or two, from an injury he encountered through a fall. Uncle Phillip, her father — a fine looking white haired old negro, tilled the garden-patch near the shanty, for their benefit, a privilege allowed them by farmer Blount without rental in consideration of the old negro's former services on the place.

The colored family thus dwelt " under their own vine and fig-tree," virtually. But Uncle Phillip had got past toiling very hard, for he was over seventy years of age — and his daughter, who did good service daily at the farm-house, earned sufficient to keep them all quite comfortable, in their small way.

Chloé's baby was this old gran'ther's pet, and while she was away about her work up at the mansion, the care of the little one was frequently left to Uncle Phillip — who took great pleasure in amusing and looking after this sable young 'un.

It required little to gratify the old man, now! In his younger years, Uncle Phillip had been quite an artist with the violin — for those days — and many a village dance had been enjoyed by the rustics, with darkey Phillip as chief fiddler. But he had long since laid down de shovel an' de hoe, so far as any very hard work went; and, for the most part, he had hung up de fiddle an' de bow, too — except when he occasionally took the latter in hand for his own recreation, or to please the round-headed pickaninny that called Chloé " mam'."

Sometimes he would set this darkey child in his high chair, beneath the vines in the shadow of the hut, and with his old violin in hand, for himself and the baby he would recall past hours — and realize " that simple pleasure which in memory lives, and unto age or childhood equal pleasure gives."

Occasionally a Yankee neighbor would halt at the hut, or the passing drover would seat himself for a few minutes' rest, as he was going by with his flocks or herd to market; for everybody knew the gray headed old darkey, and respected him for his rare good character and genial habits.

Poor old Uncle Phillip! He was a kindhearted sterling man — and long since went " where all the good darkies go," when they quit this sphere of toil and trouble! A likeness of the good old pilgrim, who for the nonce calls up the memory of " the days long past and gone," while he strikes the bump of harmony in the youngster darkey's cranium, until it thrills the young un's little great toe — will be found facing page 106.

The next year, (after Morris and Blount had had this talk,) opened prosperously. Young Deans did not forget his employer's earnest suggestions, and he carried out his proposed plans, to the letter.

The following summer, the young man had accumulated over three hundred dollars more, which he added to his previous Christmas two hundred, in the Savings Bank.

He sold more lambs of his own raising, a two-year-old colt, whose life *he* had saved, after he had been left to die with colic, (and which old Blunt gave him, outright), more fancy fowls — and he saved the bulk of his wages.

The interest on his little accumulations amounted to something. He husbanded every thing, for himself and for his employer. He worked hard, earnestly, duteously, and cheerfully.

His health continued excellent. He grew in stature and comeliness. And at twenty-one, Morris Deans had sixteen hundred dollars in cash, that he had *earned* with his own honest hands and intelligent brain.

"Twice as much as *I* had, Morris, at your age," said the old man, kindly.

"I have followed your advice, sir —"

"And you have won!"

"Thus much, sir; thanks to your kindness, and that of your excellent family."

"Now — what do you propose to do? You are 'your own man,' from to-day, lad."

"I intend to go right on, Mr. Blount, unless *you* desire a change," responded Morris.

"No! Remain. You shall name your own terms for the future, my lad. I can't well do without you, now. I am getting in years, boy. Fifty, next summer."

"You don't look it, then."

"Ah, well. Never mind."

Morris Deans did remain at Sunnyside. And, with his sixteen hundred good dollars, he 'went right on;' — where we will leave him, to learn what became of Fordham, Meyers, Ely, and the rest — since we have seen how the boy 'began to make and save money' among the fancy live stock on old Blount's farm.

CHAPTER VII.

A "BIG THING" FOR ELY HAWES.

How Frank Meyers made and used his earlier earnings, we have seen.

Born and reared in Boston, he had been bred in a retail dry-goods establishment there — to sell ribbons, tape, and domestics.

He was a whole-hearted, generous fellow — as we have shown — ready, when called on, to part with his watch, shirt-studs, or boots, if need be, to help a friend in adversity.

But he was quite as competent as the average salesman of his day, and as ambitious as the best of them; though, like a thousand others at the time of the panic, he was thrown out of business and could not get into position again, in the city where he had been educated.

So he took himself to New York — at a venture — where he hoped to find some opening, in which his good services and admirable talents might be appreciated.

With all Frank's kindness of disposition, and ready will to perform any gracious offices for those he esteemed —

with all his natural tact, and goodly rearing — he unfortunately lacked one valuable and important constituent in his composition, to wit, a business balance-wheel.

Frank could say "Yes," a hundred times in a week, if his friends and acquaintances asked his help, (when he had the ability to comply with their wishes for "a trifling loan," for example), but he never could say "No!"

He was always 'flush' — or appeared to be, in prosperous times — and he had hosts of borrowing friends who, naturally, had informed themselves touching this weakness of "clever Frank Meyers."

But the end came. The panic wound up his employers, and Frank went to the wall, for the time being, with the other unfortunates who were "thrown on their oars," if they happened to have any such handy implement to fall back upon.

Morris Deans had seasonably refunded the money Frank had advanced for his unpaid board-bill at the Widow Bean's. Ely Hawes had not been able to accomplish this little affair, conveniently, so promptly. But Ely was as honest as the sun, in his good intentions, and he too at last one day paid up. When he succeeded in maturing his invention, and had got his valuable patent out, for that same, he had calculated upon a harvest.

Meyers went to New York, after beating the bush thoroughly in Boston, and catching no bird. And there he encountered an agent in the Domestic Goods trade, largely connected with the leading cotton mills at Lowell, Manchester, and Lawrence.

This party desired the services of a *buyer* of domestics — who knew what this class of goods was; and he was aware that Frank had had good opportunity in previous years to make himself acquainted with these fabrics, thoroughly. Indeed, there were few young men in Boston, at that period, who really were so conversant with the styles and manufactures of the great New England factories.

Thus Frank stepped into a splendid position, almost directly on his arrival at the leading metropolis of the country, at a salary of four thousand dollars per annum. It was a god-send, to be sure! But Meyers was quite equal to the place proposed to him, and he entered upon his new duties with wondrous energy and corresponding success, as it eventuated.

But the city of New York is very unlike the city of Boston. The Boston-bred clerk (as a rule) is not the sort of man that gets on, always, in Gotham.

Some *do* — we admit. But more do not. And Frank Meyers chanced to be one of the former. So far as the satisfactory performance of his business duties was concerned, he filled the full measure of his employers' best anticipations. And so far as his knowledge of his business was involved, none could do better than he did, to the end.

But ———

Well, we will explain what happened to our friend Frank Meyers, the dry-goods clerk; how he made money — and lent it.

Frank had always been a money-lender, at home, in his small way. Not inconsiderable for *him*, however, because he contrived through one " friend " or another, to lend all he had, from time to time. And this was not a heavy surplus in the early days — in Boston.

When he got to New York, his salary was immediately increased sevenfold in amount, annually! What should he do with his money? he queried.

He had few acquaintances in Gotham, at first, and his funds accumulated on his hands, for he was addicted to no bad habits. He did not drink, or smoke, or gamble. But he was flush, again; and he was willing to do all the good he could — in his thoughtless way — for others, with his surplus means.

He had redeemed his Adams watch, he had paid every debt he owed in the world, and he had a thousand dollars over, in cash, at the end of eight months from the time he parted with Morris Deans and Ely Hawes, in New England.

Now he had located himself permanently in New York.

He frequently visited Boston however, in the way of business. He went to Lowell, to Nashua, to Manchester, etc., and purchased enormous quantities of cotton goods for his New York employers, to great advantage.

Still his money accumulated, for he had never enjoyed such a liberal salary before, and he couldn't (or didn't) expend a fourth part of his annual income of four thousand dollars, upon himself.

He sought out poor toiling anxious Ely Hawes, at length — during one of his Eastern visits, and the two former companions had a generous sit-down at Parker's, where Frank told his impoverished friend about the rare good success that had attended him, through the change he had made in quitting slow Boston, and locating in fast New York.

"Glad to hear of your good fortune, Frank," said Ely, sincerely. "You must be getting rich, too — as Morris Deans is. And it will not be many years before you will realize your former talked-of hopes, I suppose. Do you remember?"

"Ah, yes," returned Frank. "What was our mark?"

"A hundred thousand dollars, in gold," replied Ely, with a long-drawn sigh. "Egad! It's a good way off in the dim perspective for *me*, though, Frank. But you are really beginning to approach the goal of your anticipations, I judge."

"I am doing splendidly, Ely. I wish you were also on the high road to fortune. And I am rejoiced to know that our young friend Morris has made such a hit as I hear he has, with old Blount. He is a deserving good fellow."

"Yes. Deans is getting on finely, and the rich old farmer thinks there's nobody like the broker's lad he picked up in Boston, two or three years ago," continued Hawes. "He *saves* his money, though — as well as makes it. What do you do with yours, Frank?"

"Nothing, much. I bank it. And loan it "on call," sometimes. And I get round interest, too. But this is risky, I suppose. And I tell my brokers to keep an eye open to the paying securities that are being offered, nowadays. I'll make my pile, Ely. I'll have the hundred thousand, sure. But it isn't accomplished in a year — you know — or two, or three; except in especially fortunate instances."

"You are prospering, Frank."

"So I am, Ely. I know it. This year, my salary has been increased. Did I tell you?"

"No! How much?"

"Fifty per cent."

"Six thousand dollars a year?"

"Yes. Formerly, I thought six hundred good fair pay, in quiet steady Boston."

"I remember — yes. If I had but a sixth part of that income, Frank, I'd be a man of wealth in ten years' time, as sure as you live."

"How, my boy?"

"With my patent lock, of course."

"O yes. I recollect your hobby, Ely. You haven't given that over, yet — eh?"

"No, my dear fellow. And I never will. I shall win *my* fortune through this means. But the time has not yet come for *me*. It costs too much to put it through, you see."

"How much, Ely?"

"Eight or ten hundred dollars, at the least — to patent it and put it on the market. And it takes time, too. But I'll *do* it — be sure I will — sooner or later;" exclaimed persevering Ely Hawes, with emphasis.

"How much money have you got towards accomplishing this enterprise, to-day, Ely?"

"Not one third, as yet. But I have filed my caveat, got my first paper out, and the thing is all secured against infringement, for a few years. Meantime, I am pegging away — saving all I can from my moderate earnings — laying by a little, year by year — and by and by I'll have enough to take this bull by the horns. When I can get this lock of mine upon the market, and make it known, there's a good hundred thousand dollars in it, Frank, as sure as my name is Hawes."

"That's talking it right smartly, Ely."

"Just as I mean it."

"And you ought to know."

"I *do*, my boy."

"And you want only a thousand dollars to make every thing work smooth, and lovely?"

"Ah, that would be ample. But I must wait. I can afford it. I'm one o' the staying kind, as you know, Frank. But I'll creep up alongside o' my friends, after a while — be sure of it, old fellow."

"No doubt of it, Ely. But you ought not to remain *here* with it."

"Where — else, then?"

" New York is your field, my boy."

" No. Not at present."

" Why not ? "

" I can't afford it, Frank."

" But there is where you may find a customer, if you have really got what you think you have, my dear fellow."

" A customer? For what ? "

" For your patent."

" It isn't for sale, Frank."

" Not at a price ? "

" Well. Yes — of course."

" How much, for instance ? "

" A hundred thousand dollars, in gold. Not a dime less."

" Ah, I see. Yes. Well — I suppose you prefer a long price, and time to make it in — in lieu of a quick penny, shortly earned."

" It is worth that to *me* — in the end. That is my mark, and for that I am toiling, and shall continue to toil, until I achieve it, Frank."

" Come to New York, Ely. And I will help you to gain your object," said Meyers, kindly.

" Not now. No — thank you, Frank. O, I am getting on. It will all come out right, by and by. I am not impatient, but I am poor. I *know* what I have got, my boy. Come! We have dined sumptuously. Go with me to my rooms. I will show you my working model. It is completed — and in perfect condition. I cannot improve it. But I have not the means, as yet, to push it. So I must wait."

The two former associates went to Ely's cosey lodgings at once, and the young inventor exhibited his achievement with glowing pride to his friend — which he briefly described.

Frank saw a square dummy safe standing in the centre of Ely's apartment, and Hawes thus expatiated upon the hobby of his life. It was of wood, painted dead black, in imitation of the real thing — and the lock was attached, in form, upon the inner side.

"I call my invention the "Impenetrable Bank-Safe Lock," said Ely. "The original device is upon this imitation safe, which is now closed, as you see."

"Where?" asked Frank, walking around the square box, each and all sides of which were precisely alike, outwardly.

The machinist smiled.

"That is what I want you to ascertain, my friend! You are supposed now to be a lock-picker — an expert — a burglar, or whatever you please. Now, get into that safe. It is secured with my new lock. I undertake to say that it is just what I have named it. A bank or counting-house safe fastened with this lock of mine, is simply *impenetrable* to burglars. You can't get into it — without *my* key; and only then, with a knowledge of *my* secret mode of opening it."

"Where is the door handle?"

"There is no handle."

"How the deuse can I see where to begin, then?"

"You can't, my boy!"

"Open the door, then — and let me see the lock, Ely."

Hawes passed around the rear of the dummy, touched a concealed spring, and the outer casing flew open, of itself.

"That is very well," observed Meyers.

"Now proceed," returned Ely.

Frank sought for the lock described.

"What is the matter?" asked his friend.

"Nothing," said Frank.

"Go on, then, my dear fellow."

"This is a sell, Ely — eh?"

"Not at all. It is right before you."

"But I don't see it, nevertheless."

The inventor smiled, again.

"It is a wheel within a wheel, Frank."

"A lock within a lock, you mean?"

"Well — yes. If you choose to call it so," returned Ely, amused at his companion's remark. "But it is all there."

"Very good," exclaimed Frank. "Now, where *is* the lock?"

"Here, before you," returned Ely. "And here is the key. Now oblige me. Unlock that safe, my good fellow."

"You call this a *key?*"

"That is the key to my secret lock, Frank."

"But it is simply a knob — and it turns round and round, interminably," said Meyers, working it about.

"I know it. That is a part of the patent combination I have invented. And you may turn it round, till doomsday. Until you have the secret, you can't unlock it. Try it on, Frank. Turn away."

Meyers did so — but made no progress, whatever.

"Now — let me help you," said Ely. "And I will do just what you have already done, precisely, as you shall see. But probably with a different result."

Ely stooped forward, took the knob in his hand, and turned it round, as Frank had done.

The same click-click followed the motions of his fingers as had occurred with Meyers. And suddenly the inventor drew upon the handle, and the interior of the safe was exposed to view.

"That's a big thing," observed Frank, delighted. "How'd you do it, Ely?"

"That is my patent, my dear fellow!"

"But it appears a very simple thing to do, though."

"So it is — when you know how it is done, Frank."

And with these words, Ely closed the safe-door again.

"Now, Frank, I have shown you how to do it. You have seen how I did it, and you mustn't expose my secret, you know. There! Open it, now, please?"

Frank turned the knob again — pulled it forward with all his strength, turned it back, twisted it, and tugged at it fiercely, — but made no headway. And he gave it up.

"It is very simple," said Ely, ironically. "Why don't you open it, my dear boy?"

"Ah, I am not a professional burglar, Ely. I make no pretensions to skill as an expert in this kind of operation."

"Of course not. But anybody can manage it, as soon as he knows how, I tell you. A child could open it, with the true key to the lock."

"Sleight o' hand — eh?"

"Oh, no. Simplicity itself. In this consists its beauty, as well as its utility."

"It could be blown open, with gunpowder, though?" suggested Meyers.

"Could it? Here is half a pound o' powder, my boy. This very objection to its probable security against a desperate thief, has been suggested before. Let's see you 'blow' it open."

"I shall destroy your machine, Ely."

"That's exactly what I would like you — or any other man, thus inclined — to do! What is a safe-lock good for, my dear fellow, if it can be blown open with a charge of powder, pray? Go ahead, now."

"Give me a match, then."

"Here is something better, Frank. The finest effective wire-fuse manufactured. Now!"

Meyers went to work, with a will — and said he could do it. But, in spite of his earnest efforts, there was neither seam, cavity, hole, opening, or vacuum visible — into which he could force the point of a fine cambric needle!

The smallest grain of powder could not be pricked in, around, above, below, or beside the lock.

"If you will observe," continued Ely, "this arrangement is but the outside of the inside. Within *this* casing, the principle is duplicated. Thus the lock, and safeguard is double. The cases are to be of steel plate, and only by cutting through the sides of the safe, could powder be introduced. This would blow open a safe, I understand; but it would not affect the security of the *lock* — while such a process requires time, and is attended with a deal of noise, in exploding, you know."

"I see — yes."

"Now! How will you blow out that lock, Frank?" demanded Ely, triumphantly. "How will you insert any powder?"

"It is well named, my boy. It is impossible to penetrate it," rejoined Meyers.

"Of course it is. Otherwise, it would in this respect be a failure."

"Well, it is a good thing, Ely."

"I know it, Frank. I always told you I had it here, my boy," continued Ely, tapping his forehead, in the old way.

"Now what do you say to my 'Patent Impenetrable Bank Safe Lock,' Frank?"

"You've got a fortune in it, Hawes — as sure as we are here, to-day," returned Meyers.

"Now, then. The tumblers of this lock are self-acting, or independent of the levers — and the barrel or cylinder supports the rotary motion," began Ely.

"Well, all that is Greek to *me*, Ely. I don't know a lock-tumbler from a segment of a stove-pipe, you see," responded Frank. "I can tell you how many threads a yard-wide Manchester print of ordinary weight requires, to make it presentable, or how many go to fill a three-quarters width Lawrence Mills cambric — of any given fineness. But these mechanical technicalities of yours would simply make me sick at the stomach. You've got a *good* thing here. That I can see — provided it be original in design."

"Have you ever seen any thing like it?"

"No—I haven't, Ely."

"Nor I. It is novel, practical, ingenious, and impenetrable, my boy."

"And you have got your hundred thousand dollars in it then, as you say — in time, Ely."

"I hope so, Frank."

"Come to New York with it; and I will aid you to put it in the market," insisted Meyers.

"Perhaps I may do so," returned Ely at last — as the two friends finally separated.

CHAPTER VIII.

HOW FRANK MEYERS MADE, AND LENT IT.

Frank Meyers went back to New York city, deeply impressed with the conviction that plain plodding quiet Ely Hawes was a genius.

"That boy is a trump," said Frank. "He has been delving, and studying, and struggling with that invention of his, for years and years; working from hand to mouth as he went — pinching himself for the comforts of life — and persevering in his chosen purpose, with wonderful tenacity — until he's *got* it, now, as I'm a sinner!"

"How true it is," he continued, mentally, "that the great inventor after all is he who has walked forth upon the industrial world — not from the college, but from the hovel, comparatively. Not clothed in fine broadcloth and decorated with honors, but clad in homespun or fustian, and grimed with soot, dust, and oil.

"Here is a poor unknown young man, that seven out of ten who have watched his course, hitherto, would set down as being a very fanatic, or a hair-brained idiot, at the least. But, during all these days, he has been simply laying up material in his busy brain. And now he has worked out this "patent lock" problem, that will prove the means, unquestionably, to lead him on to a fortune such as may hardly be calculated to-day, in magnitude. Bravo, good honest Ely Hawes! You shall not want for the means to prosecute your scheme to eventual success, if the paltry sum of a thousand dollars only is required to push it to a climax."

Frank had his own little plan in his head, already, for Ely's relief. He would liked to have had his old friend with him in New York, where he could advise and consult with him. But upon his arrival there, he determined to write to Ely, and place the sum he needed to get his patent out, at once at his disposal.

Within a month from the time they parted, (after Meyers had seen the new invention,) Ely was taken quite aback, one morning, to receive by mail from New York a mysterious looking envelope thus addressed : —

To Ely Hawes, Esq.,
    Inventor of the Patent
      "Impenetrable Bank Safe Lock,"
        Boston, Mass

He opened this missive with a nervous hand, and read the following lines, after noting its bright **clean** enclosure :

"*Ely, my Dear Boy* — Enclosed find draft on Merchant's Bank, Boston, for One Thousand Dollars. I want you to use it forthwith, towards the prosecution of your *patent* matter. I know you didn't ask for it, mind. That is my affair. I've got it, you need it; and it will come round all right. Take it — and if you want another thousand, say so. I've got that, too — and it is at your service, any day. If you can repay it, all right. If not — ditto. Don't be afraid of it. When you get your 'hundred thousand,' you know, you can return it. And I shall be the happiest fellow alive to remember that it was in my power to aid you. What are friends good for, Ely, if you can't use them, in need? Go ahead with your new lock, now. I tell you you've got a big thing. And believe me always — money, or no money — Yours truly, FRANK MEYERS."

Ely Hawes was not given to the melting mood, very often. But upon finishing this generously worded epistle, and glancing again at the munificent draft before him, tears of profound gratitude rolled down his cheeks, and he thought he never before knew what true friendship was.

"Ah, my dear Frank," he murmured to himself, "you can never know how I appreciate *this* timely favor, indeed!"

Ely immediately replied to his friend's letter, thanked him in downright good earnest, expressed his utter surprise at this generously conceived act, and sent him his note on demand for the thousand dollars, with interest; to be retained by Meyers, as the sole condition of his acceptance of this favor.

Then he resolved to proceed at once to Washington, in person, to obtain his Letters Patent for the lock; and then he would begin to count upon his future fortune, he thought.

Frank Meyers had been doing this same kind of thing (in a smaller way,) all his life. He had rarely lost money by this usage — strange to say. But whenever he had cash in hand, he was noted for his willingness to help those of his friends who happened to be 'short.'

In this way, and through this careless means, he did many real favors. But this chronic affection in his constitutional make-up, while in spirit one of the best, was the worst feature in his composition, in a business view. He was always happy in being able to say 'yes' — and he never could bring his lips to utter 'no,' if he had the means in his possession through which another could be aided, or relieved, pecuniarily.

Thus Frank lacked the money-making balance-wheel alluded to in his case. And thus he did not flourish, as he *ought* to have done, with his generous income; which might have been saved, to his own credit, betimes.

Contingent upon this weakness in Frank's character, was his strange credulousness. He was fain to believe all men honest and truthful, because he had been so himself, from boyhood. And before he had been a resident in New York city two years, there were those who had measured him, and found him easily induced to enter into their little schemes, where ready cash was needed to help along their ventures.

Still, Frank Meyers was no man's fool. He was liberal, and careless in the use of his money perhaps, at times; but he was nevertheless keen in his perceptions, and knew a hawk from a handsaw, every time.

He had learned to demand security upon his open business loans. If he lent an acquaintance or a companion a hundred dollars, to accommodate him temporarily, he did it in the way of friendship. "If it comes back," he would say, "all right. I have not injured myself, and I have helped a poor fellow in need. If I lose it, altogether — the loss is mine, in purse — but I have the satisfaction of knowing I have performed a good act, unselfishly, and that is sufficient, for this occasion."

In course of time, as is not an unusual thing, there, the New York sharpers got hold of simple-hearted Frank Meyers, from Boston.

After three or four years' service in the great house he purchased cotton goods for, at so generous a salary, it became known, through his small brokers in Wall Street, that this young man had money 'lying around loose.'

Frank accumulated — notwithstanding his easy way of doing business for himself — in about four years, some fourteen thousand dollars, in cash. He was going along, swimmingly.

He had loaned and re-loaned this money, from year to year, and it had paid him handsomely, at a fair current rate of interest for his style of accommodation. He had never speculated. This was not his forte. But he was desirous to make money. And he accomplished this.

He kept steadily at work, however, and as fast as his means increased, he made new loans, and added rightfully to his gains.

At the beginning of his fifth year, his salary was again advanced — for he proved himself immensely valuable to the cotton-buying house. And no man's judgment excelled that of active, shrewd, well educated Frank Meyers.

And so — with fourteen thousand dollars at good interest, at the beginning of his fifth year in New York, and a prospective salary thereafter of eight thousand dollars per annum, Frank felt quite at his ease, and hopeful as to his future.

Thus he quietly argued his case.

"My invested funds already bring me in over a thousand a year, at this time. I can live as I wish to, upon that sum. Eight thousand — from my future salary, then — is so much clear gain. Eight thousand per annum in principal, amounts in five years to forty thousand dollars. I will invest this, quarterly; two thousand dollars replaced, every three months, will give me returns equal to eight thousand more yearly, to be put at interest, after the first quarter. This sum, annually added to the other, will in five years give me an invested capital of nearly sixty thousand dollars — at ordinary rates, upon good security. At better interest, *more*. The accumulations upon this forty thousand hereafter, in five years should reach at least eight thousand more. My hoped-for hundred thousand dollars is not so far off in the distance — after all. In ten years from the day I left old Massachusetts, I shall have earned it. Then I will go back there, and end my days in the enjoyment of my *otium cum dignitate*, if I live. And if I die — I shall not want it."

Thus sanguine Frank Meyers built his airy castle, and hopefully looked forward to the easy accomplishment of his purpose, within the next succeeding half a dozen years. And not without fair promise, from the outlook.

Frank had begun right. If he had gone on as he thus laid out his future plans in his fancy, all would have been well. And *he* would and could have been the master of his coveted hundred thousand dollars, in ten years from the beginning, as he had calculated.

But, as we have hinted, Mr. Frank Meyers of Boston fell among the Philistines of Wall Street, unexpectedly; that horde of cormorants, who like the warrior-steeds so readily " snuff the scent of the battle from afar," and who, once upon the trail, pursue their intended victim to the death, unless he chance to prove the longest-winded and the swiftest-footed in the chase!

Before the fifth year expired, Frank had twenty thousand dollars in the hands of his Wall Street brokers. And they had induced him, through flaring promises of brilliant success, to join them in a bout at stock speculation.

In this sort of enterprise, our ambitious young friend had never had the slightest experience. His money had hitherto been mostly loaned upon legitimate risks, accom panied with sound collaterals; and he had received but fair current returns, in the way of interest, with which he was satisfied.

But through the importunities of those who had served him at first to place these loans for three years and more, and the promise held out by them of a rapid increase in his gains, he assented to their proposals. And so placed within their control the twenty thousand dollars he had earned and saved, to "operate" with, for their joint profit.

At that early period — then 1843 or '4 — the palmy days of the Wall Street Stock Exchange had not come to be known, as in the later time. Still, millions in "transactions" occurred there every day, among the great or lesser commission brokers, who bandied the funds of their over-reliant patrons about, who furnished the cash means by way of 'margins,' or otherwise, for the bulls and bears to gamble with.

It was in this identical institution (then in its first stages of development,) where, but a few years later, the 'Napoleon' of Wall Street, Jacob Little, made and lost nine splendid fortunes, successively, in half that number of years. It was under the rule of this same management afterwards, that the Mac Vicker, the Jerome, the Drew, and the Travers slaughtered their scores and hundreds of innocent victims, without mercy or compunction!

And this was the bustling arena which the poor clerk Anthon Morse entered, at that same period — with his seven hundred dollars, only, in cash that he had earned and saved from his salary; and who for a few brief months, (in combination with Little and another Wall Street king,) cut such a dashing figure and so startled the money-broker-world, with his monstrous daring and prowess.

The curious rocket-like career of this youth was the most extraordinary upon the American financial record, in its mutability — and folly.

Anthon Morse was known only as a sharp accountant, who possessed the faculty of being able to add up at sight, correctly, four columns of figures at the same time, and as promptly as his compeers could add but one.

He went into Wall Street bent upon making a sudden fortune. He had just seven hundred dollars to his name; but he carried with him into the ring a clear head, a subtle will, a heart of courage, and a firm resolve to win. When he retired, he took away with him neither money nor brains, unfortunately!

Upon this paltry capital of less than one thousand dollars, Morse operated so skilfully that within six weeks he had in hand in gold upwards of one hundred thousand dollars — which he had made in stock speculation.

Did he keep it?

Yes — for the hour. And then he launched out, with frightful strides — and gained, enormously, upon this sum. In six months thereafter, he was the heaviest stock operator in Wall Street, beyond comparison. He bought and sold and gambled for millions.

The old heads stared, the younger men were astounded. Jacob Little himself was 'nowhere,' beside this bold young adventurer. And ere eight months had gone by, Morse had in hand seven *millions* of dollars in cash, stocks, and bonds!

Did he save this colossal fortune? Did he retire in season to enjoy this huge wealth, that had been literally poured into his lap, by the million? Was he really the shrewd, keen, able business man that everybody believed him to be?

No! There are certain people in this nether world fated to be fools. And he was one of these.

Before that year had closed, Morse had lost every dollar of his seven millions, and became a hopeless, helpless bankrupt. Within twelve months from the day *he* ventured into Wall Street, with his seven hundred hard-earned dollars, he went out again, seven hundred thousand dollars worse than nothing!

Frank Meyers had not then this example before him, or it might have proved a wholesome lesson to the ambitious dry-goods salesman. But this was an actual occurrence, which took place within the New York ring in Wall Street, but a few years after he tried this mode to acquire fortune unwittingly, through similar means.

We have thus shown, in this chapter, how Meyers "made and lent his money."

In the next, we will inform the reader how he succeeded in his subsequent plan; and how this young man improved the teachings he acquired in his experience.

CHAPTER IX.

FRANK LEARNS HOW NOT TO LOSE IT.

It was John Randolph, I think, who startled the House of Representatives one day in Congress, when he broke out with this text for his intended subsequent speech, on the Treasury appropriations bill;—" Mr. Speaker, I have found the philosopher's stone! *Pay as you go*"—added John. And then he halted to take breath.

Another recommendation as good as this, was the advice of Cornelius Vanderbilt, to a cloud of sufferers who gathered around him after the explosion, but who went in to win against him and Jay Gould, last year.

They had slipped up, with a heap of heavily depreciated stocks on their hands: " Never attempt to get rich, gentlemen, in a hurry. Take your time. If you had bought a hundred instead of a thousand shares, for a rise —you might have held on," said Vanderbilt, with a chuckle. The sly old fox had " unloaded " at high tide, himself!

Frank Meyers' twenty thousand dollars were in his brokers' hands, and they went into the market, 'flush.'

A great deal can be accomplished with twenty thousand dollars in cash, in buying and selling stocks upon the depositor's "margin."

The broker takes no risk, individually, in this game. He buys, or sells; and, as stocks go up or down, he takes his profits for his patron, or (out of *his* deposits) pays the losses that accrue upon the several operations, so long as the depositor's margin holds out.

Some men are constant gainers, in this traffic; but the mass, and the lesser capitalists especially, are the aggregate losers. A "corner" brought about by a Vanderbilt, a Drew, a Gould, or a Little, in any chosen fancy security, swamps all the small fry who are caught in this net.

And notwithstanding the oft-repeated warnings that are given, the victims still "go in," and are crippled or cleaned out by the more adroit heavy managers.

Meyers knew nothing of the modus operandi through which these affairs were manœuvred. He trusted his funds reliantly to his agents in Wall Street, and attended to his legitimate business, himself, with which he was thoroughly acquainted.

If his twenty thousand dollars could be manipulated to his better advantage, through the means proposed, he was inclined to accept the increased profit, and pay the brokers' commissions for doing the business and relieving him of responsibility beyond the sum he thus — at a venture — intrusted to their management, for the time being. But "I will pay as I go," he said, "and there will be no afterclap, whatever results."

The brokers bought "for a rise"—or said they did—and this was equivalent to the act; for no human being outside of the said operators' confidence, can successfully dispute this kind of statement on the part of your commissioned stock-broker.

They unfortunately purchased heavily at the top of the market, however — possibly *hoping* that the stock they invested in on this particular occasion would still go up. But it tumbled, on their hands, instead.

Next day it took another lurch, downward. A week afterwards, this first heavy purchase had depreciated six dollars and a half on the share — " with a downward tendency," at closing quotations, that day.

And they had bought a thousand shares of this stock, for account of the confident and pliable Frank Meyers, Esquire!

They trembled — but waited.

This had been hitherto a favorite in the market, and it would rally, undoubtedly — so they thought.

But it didn't.

After holding it ten days, they concluded to report progress, and see what Frank might propose, under these adverse circumstances.

"What did you say you purchased this stock at?" queried Meyers, with some concern in his expression.

"Seventy-nine," replied his agents.

"What is it worth?"

"It has touched eighty-six within thirty days, but fell.

And we stepped in at what we considered a safe figure, for a thousand shares, 79—" said his brokers.

"And now?"

"It is heavy at seventy-three."

"How much shrinkage is that, in ten days, gentlemen?"

"Six dollars and over, per share."

"Over six thousand dollars of my 'margin' gone up, then?"

"*Down*, if you please, sir."

"Yes. It has stepped down — and out — eh?" remarked Meyers, facetiously.

"Exactly."

"What is the prospect?"

"No one can say. We *thought* it would advance."

"It is not certain that it will remain steady even at 73, I presume?"

"No. But—"

"Sell it," said Frank, promptly.

"To-day?"

"At once. I had rather submit to a loss of six thousand five hundred dollars, than seven thousand five hundred. And do me the favor not to put *all* my eggs into one basket at a time, in the future, if you please, gentlemen. Good morning," said Frank, retiring.

This was short, but sweet.

"I don't know much about this kind of thing," muttered Frank to himself, as he mused over this unanticipated stroke, on his way back to his store, " but I think this, in money-making routine, is a very good way *not* to do it.

" Over six thousand dollars swamped, in ten days! One more such operation will break my financial back. And two speculations further, in *this* direction, will absorb every dollar of surplus funds I am master of.

" I was drawn into this. It is not my own choice of methods towards money-making. I know nothing about this contrivance. It is called 'respectable,' however. It certainly is not profitable — so far — to *me*."

Frank concluded that he would permit the brokers to go on. He was indisposed all at once to 'show the white feather.' In for a penny, in for the pound — he thought. We will see how they get on.

He still had fourteen thousand dollars in his brokers' hands. He was determined upon one thing: he would venture no *more* there.

" I can stand the loss of that twenty thousand dollars, and I will pay as I go — any how. I am out of debt — the money is my own — and my salary is eight thousand a year," he said.

" If they lose that sum, let it go. The test will be costly. But dear-bought experience, they say, is often the best we can procure.

" This will be dear enough to me, though — by the mass!" he continued. "Twenty thousand dollars. All I have earned in five years, and saved. A full fifth of the 'great expectations' I promised myself, a fortnight ago —

at the end of another five years, if I should live so long!"

He became anxious, for the first time in his life.

Three days afterwards, he called on his brokers again.

"Well," he said, quietly, upon entering their busy office. "How is the stock market?"

"Feverish, sir."

"Are you doing any thing?"

"For you? Yes. We bought two hundred shares day before yesterday for your account, and two hundred to-day of another. Both are rising."

"How much, so far?"

"Yesterday's purchase has advanced three dollars on a share, sir."

"Sell it," said Frank.

"To-day?"

"At once. A nimble sixpence you know is better than the slow shilling."

They sold it within the hour, at three dollars and a half advance. The other two hundred shares were sold within the week at five dollars per share advance. This gave Mr. Meyers nearly two thousand dollars profit; and swelled his deposit to sixteen thousand dollars, in his brokers' hands.

They bought for Meyers five hundred shares of another kind, at forty-one dollars — which went up slowly, in two weeks, to $43\frac{1}{2}$.

"Sell," insisted Meyers.

This gave him twelve hundred dollars more increase. And then he requested a statement of account, which was furnished him.

The balance to his credit was a trifle rising seventeen thousand dollars — over and above commissions, and charges.

"Your check, gentlemen, if you please, for this?" said Meyers, civilly.

They looked at their patron — smiled — and filled an order upon their bankers for the amount, without demur.

"No more for me," observed Frank, placidly. "I have seen *this* elephant! Three thousand dollars sunk, in six weeks. No more for *me*. I am cured. Good day, gentlemen."

Thus Mr. Frank Meyers ascertained how *not* to lose his money, for the future. It had cost him only three thousand dollars to learn this lesson — as it happened — and he thought he had escaped at a moderate figure.

So he had. It might have been seven times three thousand, or thereabouts, had he been the simpleton his brokers fancied him to be.

He took his seventeen thousand straight to his employers' bank, where he deposited it with about a thousand already there to his credit.

At the end of the next quarter, he added the two thousand received for his salary to the rest, and thus found himself the clear owner of twenty thousand dollars, once more.

Within a month he took a bottom mortgage upon a handsome brick block of four residences in twenty-fourth Street, New York — at six per cent interest, with this money.

He did not disturb that investment. And, five years subsequently, the property fell into his hands under foreclosure.

The four houses were then worth forty thousand dollars — and paid a ready rental of more than six per cent upon this value.

Frank Meyers never put a dollar into any species of speculation from the time he so narrowly escaped, on the occasion referred to. And, in the future, he went steadily forward in his career, as we shall learn, by and by.

Meantime, Ely had gone to Washington in pursuit of his papers securing him the Patent; for which he had long since filed his caveat, for early protection.

And we will leave Frank Meyers now, for a time, in the enjoyment of his income — pursuing his routine-duty as cotton-goods buyer for the New York house — while we learn how Ely Hawes the diligent mechanic got along with his admirable invention of the Bank-safe Lock.

CHAPTER X.

HOW BRAVE ELY HAWES FLOURISHED.

As soon after he found himself in possession of the thousand dollars which Frank Meyers had so kindly loaned him, as he could conveniently leave home, Ely Hawes turned his face towards Washington.

He had never yet seen the National Capitol, and had no clear idea what he was to do there, or what complications he would be called on to encounter in that city of politicians, strangers, charlatans, and humbugs.

He entertained a vague notion that the city of Washington was a kind of consecrated place — isolated from the outside world — and hemmed around with monumental memories, and the solemnest associations of the early days of our great and glorious American republic.

He procured a comely new suit of attire, and placing his safe-lock model in a neat black satchel which he suspended at his side, with hopeful animation Ely started for the Capitol, to procure Letters Patent for the pet invention upon which he had spent years of study, and which he now believed to be perfected, at last.

When he arrived there, the romance was very swiftly taken out of him. He found the national capital — in the John Tyler administration — a conglomeration of red mud, unpaved streets, seedy negroes, decayed old build-

ELY HAWES STARTS FOR WASHINGTON.

ings, indifferent public houses, idle bummers, villanous hacks, and general discomfort; where the charges for entertainment were exorbitant, the food second-rate, the water sickening, the air malarious, the foul canal (or river) putrid, and the weather 'hotter than Tophet,' to repeat his own mild way of putting it. But this was over thirty years ago. And Washington is changed, since then — somewhat!

One of the first individuals Ely met in Washington was a wandering native of that metropolis, whom he encountered not far from the Depôt where he landed — a Mr. Scrane.

This young man stood at the street corner, smoking, as Ely came along. Being a stranger at the capitol, the latter inquired the way to the Washington House, where he desired to halt.

Mr. Scrane was very civil. He was puffing away inordinately at a long cheap cigar. Near by him, sat a hammer-headed dingy gray dog, with a large black patch around his right eye. Hawes noticed this brute, but did not take a serious fancy to him. He was an ugly looking customer, and his master was not much more agreeable to look at.

This lively pair were waiting for "something to turn up," evidently. Ely shied the bull-dog, but civilly inquired the direction to the hotel he sought. The owner of the beast said "Yer needn't be afeered o' the dorg, sir. He don't meddle wi' nobuddy 'nless he's pick't on. Washint'n 'ouse? Yas. I'll take yer bag, an' show yer, sir. It's a good bit o' distance ter the Washingt'n 'ouse. This way, sir."

The accommodating corner-man took Ely's bag, without

further parley, and the two men moved on — the black-eyed gray bull-dog following his master's heels, closely, without invitation.

"'Ee's a werry good dorg, that," observed his owner. "I calls him 'Uncle Sam,' fer short, sir. 'Ee won't worrit nobody, ef 'ee's lef' alone — leastways ef 'ee hain't no-think ag'inst a pusson."

"He's a dreadful creature to look at," suggested Ely, putting it gently.

"We thinks 'ee's a 'ansome cretur, sir. Ther's on'y one man 'at that purp don't fancy, 'ere 'n Wash'ntun. That's Mr. Topley."

"Topley? Who is he?" asked Hawes, disposed to be social for the moment, though his eye was frequently turned anxiously towards the dreadful dog behind them.

"Mr. Topley? Wal, sir, I don't know edzactly. Nobody don't know Mr. Topley, I reck'n. Ee's a gen'le-man as comes ter Wash'ntun, and — an' *goes away ag'in.* That's about all we knows o' Mr. Topley."

"What does he do?"

"I railly don't know, sir."

"Is he in the Department?"

"O yas. That is — ee's in, an' out, an' up an' down, an' 'round, gen'ally. Nowheres 'n pertic'lar. They calls 'im 'a mysteer'ous man.' But the dorg don't like 'im — some'ow, an' I reck'n 'ee don't like the dorg," remarked Mr. Scrane, glancing down at the beast with the black eye and elongated under jaw. "But 'ere we are, sir!"

Arriving at the Hotel, this man accepted half a dollar for his services, and Hawes gladly got rid of owner and dog, without comment, as he entered and registered his address upon the hotel book.

Among the sights he saw in Washington, common at that period, Ely was especially struck with the represen-

OUR "CULLUD BROTHER,"   AND HIS "MASTER," IN 1840.

tative Southern colored man whom he met there, at every turn, as well as his then legal lord and "master;" the former poor, degraded and enslaved by American statute, but portly, talkative, ill-dressed and good-natured — while the latter was rich and well clad but lean, imperious, and constitutionally sour in aspect, in temper and intercourse. But this was anterior thirty years to "reconstruction."

Ely had conceived an indistinct impression that he had a colossal job before him, to procure his desired papers at the Patent Office. He did not know exactly why.

Other inventors had taken pains to din into his ears the most discouraging suggestions as to his probable future prospects, in this direction.

But he had hitherto charged all this volunteered advice and disheartening information to jealousy on the part of those who offered it; since he was aware that most of his gratuitous informants were, directly or indirectly, competitors in his line of invention.

He had a generously replenished purse, however, and a good square backer, too, in Frank Meyers — should he find himself getting short of funds.

He did not know what the cost of his present project would be — first and last — but he made up his mind that it would be expensive, as well as troublesome to accomplish. And he went to the capital prepared for all contingences, as he believed, determined to remain there until his work was consummated.

On the second morning after his arrival, he went straight for the Patent Office, hopefully.

He found a large building, where there were more rooms, and apartments, and "departments" in the pile, than he had ever before encountered under one roof in the whole course of his life. Big enough, he said, to answer the purposes of three huge hotels.

And every room was filled with servants, too — clerks, waiters, janitors, messengers, by the score; all busy as beavers, apparently, and each devoting himself to his work — such as it was — with remarkable outward show of assiduity.

So deeply engaged were those to whom he at first courteously introduced himself indeed, that he found it quite impossible to get either himself or his business taken the slightest notice of!

It was quite noon when he first presented himself at the office where he sought some initiatory information as to how he should proceed, and learn whom it was necessary he should apply to, in form, for particulars of the requisite mode of procedure in his case.

A pot-bellied man — Mr. Julius Puffborl — who appeared to be in the last stages of dropsical inflation, from his extreme obesity, informed the stranger in wheezing accents that he'd " better try nummer vifteen, on the zecond vloor, vust ; *he* could put him on the right drack," he reckoned.

And Ely sought out room fifteen, upon the second floor, accordingly.

He knocked at the door of this apartment, thrice. But no response was accorded him.

" There's nobody *here*, at all events," said Ely, quietly. Then, opening the door at a venture and peeping in, to his surprise he discovered that there were four or five able-bodied individuals inside ; all busy, like the rest he had seen.

"They must be hard o' hearing," concluded Ely. "I knocked three times."

Then he entered.

"If you please sir, I wish to get a Patent," began Ely, respectfully addressing a tall red-haired man, perched in a comfortable high chair, *very* busily absorbed in reading the "Constitution" newspaper.

He was so deeply engaged in this arduous morning work that he did not raise his eyes, even, at this civil salutation.

"If you please — did you hear me, sir?" said Ely, cautiously.

No answer.

"I want to get out a Patent —"

"What are you talking about?" asked the Department man, severely.

"I want a Patent, sir —"

"Why don't you go where they provide 'em, then?" grunted the other.

"I was directed here, sir."

"For what?"

"To procure my papers. I have a new invention —"

"You must go to the Patent Office, to learn about that, man!"

"Isn't this 'the Patent office building,' sir?" asked Ely, somewhat confused.

"This is the War Department — the Commissary General's office."

"Where *is* the Patent Office, if you please?" queried Hawes.

"It is easy to make money," observed old Blount to Morris Deans, "but not so easy to *save*, and keep it. It is harder still to learn how to enjoy it, wisely and rationally."
[CHAP. vi. page 106.

"Half a mile from here."

"Which way, sir?"

"Now I can't give you any more of my valuable time, sir. I am not a walking Directory. You must *not* tease me any farther," insisted the tall clerk.

And he went on, with his morning paper.

Ely moved out of " nummer vifteen," and slowly down the stairs — away from the War Department, to seek the place which he supposed he first had found correctly.

And after some inquiries on the Avenue, he discovered the building he was in search of.

By the time he had contrived to propel his tired body up to the great portal of the Patent Office building, it had got to be quite two o'clock.

In those days, "two P.M. sharp" was the hour for closing the arduous labors of the day, in the several government Departments. These hard-toiling clerks commenced at nine or ten o'clock in the morning. And it was scarcely to be expected that they could stand it to continue a moment beyond the required 'regulation time,' on duty!

So, as Ely went up the broad steps, there came rushing down a hundred or two tired clerks — all 'done, for the day' — on their way home, to dinner. For even government employés must *eat*, you know. How else could they sustain life? They couldn't, of course.

So great was the outpouring, and so earnest were the hurried movements of this horde of released Department operatives (for, Washington clerks do hurry, on the way *from* the Departments, to dinner! though they are habitually prone to make haste very slowly in going *to* their daily work) that Ely supposed the building to be on fire, at first sight.

"What's the matter?" he asked, innocently.

But no one stopped to answer this interrogation.

"What has happened?" he repeated.

Away pushed the fast retiring clerks.

"Say, what's up?" he reiterated.

And another fat man, of five-and-forty, who through physical infirmity couldn't hurry, replied "Did you speak to me, sir?"

"What is the row, here?" asked Hawes. "Is the house on fire?"

"I think not, sir. I don't smell no smoke, do *you?*"

"No! But, where are all these people running to, sir?"

"Dinner, my friend. Time's up, you see. Two o'clock. Work is over, for to-day, thank God!"

"Don't you come back then?" inquired Ely, innocently.

"O, yes. We return — regular as clock-work, my friend. That's the rule. We can't break over the regulations, o' course."

"Then you *do* return?"

"Yes. To-morrow morning."

"Not to-day?"

"No — bless you! You don't suppose we can work *all* the time, do you?"

"I didn't know what your office hours were," returned Ely.

"They're enough, heaven knows! From ten till two. And the best of us have but precious poor pay for that."

"How much?" queried Ely.

"None of us get over twenty-four hundred a year.

HOW HARD THESE MEN TOIL, IN THE PUBLIC SERVICE!

And many not more than sixteen or eighteen hundred dollars per annum," said the fat man — moving away.

"Poor devils!" exclaimed Hawes, with mock sympathy. "How hard they do have to work, here, to be sure! And only five to eight dollars pay for a service of three or four hours, daily! This is really too bad. And yet, strange to say, these laborious and ill-requited places are always filled — while among the occupants few die, and none resign. The amount of real patriotism and self-sacrifice among these willing office-holders is certainly not to be commuted!"

Then a well-fed fellow of over fifty who was evidently at home in this locality, came very slowly down from the interior of the building, to whom Ely inquiringly addressed himself, in the hope of obtaining a hint that might serve him, at the moment.

"A MATTER O' TWO AN' THIRTY YEAR."

"This is the Patent Office, I believe sir?" asked Hawes.

"Yes," replied the stout man, without halting in his measured steps.

"You are an official here?"

"Yes — I should say so —" still proceeding toward the outer portal, unconcernedly.

"Been here long, sir?"

"A matter o' two an' thirty year," returned the pursy old clerk, thrusting his hands into his coat pockets, and moving along.

"Ah, then you can tell me — if you please, to whom I should apply for a ———"

The man had gone straight on — and away. He was out of sight. *He* hadn't time to stop, on the way to dinner, to vouchsafe a stranger information, gratis, verily. He was too old a settler for this!

"The long and the short of it, is," observed Mr. Puffborl, wheezingly, alluding to the confused stranger, as he stood before a tall dapper whiskered chap who left the building last, "this young man yender's a new-comer, altogether. 'Ee's arter an app'intment, I reck'n. An' so I zent 'im up ter nummer vifteen. They'll take keer o' 'im in nummer vifteen, I reck'n."

"Wants an appointment, eh?" drawled the tall youth, slowly.

"So I dhink, from 'is eggsitement, and airnesdness. 'Ee don't appear to know edzac'ly wot's the matter wi' 'im. But nummer vifteen' ll set 'im all right."

THE LONG AND THE SHORT OF IT.

"I wish he may get it," returned the long young man.

And Mr. Puffborl with his elongated friend turned away leisurely, dinner-ward.

The anxious young inventor was standing alone, upon the steps of the great Patent Office building, now.

The hive had been emptied.

Desks were closed. Doors were being fastened. The

busy bees and the humming drones were all gone, now. — It was three minutes past two o'clock, P.M.

Ely stood a few minutes gazing over at the sluggish Potomac, as the River glided silently and turbidly down toward the ocean. Then he descended to the deserted sidewalk, contemplatively, en route to his lodgings at the Washington House, where he had engaged accommodations for a week or two.

There was but a single human being immediately within sight, when he reached the walk in front of the Patent office, and temporarily halted there. This was a decayed looking darky — who evidently saw that Ely was a stranger in the capitol. The colored man touched his torn hat respectfully and bowing, said —

"Want ter fine sumfin', Mass'r?"

"What?" returned Ely.

"Lookin' fer sumfin', sah?"

Ely eyed the sable inquirer an instant, and answered "No. Who be you?"

"I'se Mass'r Greene's boy, I is, sah."

"Master Greene, eh?"

"Yis sah."

"Who is he?"

"Mass'r Greene? 'ees der boss yere, ober nummer tirty-tree. I'se gwine up dar ter fix up der room fo' 'im. Dar all dun gwine fo' to-day, sah."

"I know it. You're employed here, eh?"

"I cleans up Massr's room, w'en he's gwoin away in der art'noon; dass all, sah."

"Who is your master, then?" inquired Hawes, interestedly.

"'Ee's der boss 'zaminer, sah," replied the colored boy.

"The boss examiner, eh?"

"Yis, sah," said the good humored servant.

"Of Patents, do you mean?" continued Ely.

"Yis sah."

"What time does he get here, in the morning?"

"Mos'ly at haaf arter nine about, sah."

"Half past nine? And he is chief Examiner, you say?"

"'Ee's der boss, sah."

"Room No 33, you said?"

"Yis sah — tirty-tree, fuss flo', leff han' side — wid der glaass pannels ober de top."

"He is the very man I want to see," said Ely — "the Chief Examiner. I will come over in the morning. Thank you. What is your name?"

"I'SE MASS'R GREENE'S BOY, SAH."

"Me? My name's Dick — Massa."

"Well, Richard — I will — "

"*Dick*, sah."

"Ah, yes. I'll come round in the morning, Dick. Much obliged to you."

Dick grinned broadly — went up the long steps into the building, with his broom under his arm — and Ely returned to his hotel.

Nothing had been done, so far. Hawes had not made the first move in the right direction, as yet, towards procuring his papers for the patent.

He had been at last in Washington five days. And he was as far from his object, or from any knowledge of what he had yet to undergo, as he was when he arrived.

He dined that evening, however, went to bed, and slept soundly. He was very tired. But, on the morrow he would find and confer with Mr. Greene, the chief Examiner.

"Mr. Greene is my man," murmured Ely, as he threw himself upon his mattress, tired out at last. "I'll walk into his affections, early to-morrow morning. He's the Chief Examiner — the man I want to meet. He must be one o' the twenty-four hundred a-year chaps. Not bad to take, that salary — fact!"

His model machine stood upon the table, beside his bed. He thought over all the past toil and contriving he had bestowed upon his pet invention; and congratulated himself that he had at last arrived within sight of the receipt of his coveted Letters-Patent — which he would no doubt have in hand, now, in a few hours, or days, at farthest.

Poor Ely! He had never before attempted to accomplish this undertaking, the conclusion of which in his case was yet so far away in the dim distance. But still he could not but declare to himself that the movements of all these people were strangely dilatory, and that the progress they made was "slower than that of a turtle with a slow fever."

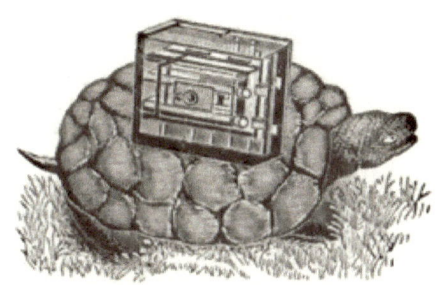

THE AVERAGE RATE OF PROGRESS IN GETTING OUT A PATENT!

CHAPTER XI.

MR. GREENE AND MR. POMPUS: EXAMINERS.

The name of the Chief Examiner, at this time, was not Greene, at all — but Mr. Zintsing Pompus; quite another personage.

Mr. Greene was a prominent subordinate, or Assistant Examiner, only.

Pompus was of German origin. A short enigmatical man — who no doubt was an expert, in his way. But his cognomen was not euphonious, though it was altogether appropriate.

He knew a heap o' things, so Ely declared, that the generality of mortals had not yet acquired: mostly in technicalities, however. And he had a mannerism in displaying his "scientific attainments," which was simply astonishing, to those who had not devoted themselves to the study of the dictionaries of inventive art.

Bright and early next day, Ely took his model Lock under his arm, and found his way to "Room 33, first floor, left, with the glass pannels over the door," as described by obliging Dick, the darky.

This was a spacious apartment, into which Hawes pushed his way at early ten o'clock, where he discovered at least a dozen men, hard at it — reading the daily papers, again.

All these people were politicians. And it seemed to Ely that a careful perusal of the public journals was the *first* duty of these gentlemen — any way. So far as his observation went, at any rate, they attended to this branch of their business faithfully, and universally, at all hours!

"Mr. Greene?" queried Ely, addressing himself to the first individual he encountered, in No. 33.

The gentleman was

"MR. GREENE — ONE WORD, IF YOU PLEASE."

busy. He was poring steadily over the long "leader" in the Constitution newspaper.

"Ahem — Mr. Greene?" repeated Ely civilly, again.

But, whoever he was, this gentleman vouchsafed the visitor no reply.

"I believe this is Mr. Greene?" repeated Hawes, raising his voice, audibly. "I would like to trouble you one moment, if you please, Mr. Greene."

"What do you want?" yelped this functionary, sharply.

"I wish to confer with Mr. Greene," returned Ely.

"Why don't you go where he is, then? What the devil are you badgering *me* for, I'd like to know?"

"Aren't you Mr. Greene?" asked Ely, a little startled.

"*No!* I am not."

"Is he here, sir?"

"Tom!" yelled this civil clerk, hailing a messenger. "Take this man away. See what he wants."

Tom came outside of the rail, and asked, "what is it?"

"I want to find Mr. Greene," said Ely.

"What Greene, sir?"

"I don't know that."

"There's six of 'em," said Tom. "Which one is it?"

"I really don't know."

"How can I direct you, then?" rejoined Tom.

"It's the Examiner, Greene."

"Of patents?"

"Yes, sir."

"This way, then."

And Tom brought Mr. Hawes to Mr. Greene, directly.

Greene proved to be rather an accommodating person, but a very precise and methodical man — who never permitted himself to move out of the department ruts. He bowed stiffly to Ely, who said —

"Good morning, Mr. Greene. I want to get out patent papers for my new invention."

"Name, sir?"

"Of the invention?"

"No, *your* name."

"Hawes, sir."

"First name?"

"Ely. Ely Hawes, sir."

Greene wrote down the address, as he understood it, and replied—

"Now, Mr. Orze — what is this invention?"

"Impenetrable Bank-safe Lock, sir, I call it."

"You are at liberty to call it by whatever name you choose, Mr. Orze. You are an American citizen, I presume, and every citizen of this free enlightened Republic has the inalienable right to call his own invention what he likes. But this title, allow me to suggest, Mr. Orze, is a very elongated one, and quite unpronounceable, by persons possessing only the ordinary length of tongue, and breath."

"I think it a very good name, sir — and appropriate, as well. It *is* impenetrable."

"We will not argue the point, then, Mr. Orze."

"*Hawes*, if you please, sir."

"I comprehend you, sir. I understand *your* name, perfectly. I did not allude to that, Mr. Orze, but to the singularly lengthened title of your proposed new patent safe."

"It is a lock, sir."

"Did you not say it was a Bank safe, just now, Mr. Orze?"

"Bank Safe *Lock*, sir."

"Ah, yes. I have it so, Mr. Orze. Now, then — what have you done about it, so far?"

"It is all completed, sir. I have it here, with me."

"I mean what have you done already towards procuring Letters Patent for this safe?"

"Nothing, sir."

"Then you must begin at the beginning, of course, Mr. Orze."

"I filed a caveat, some time ago, sir—"

"Yes. That was right."

"And now I want my papers."

"Is this all you have done?"

"Yes, sir."

"Well — you now apply to *me*, I presume, for information as to what you need to do next, Mr. Orze. Is that it?"

"I merely want my papers — that is all, sir," said Ely. "I've got the model, and the money to pay the fees, and I desire to take the documents home with me, when I leave Washington; which I hope to do to-morrow or the next day, if possible."

Mr. Greene looked cautiously into Ely's honest face, as if he deemed him loony, and said "Mr. Orze, you have never taken out a Patent from this Department yet, I presume?"

"No, sir."

"I thought so," ventured the clerk.

"*Why?* That doesn't prevent me from doing so, in this instance, does it?" queried Ely.

"Oh, no. But there are certain forms to go through, Mr. Orze — certain Departmental regulations to be observed — in *all* cases, in this sort of proceeding, of course."

"I know that, sir. But I want to push it through — that's all."

"We never permit any pushing, in this Department, Mr. Orze. There is just so much to be done here, and it must be done, *in form*, before any thing official emanates from this Department, in the shape of Letters Patent."

"That is what I am here to do, sir, when I can learn *what* I am required to do."

"Precisely, Mr. Orze. Now then, you have filed your caveat — "

" Yes sir, long ago."

" Very good. It will be necessary to have drawings of your Bank-safe made — "

" *Lock*, sir," said Ely, again.

" Lock, I mean. Yes. You must have drawings made — in whole, and in parts: sectional, elevatory, longitudinal, horizontal, and perspective, for the use of this Department. Then you will file your specifications of claim too, and record your declaration, etc. Then your working model must be submitted, and examined, to guard prior inventors against infringements. Your papers, specifications, drawings, and machine will then be in readiness — as soon as they can be reached — to be "filed" in this Department, for due reference at the proper time to the Examining Department. That Department, though connected with this in Departmental business, is a separate Department, nevertheless, in effect. Because, you perceive, Mr. Orze, that the incipient manipulations of the to-be-examined documents are all conducted in this Department before they can, by the regular course, be recognized in the Department to which I have alluded. The Examining Department will await the official Report in your case, Mr. Orze, before it can act, therefore — at all. Then that Department, upon receiving from this Department, (through the intermediate Department, where every thing from this Department is engrossed before it goes to the Examiners' Department,) will — as soon as it comes up, in regular routine — report back to this Department whether, or not, your proposed new Safe, or Lock, or whatever you conclude to call it, is patentable, at all. Mind you, I do not say it is, or is not. If it *is*, the Examining Department, through the Intermediate Department, will notify this Department of the fact, pro. or con. and then this Department will be able to make such report to the upper Department, upon the merits of your case, as upon final Examination in this Department, the facts may seem to warrant. All this takes time, Mr. Orze, as you will now comprehend, after the lucid explanation I have given you, briefly. If your proposed invention is *rejected* by the upper Department, for any cause — (and this is a very common occurrence I assure you, for various causes) the report from that Department is forwarded to the engrossing Department, and from that to this Department; whereupon, as soon as it is reached in regular order, this Department will notify the nominal inventor of his non-success; and there the matter terminates. But no case goes from this Department to the other Departments, until it falls into the regular channel, in course. We do all we can — but we cannot move any faster, Mr. Orze, than the Departmental force can accomplish the work assigned to it — in the regular order of receipt. You comprehend me, I presume, Mr. Orze?"

"And *my* case goes into line, then, from to-day?"

"Yes, sir."

"How many are there before me, on your lists, Mr. Greene?"

"I could not answer that question, Mr. Orze, without a reference to the Departmental records. But I should say, at a venture, there were twenty-three or twenty-four hundred."

"Twenty-four hundred before me?"

"At least that, Mr. Orze."

"When do you imagine mine can be reached?"

"I couldn't say, really, Mr. Orze. But just as soon as we can arrive at it, in due course. Now, I will file your application, duly — and you must excuse me; for I have a great deal to do, to-day. You can call again, in the course of a month, say — and we will then inform you what has been done in your case, in this Department, and when it will be worth your while to — call again."

Mr. Ely Hawes was a modest man, though his talent was genuine, and he bore every appearance of the well-dressed comely intelligent gentleman — as he was.

The supercilious clerk who had him in hand turned up his supercilious nose, at last, and inquired in his most offensively officious way, as he pushed a big book before him towards Ely — " Ah, I say Mr. Orze, you are able to write yer name, I sp'ose, eh ? Yer can *write*, I take it ? "

"AH, YES. YOU CAN WRITE YOUR NAME?"

Ely made no reply, but taking the pen, he signed his name as required in the impertinent clerk's book, and left this hopeful government pimp to his leisure.

Mr. Greene then took up a printed blank, upon which he scribbled these words : — " ELI ORZE — application July 7 — *Portable Bank Safe* " — and bowed the young inventor toward the door.

This precious document was thrown into a pigeon-hole among the O's, naturally, and the Departmental underlings, when they "reached it" some weeks afterwards, filed it away, hopelessly — since it should have been indorsed Ely Hawes, and been placed among the H's. of course !

Ely had listened to this long story, but could not comprehend much of it, and remembered less. But the desks began to be closed again — the clerks were hurrying away

— and he found that two o'clock had come round again, as he mournfully left this foggy " Department."

Not until the following day, at noon, was he able to bring himself into contact with the party with whom he intended to make direct communication in the first instance — to wit, the *Chief* Examiner, Zintsing Pompus, esquire.

This man after all, so Ely fancied, was the proper person to see in his case — which he deemed a very simple affair, albeit Mr. Greene had surrounded his matter with a wondrously complicated veil of unmitigated haze, during their late interview at Room No. 33.

After numerous rebuffs and many more inquiries, the patient inventor found the private office of Mr. Pompus, to whose notice he concluded he would address himself without circumlocution, and without reference to what Mr. Greene had stated to him — satisfied that it would have been more to his profit had he at the outset applied to head quarters.

" You are Chief Examiner of Patents, I think," began Hawes, upon being shown into the august presence of this important personage.

Ely had his small model lock in his hand, and was obliged to wait some minutes for Mr. Pompus to attend to him. When that pursy and fussy gentleman came round to it, he approached Mr. Hawes with an air of consequential civility, as the inventor stood at the end of the long table in readiness to make his appeal to the Chief, but that big-bellied functionary anticipated the humble applicant as he came forward, with the common-place inquiry, in a patronizing tone —

"Well sir, what have *you* got?"

"I am desirous to obtain a patent for a new bank-safe lock, if you please, sir."

"Ah, yes. Come in — come in, sir. We'll see about it," responded Pompus, dubiously.

And Ely gladly followed the portly Mr. Pompus directly to his desk, in the rear of the great room.

"WHAT HAVE YOU GOT?" ASKED MR. POMPUS, POMPOUSLY.

"You are Mr. Pompus?" said Ely.

"I *am* that individual," returned Pompus, gravely and majestically. "Who have I the honor of meeting, to-day?"

"Me? I am Mr. Hawes, sir — inventor of the Impenetrable Bank-Safe Lock," replied Ely.

"Ah, yes. Sit down, sir. I have never heard of this invention. You said Orrs, I think. Not Hobbs — "

"Hawes, sir. Ely — of Boston."

"I know a Mr. Ely, of Boston — a Patent lawyer there, if I remember. A very able man, in his way. Any relation, Mr. Ely?"

"My name is Ely Hawes, Mr. Pompus," returned the inventor, wondering how all these people should be perpetually mistaking his plainly pronounced name.

"Well, Mr. Orrs, what can I do for you?" rejoined Pompus, mechanically.

"I wish to procure Letters Patent for my Lock, sir."

"Oh, that is it, eh? Well, the process is very simple, sir. It is only necessary that you proceed in due form. There is a right and a wrong way, in most concerns of life. But in this kind of transaction there is but *one* way — that is, the legal, regular, established, routine course, Mr. Orrs."

"Hawes, if you please, sir."

"How do you spell it?"

"With an H."

"Ah, yes. Well, Mr. Hawes, you must begin *en règle*."

"What is that, sir?"

"In order — in form — in due course — in regular routine."

"And that course ———?"

"Is to begin at the commencement, Mr. Hawes."

"I have already filed my caveat, sir."

"Now you want to go right on, then, if you are ready."

"I am waiting, sir."

"Yes. You must necessarily wait. Your papers cannot issue from this Department until your invention is described, model submitted, case examined, same reported upon, and facts determined whether it is an original and patentable article. All this will be decided upon and acted on, in due course — beginning at the beginning. When your proposed implement is thus specified, submitted in model, examined, decided on as to its patentability, and reported on, favorably — it will in due course reach this Department. This Department will return its official approval and instructions to the Intermediate Department; that Department, when able to pass upon it, will report it to the Examining Department; then the rightful Department through which all Patents are promulgated, finally, will issue notice to the inventor, accordingly; and he can then proceed, in regular order, towards obtaining the Letters Patent applicable to his individual case. I say individual case, Mr. Hawes, because each case must stand or fall upon its own intrinsic merits, you observe. To bring about this result in order, and with due consideration for the claims and rights of all parties, Mr. Hawes, it is necessary that the utmost care and deliberation — as well as circumlocution should be observed — in all the Departments of the Patent office."

As Mr. Zintsing Pompus at this point halted to take breath, and swallow a glass of colored water, Ely availed himself of the opportunity afforded to ask a question.

"How much time does all this formidable manipulation involve, to consummate the applicant's wish, in a given case, Mr. Pompus?"

"Well, Mr. Hawes — that depends," said Pompus, pompously.

"Depends? Upon what, sir?"

"Upon the palpability of the case; the character of the invention — the complications that ordinarily arise in *all* cases where there is any peculiarity in the design — the pre-eminent probabilities that the device is an infringement upon prior creations of a similar nature — and a hundred technical et ceteræ that I have not time to particularize; such as the general elimination of the principles involved, the elucidation and scholium requisite to be observed regarding its intricacies, the disintegrating and severance of the combinations, and the final distribution of its orders of excellence, or otherwise."

Ely Hawes had got into a profuse sweat, by this time, while his informant appeared perfectly cool and serene.

The profundity of the intellectual dissertation he had listened to, quite overcame the youthful inventor; and he began to make up his mind that his simple but really ingenious contrivance would never bear any such conglomerated investigation and tautological assault as seemed to be contemplated in these sagacious but long-winded suggestions.

"Is there no shorter way than this to obtain Letters-Patent, for a simple device like mine, Sir?" asked Ely, in despair.

"There is but *one* mode, Mr. Hawes. Whether it be for a pen-holder or a steam-engine, it is the same."

The poor mechanic bowed his head — and threw up the sponge!

As he was turning away, Mr. Zintsing Pompus said "perhaps, Mr. Hawes, if you should employ a Patent Solicitor to attend to your little affair with this Department, it would materially assist you — sooner or later."

"Would this expedite matters, Mr. Pompus?"

"I don't say that, sir. I merely suggest that you are quite unfamiliar with the modus operandi and the ramifications of the routine of this Department. A Patent Solicitor will give *us* less trouble, and you *no* inconvenience — except to pay his charges; which are independent of the legitimate fees of this Department, of course."

"Where can I find this gentleman you mention, sir?" asked Ely, somewhat relieved.

Mr. Zintsing Pompus handed Ely a card, several of which he seemed to have close at hand, on which he read the address of "ELTON SHROOD, *Attorney* — C Street."

And Mr. Hawes 'went for' Mr. Shrood, without farther comment, or delay.

"On C Street, Mr. Orrs," advised Pompus, handing Ely the bit of pasteboard. "You will find Mr. Shrood an educated gentleman, and quite *au fait* in his calling."

"Thank you," returned Hawes, looking at the address.

"You comprehend, Mr. Orrs, that the necessities in your case are not exceptional, at all. This Department is in no wise complicated in its ramifications, when once its formula is appreciated. Mr. Shrood is an experienced Solicitor, and he will understand precisely what to do in the premises. It takes time to acquire this knowledge. *He* knows how to do it. Good morning, sir."

"Good morning, Mr. Pompus," returned Ely, more hopefully — as he was thus bowed out of the solemn presence of this dignitary, who had so completely astounded and perplexed him.

"I trust that Providence will kindly permit me," observed Ely, reverently, "to get out of this place, alive. I want my Patent papers. And I will have them, before I leave Washington. But, once clear of the limits of this departmental city — with those documents in my hands — if I am ever caught in this burg again, it will be after this!"

He went on, hunting for Mr. *Elton*, on C Street, for a time. Then he discovered that it was Mr. Elton *Shrood* he desired to meet.

And after pacing down and up the elongated street upon both sides, and half way back again after he discovered the mistake he had made, his eye fell upon a little tin sign bearing the address of " E. Shrood, Solicitor and Claim Agent."

Ely entered this gentleman's quiet office, and thanked his stars that he had found a man in Washington, at last, who was not so busily engaged in reading a newspaper as to be unable to vouchsafe him some show of attention.

CHAPTER XII.

OUR YOUNG MECHANIC MAKES A POINT.

ELY having adopted the advice of Mr. Zintsing Pompus, readily secured the aid of lawyer Shrood, who was a very good Claim and Patent Agent.

He was known familiarly in the Departments, and he was himself intimately acquainted with all the ropes in that ship. What *he* couldn't do — when he undertook it — was not worth doing in the management of this sort of case, it was admitted.

His fee in advance for services was two hundred and fifty dollars. If the thing were brought to a head within sixty days, Ely promised him another hundred dollars. If in forty days — two hundred more. If he accomplished the business in thirty days, Hawes would pay him two hundred and fifty dollars additional. "And sharp's the word, now," concluded Ely.

"I want to get out of this town. I have no doubt it is a very nice place to reside in — for those who like it. I say nothing against it, but I don't! For every week less than four weeks from to-day that you gain, in point of time in this business, Mr. Shrood, I will pay you fifty dollars in addition to the promised two hundred and fifty, extra. I am heartily sick of Washington. Bring me my Patent papers in fifteen days — and I will pay you three hundred and fifty dollars more than you have already charged me. Come!"

"You may rely on my best endeavors, sir," said the attorney, politely. "Still, there is just so much to be done, you observe. And these people are not easily hurried, you may feel assured."

"It is immaterial to me *how* this thing is accomplished, so that it is legally and rightfully concluded," rejoined Ely. "But I am anxious to return home, and I shall not leave without my papers."

As Ely left Shrood's office, at length, he encountered upon the sidewalk the full-blown figure of his friend Mr. Puffborl, whom he first met at the War Department, in Washington. Puffborl instantly recognized him, and wheezingly accosted the anxious mechanic.

"Ah — 'ow ar yer? Yer vound 'im 't last, eh? I didn't know wot yer war arter, to'ther day. Yas. Yer a gittin out a patent — eh? I thort it were a app'intment. Nummer vifteen warn't right. But ef yer'd a tole me yer case, I'd a put yer on the drack," continued Puffborl, grasping the Yankee inventor's hand, and passing his other palm familiarly up to Ely's shoulder, in a kindly way.

"I am getting along nicely, now, thank you," returned Hawes. "Mr. Shrood has taken charge of my case."

"Orl c'reck then. Ee'l vix it up vor yer. 'Ee knows wot's wot, in the patent line," said Puffborl, patronizingly, as he left Ely upon the walk again.

Mr. Attorney Shrood went to work directly, and heartily, in Ely Hawes' interest. This was a paying job!

MR. PUFFBORL GROWS AFFECTIONATE.

There was a prospect of round remuneration for his services, and he soon ascertained that the young inventor had really devised a good thing, in his "improved combination lock."

At first it was thought that the principle of action was not altogether new. But this objection was overcome speedily, through Shrood's management and arguments, since he was well conversant with previous American inventions of this character, and his legal opinion was highly respected at the Department.

Besides this, Shrood was in earnest. Through his zeal in pushing this affair, personally, (and a little extra work and pay among the proper parties), a few "over-hours" were devoted to this matter, in the examinations and forwarding of the official documents in the case.

And thus the affair of Mr. Hawes took a fresh start immediately, and went along, glibly — for the time being.

Ely wandered about the city — saw what was to be seen — visited the different points of interest in the immediate vicinity — went to Mount Vernon the estate of George Washington, to Arlington the Lee estate, to Bladensburg, Silver Springs, Alexandria, Georgetown — and visited the monuments, the Capitol Buildings, the White House, the pictures, statuary, and the theatres. And finally wore himself out with the heat, and trudging up and down over the "magnificent distances" that separated the different notable locations in and around the great Federal City.

Thus fourteen days expired, and he had been able to obtain from his Patent Agent, Shrood, only the stereotype report "We are getting along, Mr. Hawes, as rapidly as possible. But it takes time, and needs patience to get these Patent papers through."

Ely had gone out of Shrood's office that day but two or three minutes, when the Attorney on looking up at his front window saw the passers-by hurrying down and across C Street, furiously; as if some unusual object attracted them from their customary habit of lounging leisurely along in the heat.

He stepped down to see what had occurred, and found three or four men in the act of raising and bearing aside to the grassy square, the figure of a man who had been thrown down at the street-corner by a furious runaway team, that was flying away in the distance, as he came up.

The poor fellow was bleeding at the mouth and ears, and his appearance was indeed deplorable.

"Who is he? He's dead, I reckon."

"Does anybody know him?" asked the crowd.

"I do," says Shrood.

THE ACCIDENT. — "HE'S DEAD, I RECKON."

"Where does he belong?"

"Call a surgeon," replied the Attorney, briskly. "Here! Take him into my office. He is stopping at the Washington House. If he isn't dead, we'll get him down there, directly, as soon as the Doctor arrives. Hurry up!"

The active directions of Shrood were humanely followed, and Ely was quickly stretched easily upon the lawyer's sofa — where medical aid was soon summoned beside him.

He was utterly unconscious, however.

The surgeon arrived, stripped his outer garments off, examined his breast and limbs, and found no broken bones, fortunately.

His head was bruised, but the skull was not fractured, it was ascertained. But he lay speechless for half an hour, and the Doctor having bathed his temples and injured scalp, concluded the shock or blow he had encountered had affected his spine, probably.

At the end of nearly an hour, the young man opened his eyes, glared about him, and asked —

"What is it? What did it?"

"Quiet, now," suggested the Doctor, kindly. "You have been hurt — but I trust not seriously."

"What happened? Ah, Mr. Shrood — I see you. Did I fall?"

"No. It is all right," returned Shrood, encouragingly. "You were stricken down, they tell me, as you turned the corner, by a runaway team. But you will come round right, I reckon, if you don't fret over it — eh, doctor?"

"Yes. Let him lie here, at present. I think it is only a temporary shock, luckily. Keep him quiet, but don't allow him to sleep, if you can avoid it without worrying him. I will be back in an hour. I am obliged to call on a patient, who is taken ill, suddenly — but will return at the earliest possible moment."

Shrood sat down by the side of the sufferer, talked to him, softly, at intervals, fanned him, and bathed his head and face — and within the next hour, Ely was sitting up, — quite recovered, seemingly.

When the Doctor returned, he pronounced his patient safe. Before sunset, he was taken to his hotel lodgings. And there he remained five weeks, before he was permitted to ride out, after this unfortunate accident occurred to him. A violent fever succeeded the wretched shock, and he was greatly reduced in physical condition, ultimately.

Jimmy Buck, the young Washington carriage-driver was close at hand, after the accident to Ely. He had witnessed the knock-down, and his mud-spattered vehicle was brought before the lawyer's door, instanter, when he observed that the fallen traveller had been borne into Shrood's office.

There was a job in prospective, he fancied, whether the victim were dead or alive, after this occurrence; and Jimmy, who was of an enterprising turn of mind in his business, proposed to be on hand seasonably.

He hung round the door, smiled at the doctors and visitors who came and went, and remained at his chosen post until Ely's friend desired the services of a whip — when he stepped cheerily up, with the salutation, " kerrige, mass'r? It's rite yere, afo' de do'. Been yere a waitin' fo' de gemmen dese tree 'ours, sah."

And Jimmy bore the wounded Hawes away to the Washington House, at a cautious pace, charging the unlucky stranger for the time he had been lingering before the lawyer's door.

Ely paid the grinning darkey driver six dollars for his attentions; which Jimmy declared was "dog-cheap, mass'r."

The sufferer was in no condition to bargain or higgle with his cullud friend, on this occasion. Had he been posted regarding the nominal city carriage-hire regulations, however, he would have known that the smiling Washington whip was legally entitled to but six York shillings for this service.

He entered his hotel, and Jimmy Buck disappeared with his plunder, perfectly satisfied with this bit of sharp practice.

But Ely was stout of heart and strong in natural constitution. He rallied, at last, and came out of his jeopardy in safety — thanks to his own previous good habits, and the zealous care he received at the hands of attorney Shrood and the skilful surgeon who attended him.

JIMMY, THE WASHINGTON WHIP.

About a week after the fever took a favorable turn in

Ely's case, he convalesced rapidly, and Mr. Shrood said to him "You are getting along nicely Mr. Hawes, I am happy to learn from our physician."

"Yes, I am quite strong, I think," returned Ely. "How do we get on with the Patent papers, sir?" he inquired.

"Well, you mustn't bother your head about that subject, the Doctor says — for the present. We have done very well."

"Not completed yet, eh?"

"When you are able to hear good or bad news, my dear sir, it will be quite time to discuss the Patent matter."

"I can take it as it comes," said Ely, courageously.

"Equal to either fortune, eh?"

"O, yes."

"Well, you mustn't get excited about it."

"No. I am very calm. Has our application been rejected?" asked Ely.

"Not at all."

"What then?"

"The report was concluded near a week ago, Mr. Hawes — but you were too ill to hear about it."

"Favorable, then?"

"Yes. And your Letters Patent are already issued. I have them at my office."

"Thank you — thank you —" said Ely, earnestly. "I am really *much* better, now, Mr. Shrood."

"I say, Frank, come down!" shouted Ely, hurrying to the stairway, in Meyers' lodgings, on his return from Washington. "I've got the papers!" [CHAP. xii. p. 191.

"I will bring the documents round in a day or two," added the Attorney. "And as soon as you are physically able, now, you can leave town, with the coveted papers in your pocket. Your invention is a good thing, Mr Hawes — a very good thing," concluded Mr. Shrood, in a congratulatory tone.

Ely came up, with rapid strides, after this friendly announcement. And within three weeks he was out of doors, well recovered.

He paid Shrood liberally, discharged all his bills, and finally left Washington, in recuperated condition and excellent spirits, for New York city, where he had written Frank Meyers and appointed to meet him, on the way to Boston.

Ely made the best of his way back to New York, in good earnest. On arriving there, he lost no time in looking up his friend Meyers; and reaching his lodgings, he hurried into the house.

Taking his Patent papers from his breast-pocket and flourishing the documents in one hand, with his carpet-bag in the other, he approached the foot of the second stairway, and cried out, joyously,

"I say, Frank! Where are you, my boy? Come down! I've got 'em. And it's all right, at last!"

Meyers received Ely enthusiastically, and congratulated his friend right heartily upon his assured success — so far.

Ely told his story to Frank Meyers, feelingly, when they sat down together, and the two old friends had a grand time in discussing the details of this late Washington trip.

"Were you ever there?" asked Ely.

"No," said Frank. "But I have heard a good deal of the Capitol. It must be a nice place."

"For a small party, yes," returned Ely, "it is. When I go there again, it will be —"

"When you seek other Patent papers, I suppose?" suggested Frank.

Mr. Hawes smiled.

"Now it is all over, Frank, I don't regret it," he continued. "But if you ever happen to require a similar service, let me recommend you to stay at home, and employ a Patent Office Solicitor to do your work, if you can raise the money to pay him for the luxury. *I* have had enough, in my experiment, I assure you!"

"Well, you triumphed, at last, Ely. And through your own determined application and perseverance, it would seem."

"Yes, I have labored for it, and I've got it, Frank — so far. Now, I am going to work to make my hundred thousand dollars out of it."

"And I will help you, Ely — every time," returned Meyers, cordially. "You shall come to New York, and together we will make your fortune, out of your splendidly contrived Bank lock."

Ely had made a point, finally. He had obtained his Patent papers, and he accepted Meyers' suggestions, gratefully.

Thus then it was decided.

And by and by we shall learn what came of this resolve.

Now we will turn to the history of our friend Reuben Downer, the printer; who, like the rest of our characters, had his aspirations, and his eye towards a fortune.

CHAPTER XIII.

HOW REUBEN DOWNER MADE AND SAVED IT.

REUBEN DOWNER was not a native of this country. He was born in Ireland. When he arrived on the shores of America, he was thirteen years old.

He was never of the boastful sort. When he touched the soil of his adopted land, *certes* he could not have boasted of an over-burthen of this world's goods! Under one arm he carried his bundle of coarse apparel, and in his odd shaped hand-basket he had a change of underclothing, only. He soon earned an outfit, however, and comfortable shoes to his feet.

He had no friends in America, then, but he was stout-limbed and stout-hearted, both. His health was robust, and his will of the best. He looked cheerfully before him — though his prospect was none of the most encouraging, to be sure. But he was made of the right stuff, he resolved to do his highest, and he believed that honest industry and dutiful vigilance would surely bring its reward — in the end.

Of all the representative personages introduced to our

readers in these pages, as we have already hinted Reuben Downer was the poorest boy of our chosen characters; a printer's apprentice, in one of the New England States.

He had experienced a hard life in his earliest years, but he was peculiarly constituted, and took the rough portion of his existence with graceful resignation to what Fate had ordained his lot in life to be.

He was conscientiously scrupulous in all his dealings and intercourse with those with whom he associated, or came in contact, and from his earliest years he proved himself thoroughly reliable and trustworthy, in every undertaking he entered upon.

His genius was remarkable and his manliness irreproachable. But poverty followed him for years, and he found it difficult to surmount the many obstacles that continually seemed to crop out in his path, until he reached his majority, in years.

Then he had acquired the trade of a printer, only — and at this profession he was able to gain barely a decent respectable livelihood, like thousands of others, in the routine of the portionless mechanic.

He had declared to Frank Meyers and his companions that he would one day be rich. How this desirable object was to be attained, he never stated.

"But I shall conquer fortune, sooner or later, lads," he insisted. "You talk of 'a hundred thousand dollars in gold,' as your maximum. This is a very respectable sum to aim for. If *I* ever get that amount, or half that sum,

I will make it five times a hundred thousand, before I make it less than one hundred. This is *my* figure."

Reuben was a good workman. Tasteful, swift, correct, and apt as a compositor, and competent at last in any branch of the trade to which he had been educated.

His duties for a few years required his constant employment at the case. But occasionally he became a correspondent for the daily journal upon which he was for a long time engaged as printer.

During the latter portion of John Tyler's administration in the Presidential chair, Mr. Downer went from New England to New York — where he found his former friend Frank Meyers flourishing.

He was thoroughly ambitious, but he possessed no ready capital to launch out in his vocation, upon his own account. Besides this, though he felt himself competent to the management of such a business as a weekly or a daily paper, (which he hoped one day to be at the head of,) the competition in this kind of enterprise was too great for him to risk embarking in such an enterprise with the limited funds at his command.

"I will not run in debt for any thing, at all events," he insisted. "I will earn my capital first, and then I will so place it, upon opportunity, that it will give me what I desire, and yield me a goodly return in the end. I know what I want. My scheme is all developed, theoretically. I can win a fortune with it, after a while — but I have no means, as yet, to venture upon my long-considered experiment."

When toiling as a printer's lad in the New England news-paper office where he began his career, Reuben looked forward hopefully to future advancement in some other field than that where he was thus plodding along so unpromisingly. What it might be, he had then no clear idea. Yet from his very youth, he felt that he was some day bound to be honorably at the head of his profession.

He toiled early and late, but made slow progress. Yet he never was discouraged. His course was marked out. He placed his resolves squarely upon *principle* — in all his undertakings, small or great — from his youth upward.

Honest, industrious, enterprising, talented, sober and persevering in his purpose, he went steadily forward, and always established the rule in his life, to pay for every thing he received, as he went along. If he could not do this — however much his need or fancy craved a thing, he would deny himself the possession or enjoyment of it. He never would borrow money, but always earned it. He never expended money that was not his own, and never accepted a loan from a friend, however " short " he might be, temporarily.

" I will not run in debt," he declared, " whatever I do. Until I possess the means to accomplish my wishes, or objects, they will go unattained. When I have the cash in hand, I will buy what I want, and pay for it. Then if I lose it, it is my loss, and not another's ; and I can go to work and earn more — as I did the other."

His tenacity in purpose was notable. Once he made up

his mind in any particular direction, considerately, he never gave up the pursuit of that aim, until he had accomplished his wish. And in all the plans he ever so undertook, he never failed of final success.

A few years after Reuben Downer went to New York, having connected himself with a good printing house there, his superior talents as a workman were recognized. But he received only indifferent remuneration, in those days, and found himself compelled to "sail close to the wind," to meet his current expenses.

He followed up his habit of strict economy, however, and kept clear of debt — always looking forward cheerfully and hopefully for his opportunity; which he felt confident would some day open up, and through which he would be able to launch out upon 'a free course.'

Fred Gleason, of Boston, the originator of the old "Flag of our Union" newspaper, had taken the field early in this sort of enterprise, and held it — for years; out of which *he* had made a handsome fortune. M. M. Ballou succeeded him, and made another in this same establishment, which he finally sold to his successors advantageously.

But Boston and Philadelphia, at that period, controlled the leading literary weekly publications of this character, and Messrs. Harpers had not yet started their now popular periodical publications.

Reuben saw that New York — the grand centre of American commercial enterprise — had then no weekly paper of this kind. And he conceived the idea of putting upon the market, for universal circulation, a new weekly literary journal, in a miscellaneous and popular style; and quietly but earnestly he went about it, as soon as his long-considered plan was matured.

He consulted with Frank Meyers and other friends, who thought his scheme a good one. But he had little money, and his contemplated enterprise could not be carried out successfully, without funds!

His determination not to run in debt for a dollar's worth of material, delayed him, but he kept hard at work constantly, at type-setting, saved every dime he could earn and spare from his wages, and finally had a moderate sum to venture with, in his new undertaking.

Reuben had the advantage of experience in his calling, and his taste and skill as a printer were acknowledged. He bought out a small commercial sheet that had had a weakly existence, and seating himself in the editorial chair, he changed the character of this to that of the literary paper he had contemplated.

His plans were original. He resolved upon making the "Leader," as he called his new paper, the first of its class in America, as it was the first — in fact — in peculiar conception, form, style and conduct. At the outset, he printed only a few hundred copies, in folio form. Then he changed it to a quarto, and through the assistance of a thriving news-publishing house, he increased its circulation, rapidly.

Then Reuben concluded to startle the reading world with a novel style of advertising his new project. This course involved considerable outlay, for it was expensive. But Reuben was doing very well. His "Leader" had begun to sell, largely. He engaged able contributors, and paid them liberally. And he had got a start.

From a few hundred, or thousands circulation, his paper went up to ten, fifteen, twenty thousand a week. Then he went into the columns of the daily press, with his famous announcement — "*John Jones writes for the Leader!*" "John Jones writes for the Leader!!" "John Jones writes for the Leader"!!! repeated a thousand times over, in a single line each of displayed type.

Everybody said "What of it?" "What does Reuben mean?" "Who says John Jones doesn't write for the Leader?" "What nonsense is this?"

But everybody read this unique style of announcement, and all the world and his wife wanted to know directly who John Jones was, who Reuben Downer was, what the 'Leader' was, and what John was writing about, in the Leader, of course.

Then came another column, or whole page, of the daily Herald or Tribune, plastered all over with "*Read Fannie Firm, in the Leader!*" "Read Fannie Firm, in the Leader!!" "Read Fannie Firm, in the Leader!!!" And all the rest of the world and mankind generally rushed for the "Leader," to learn who was 'Fannie Firm,' and why *she* was to be "read in the Leader," and nowhere else.

"Reuben Downer is on the high road to fortune," cried the multitude. "Reuben Downer is going to the dogs," muttered the croakers — who didn't see why this late poor printer should thus flaunt his enterprise in the teeth of everybody, whether they would or no!

The astonished pedestrian as he went up and down the public streets, beheld on every hand, also, the mandatory queer injunction placarded upon the walls and corners — "Buy the N. Y. Leader! Buy the N. Y. Leader!!" And they queried why "buy the Leader?" What *is* this Leader?

And then they hunted up the dashing spicy new literary weekly. It was a success — and a grand one, indeed.

THE ASTONISHED PEDESTRIAN.

"What do you fill up all the papers in town with your nonsense for, Reuben — in this way?" asked a man, one day, stopping him in Broadway, and criticising his new style of declaring that "*Everybody reads the New York Leader!*" "Everybody reads the New York Leader!!" "Everybody reads the New York Leader!!!"

"*I* don't read these advertisements, anyhow."

"Don't you?" queried Reuben. "How did you happen to know I advertised my paper thus, then?"

Next week, all the dailies were occupied with a single line — printed over and over, sixteen hundred times in each. "*Buy the N. Y. Leader!*" "Buy the N. Y. Leader!!" "Buy the N. Y. Leader!!!"

And they did buy it — with a rush, to be sure, as the event proved.

All this cost money. Heaps of *cash* — for Reuben would never get trusted. He asked no accommodation. He was a cash man. He paid as he went along. Hundreds, thousands of dollars a week, for months and months, for advertising.

Where did he get his money?

He earned it, in his business. His sales increased. In a few months his circulation ran up to fifty, sixty, seventy-five thousand copies a week. Then he advertised again, and paid for it, roundly.

Everybody talked about Downer's Leader. Everybody bought it. Everybody read it. Everybody liked it. And within a couple of years, Reuben Downer was printing each week nearly two hundred thousand copies of his famous new literary paper.

But he didn't halt, now!

He went right *on*.

He sought the best writers in the land, and paid them munificently for their contributions. He could afford it. He was getting rich, while he did this. And already *he* had more than a hundred thousand dollars in gold at his command.

Imitators sprang up around him. His style of advertising, his form of publication, his mode of issuing his paper was adopted.

But Reuben secured the foremost popular writers of the day, and constantly announced, in his peculiar way, that "Silas Cobb writes *only* for the Leader"! "Silas Cobb writes *only* for the Leader!!" "Silas Cobb writes *only* for the Leader!!!" Or "Fannie Firm writes *only* for Leader!" "Fannie Firm writes *only* for Leader!!" "Fannie Firm writes *only* for Leader!!!"

And within another year his weekly "New York Leader" had reached a circulation of near three hundred thousand copies — and the great reading public of the United States called loudly for more!

Downer was in good spirits, now. He was rolling up his thousands. He began without a dollar. But he had brains, and pluck, and sterling energy to work with.

By and by we will learn what became of Reuben, and his splendid enterprise — the "New York Weekly Leader."

CHAPTER XIV.

HOW DAVID THE DROVER MADE HIS PILE.

DAVID MOREHEAD was born in New Hampshire, among the sturdy farmers and cattle-dealers of that ilk. He was raised by Deacon Rounds — a good pious solid old-school man — who had himself been reared also among the hills of the Granite State.

This boy had been left to the Deacon's charge upon the death of a near relative, and at twelve years old, with a meagre common-school education, David went to work upon the old Rounds place — where horses, cows and sheep were largely bred, from stock among the best that ever went into, or out of the county in which he dwelt from childhood.

David took to horse-flesh more kindly than towards the cattle kine ; like most boys, in their teens, who fancy the " nobler " animal naturally, on account of the pleasure they derive in taming, driving, and riding this leading favorite among the beast creation.

It was David's fortune however to be placed in charge of the oxen and sheep upon the Deacon's farm, mostly, for several years; and he came to be accustomed to their care and management, and had the selling of the stock, as it matured or was fattened for market, eventually.

As the Deacon's business flourished and increased, David was sent into the neighborhood as a purchaser — for he got to be an excellent judge of the merits and quality of live stock; and so, from year to year, he made the acquaintance of all the breeders and dealers in the country round, of whom he was a heavy buyer, every season, at length; the Deacon furnishing the cash means to carry on this trade, for his own exclusive benefit.

All that David could realize out of this toil and traffic, was his day's wages and actual travelling expenses, for a long time. Deacon Rounds was a very honestly disposed man, but he was avaricious, and parsimonious, both.

DAVID — THE DROVER.

He knew that David had no capital, and therefore he did not fear competition, in that quarter, even after the boy had grown to manhood, and become his own legal master. So he continued to supply him with funds to purchase for his (the Deacon's) account, and contrived to pay as little as he dared to offer him in the way of remuneration, for so competent, faithful and shrewd an assistant as David Morehead proved — in the end.

David was limited therefore to the business of buying and selling neat stock; and he went up and down the country, in all directions, in quest of the animals desired over and above those that could be economically reared upon the Deacon's premises.

He was known as David, the Drover. Far and near, his word was as good as his bond, for he was scrupulously honorable in all his dealings, and never traded with a man in such a way that he could not meet him a second time, and trade again, if occasion called for it.

After he passed his majority, David was anxious to strike out for himself. But in that country a man's earnings under such a close-fisted patron as was Deacon Rounds, gave the employé small chance to lay aside money, to any extent. And, in this respect, David Morehead was no exception to the general rule.

Still, he had saved a little, and in the later two or three years of his life he had added to his small means a few hundred dollars. He then informed his sharp old master that he had determined to go on the road upon his own account.

The life of the drover can hardly be said to be a merry existence!

On the contrary, it may safely be chronicled as a pursuit of toil and sweat and dust and discomfort — in the main.

Yet in northern New England this pursuit has for many years proved highly profitable, and thousands are engaged in the work of producing the multitude of horses, the herds of cattle, and the flocks of sheep that furnish the eastern markets with their best live stock of either kind — for pleasure, work, food, or clothing.

David Morehead had come to have "an eye for business," towards his own individual emolument.

He had served a long apprenticeship at the trade, and thus far Deacon Rounds had had by far the best of the bargain that had gone on between them for so many years.

David had been confidentially talking latterly with an infirm old man he had chanced upon, away down on the Connecticut River — in the course of his repeated wanderings — who had a dilapidated estate on his hands which bothered him to pay the taxes on, of late years.

"Buy me out, David," said Grimes, earnestly. "*You* ken run the ole place, an' make yer forten outen it. Ther's tew hunder'd acres, a'most. An' ef yer'll stock it with cattil an' hosses, yer ken make a heap o' money, wi' *yeur* 'sperience, an' grit. *I* can't. I'm play'd out. An' wot wi' the roomatiz an' the taxes together, I'm dead beat wi' it. Come — wot d'yer say?"

"I haint no money to speak of," returned David.

"Don't want much, Dave."

"It 'ud take money to stock it rightly, Grimes."

"Begin small, then, Dave."

"I should hev to — that's a fact!" returned David, reflectively.

"Well — take it. Gimme an 'greement ter take keer o' me an' my old woman's long as we live, an' yer ken come yere, an' do wot yer like wi' the place. We haint no child'en, yer know, an' yer ken jess hev' it all yer own way, Dave. Ther's parsturin' enough to keep a hunder'd head o' cattle an' colts an' sheep — an' yer kin make money outen it, I tell ye, sure's yer alive."

A bargain was struck.

David bought the place, for a few dollars, (to make a legal money consideration in the deed,) and agreed to keep old Grimes and his older wife so long as they lived, without charge, as a further valid consideration.

"In the course o' human events," said Grimes, mournfully, "we two ole folk can't live many years. It'll come to yer, David, cheap. But it ain't o' no use to *us*, 'thout somebody takes it, an' looks arter us."

The New Hampshire drover went home again, dreaming of his new prospects. He made up his mind to quit Deacon Rounds — and told him so. The Deacon demurred, for he knew David's value. But the latter had resolved, and he said "I've sarved you a good many year, an' I'm bound to go it alone, now. I want to make a little money, like the rest o' folk — an' you know how it is, yourself, Deacon," insisted David. And so he shortly left his old quarters, and began life in earnest upon his own account.

David took possession of the wasted Grimes farm, and put a score of cattle upon it, a few months afterwards.

Then he bought and traded for half a dozen Morgan colts. He owned three or four old brood mares, and, with twenty or thirty sheep, he began to raise stock on his own premises.

Within two years old Grimes gave up the ghost, and his wife soon followed her played-out lord and master, to another and a better world.

David Morehead became the proprietor of a fair pasture farm, in consequence — and he fenced it, manured it, began to cultivate it, and went on improving his place and his prospects.

But he did not leave the business of the road. He had become so accustomed to the life of the drover, that he couldn't give up the habit of going abroad every week, to buy and sell and dicker for live stock. Thus he made money, surely, but not rapidly, while he hired a good hand or two to look after the land and stables, the flocks and herds and studs at home.

In the pasturing season too, he boarded horses and mares for gentlemen who knew him, and who were glad to have their breeding or fancy animals in such good hands, upon occasion, when they were away from their estates or town residences, often months at a time, every year.

This paid David well — and he had ample room thus to accommodate a goodly number of animals, not his own.

He saved his money, too. Deacon Rounds had taught him the value of it. And he did not forget that " a dollar was one hundred cents, that ten dollars were a hundred dimes, and a hundred dollars were four hundred good round quarters — every time."

David boasted that he knew thus much of financial science, and allowed that Deacon Rounds had taught him this, from the start.

Then David got married.

He found that he needed a wife to look after his household affairs, and see to things in his absence from the place.

His courtship was brief but business-like. He met Polly White at a huskings one day, and found her "a nice good girl — capable, healthy, and willin'," he said.

Three months afterwards, they were wedded. He knew her family, previously, and Polly's father was aware that David was a clever, thrifty, honest young man, who would make his daughter a good husband.

The old Grimes house was not a large one, or in very presentable condition when David became the owner of the farm. But he fixed it up, by degrees, and when he took Polly home there as his wife, the premises had been greatly improved, and comfortably furnished.

She was content, and they lived very cosily and happily together; for Polly had been well brought up, and was just the woman for such a man as she had united her humble fortune with.

It was three years after he married, when he was flourishing nicely in his business, (which had by this time become very considerable, and was constantly increasing) that David pushed his way down to Brandville, five-and-forty miles below his own farm, on the Connecticut River.

He had a pair of very promising black Morgan colts he had raised, which he wished to dispose of — but for which he had not as yet been able to find an appreciative customer, in his own neighborhood.

David knew what a horse was. But he hadn't got his ideas up to the best market value of such a pair as these splendid colts were, yet.

His estimated price was six hundred dollars, or thereabouts, for the span — and they were beautiful animals. But, at this period, three hundred dollars for a five-year-old colt, was a very goodly figure, as everybody knew.

For Morgan horses, these were full-sized. And they were perfectly matched. They had been carefully broken to harness, and were speedy. One of them was faster than his mate, but upon the road they could trot to the pole in about three minutes, together. And they had never been trained, at all. This branch of the business of the horse-man, David knew nothing about. But he knew he had a lively pair of colts, and he took pride in showing off his handsome steppers, whenever the opportunity presented.

Now, however, he desired to sell. And he intended to go back to Polly without the black colts, but with six hundred clean hard dollars, at the least, instead.

He chanced to fall in with Morris Deans — at old Farmer Blount's place — upon halting at Brandville, on his way to Springfield; if it turned out that he did not meet with a customer for his colts previously.

Morris had by this time got to be pretty well up in the science of horse-flesh. He had been at Sunnyside almost five years. And *he* knew that such a pair of blooded colts as this New Hampshire man had brought down for a market, were " worth a farm," almost, in *his* hands. He liked them. And he didn't hesitate to say this to David — who at once pricked up his ears!

" Are they speedy?" asked Morris, looking the high-headed Morgans carefully over.

" I reck'n they're fair," said David. " I never druv' 'em separate, much. But I cal'late they're good steppers, and stylish."

" Not fast, then?"

" Wal — I don't know what you call faast, hereaways. But they can foot a mile 'n three minits, easy enough."

" Together?"

" Side an' side, any day."

" What do you ask for them?" queried Morris, indifferently.

" Wal, I want to get a thousan' dollars for the tew," said David, coolly.

Morris said — " no. I don't want them. You can travel, David."

David took up the lines, jogged down the road half a mile, and came spinning back again, up past the Blount farm, at a tearing gait — and away to the Brandville tavern stables, saying quietly to himself, "I've found a customer for the colts."

Morris watched the movements, and went over to the country tavern, where David said he had concluded to tarry over night.

In the morning he took his ponies out, to show them. Morris was delighted with them. They were really a very fine pair.

"I will take them," said Morris, after seeing their performance, in the morning.

"Wal," returned David shrewdly, "I've concluded I ken do better down at Springfield. They're *good* 'uns. But I'll take fifteen hunder'd dollars for 'em."

"You named a thousand yesterday, David," said Morris.

"So I did. An' you said 'No. You ken travel, David.' Didn't you?"

"Yes —"

"An' I travelled, Morris."

"Now you want fifteen hundred?"

"Exackly," returned David.

"Well. I hope you may get it, then."

"I shall, Morris — or I'll take 'em down to Springfield."

"Go ahead. Horses have riz, I guess, up in New Hampshire, David!"

Morris went back to the farm. He wanted that pair of Morgan colts. He knew where *he* could place them, after a while, to advantage. But he left David alone, for the day.

Towards night, the shrewd drover harnessed up his beautiful team and drove down past Sunnyside farm again. Morris saw him, and hailed him.

"Which way, David?"

"Springfield," said Dave, hauling up.

"You'd better let me have the colts, David."

"I will, Morris."

"At what price?"

"Wal, I don't mind, now — if you *want* 'em, an' I reck'n you do, Morris — I don't mind a tradin'. You know what a good pair o' Morgan colts is. An' if you want to put out sixteen hunder'd dollars on 'em, they're yours, an' it's a barg'in."

"Sixteen hundred!"

"That's what I said, Morris."

"You're risin', every time you speak about 'em!"

"Two thousand I'll ask for 'em, in Springfield, Morris."

"What is the lowest sum you'll sell them for?"

"Sixteen hunder'd dollars, *now*."

Morris threw open the wide farm-gate.

"Drive 'em in, David," he said. "They're mine. You can't raise on *me*, again, at all events."

"All right," returned David, complacently. "They're good 'uns."

The splendid black Morgan ponies were driven into old Blount's stable, forthwith.

And that night David returned to Polly, with sixteen hundred good dollars, for his fancy colts.

"Good-by, Morris," said the New Hampshire drover.

"Good-by, David. Come again."

"I will, Morris."

"When you have a better pair o' colts than these, bring them to Sunnyside farm."

"I'm satisfied, Morris. I know what *you* will do with 'em. You'll double your money on 'em! That's what you'll do."

"Mayhap I will," said Morris, smiling. "But *you've* got a good price for them, any way."

"Yas. An' now I think of it, ther's old Winkham, up above me, to home, has got a comin' six-year-old geldin' that'll travel like a rein-deer. Do you want a fast 'un, Morris?"

"Bring him down. I'll look at him," returned Morris.

"I will — some day. Good-by, Morris."

And with this, the two sharp cattle-dealers separated, mutually gratified with their trade.

OLD WINKHAM'S TROTTER.

CHAPTER XV.

STORY OF "SPOT," FARMER BLOUNT'S FAMOUS DOG.

AMONG the attractive denizens that Morris found at Sunnyside, was a splendid animal of the canine tribe, about four years old when the broker-lad went upon the Connecticut River farm — to which he became very strongly attached, and which in turn took a great liking to Morris, from the start.

This was farmer Blount's noble Newfoundland dog "Spot," a large black and white silky-coated fellow, curiously marked, for one of this species, and thus named on account of the numerous patches or spots that were scattered over his handsome great body, in clean relief.

"Spot" had been at the farm about a year when Morris entered old Blount's employ.

"He's a noble dog," said the young man to Eunice one day, when she was amusing herself upon the lawn in front of the house with this intelligent and comely animal.

"He is, indeed," returned Miss Eunice, pleasantly. "He knows as much as a human being too, about many things."

"He's a splendid fellow, Miss Eunice. Where did you get him?"

"Oh, Spot has a most romantic history, indeed," replied Blount's daughter. And then she narrated the following account of this sagacious beast's previous prowess, and told how he came to be a resident at Sunnyside farm.

PORTRAIT OF "SPOT," FROM LIFE.

"Spot" was a foreigner, not a native of this land. He was met with by old Blount, accidentally — when he was about three years old — and he, learning his singular history, made a handsome offer to the man who had him in possession at the time, and brought him to his farm; where a hundred times his cost could not have subsequently purchased the brave creature, whose record was as follows.

Upon the outer point of a sharp promontory extending seaward from the New England shore, there stands an old Light-house — one of the earliest structures of its kind erected by the United States Government.

A former Keeper of this Light, named Bazin, had had for a year or two a magnificent great dog, that came into his possession under the following peculiar circumstances, just after the occurrence of one of those terrible catastrophes that happened occasionally in his long experience, upon the dangerous reef near which his beacon-house stood.

One of those driving storms, so common on that coast at certain seasons, had raged two days, when Bazin's daughter, Alice — a stout-framed, brave hearted girl of twenty, and a worthy helper to her father — who had been upon the watch in the upper light during the latter part of the night, (as was her custom, alternately with the old man, in bad weather,) suddenly summoned her parent from his bed, with the alarm that a vessel of some kind had just struck on the rocks above the Lighthouse, amidst the fierce gale.

The daughter had also heard an unusual moaning at the base of the Lighthouse, but amidst the hurricane and darkness she could not make out what it was. As soon as she had roused her father, she hastily donned her rough-weather suit, and with a lantern sought for the cause of this strange sound, that still wailed out on the night wind. And very shortly she was startled to behold a huge black and white dog — that was mournfully howling beneath the lower windows of the Lighthouse.

Alice spoke to the great beast kindly, though at first she was not a little frightened, to see this extraordinary apparition in that out-of-the-way place. But she quickly recovered herself, for the docile manners of the dog assured her that he meant her no harm, but came there in search of help!

He whined nervously and ran out in front of her, when he saw her lantern; then turned, started off again, barked loudly, and strove to say "Come on, Miss. This way!" as he moved forward, heading towards the wreck. The girl fancied she understood the dumb brute, and followed him, lantern in hand, (as soon as her father came out) away to the inner shore of the ledge.

The wrecked vessel proved to be a brig, whose masts were gone, which had been driven stern on against the bowlders — where she was dashed to pieces, before the storm subsided.

In a few minutes, the Lightkeeper and his daughter, preceded by the dog, reached the rough beach; when the animal led them directly to a spot where lay two bodies — those of a woman, and a child some three years old. Alice took up the little boy, the father raised the woman, and though they were insensible and shockingly bruised, they were hurriedly borne into the hospitable Lighthouse living-room; the dog voluntarily taking up the lantern in his teeth, as they went, and exhibiting great satisfaction at the rescue of his friends.

The little boy died, however, before daybreak, and the

mother survived him but a few hours. She gave but slight information touching the disaster, for she was fatally hurt, among the sharp rocks, before she and her boy reached the shore.

Yet she stated, incoherently, that the vessel lost her masts at sea, was afterwards thrown on the rocks, the passengers and crew were washed overboard, and she with her baby had been dragged on shore by their dog. This was all — and she died next day, at noon, without further exhibition of consciousness.

The name of this woman or of the brig was never learned. The two bodies were buried in one grave, and Bazin coaxed the big dog to remain at the Lighthouse. He named him "Spot." And he subsequently became famous as a valued assistant there, in saving life and property, for a year or more.

The dog did not escape severe hurts during this accident. He was lame for two or three weeks, but being in robust health, otherwise, he soon recuperated. He was then about two years old, inordinately fond of the water, and was a powerful swimmer. The old Lightkeeper and Alice both availed themselves of his good qualities in this respect, and the evidence he had given in this instance of his courage and sagacity, induced them to believe that upon similar occasions of distress he would prove valuable in the frequently dangerous routine of their hard life.

So they encouraged Spot's fondness for the water, and soon found that he was intelligent, willing, and fearless amid the dangers of the sea, as well as very expert in his performances. And thenceforward he became their constant companion, whenever they ventured out in their boat to assist the perilled mariners, along the shore near the Lighthouse.

During the succeeding year, he had aided in saving several lives from wrecks; and, through his own individual exertions, he had rescued two persons, in that time, from drowning.

Early one morning in midsummer, a bark from Halifax, for Boston, was discovered by Bazin befogged in the offing, after a sharp gale that had occurred on the previous day. The sea still rolled heavily inland, beyond the Lighthouse, but the fog was so dense that the bark could be caught sight of only at intervals — when, from her drifting, she appeared to be rudderless, or unmanageable. She was nearing the rocky shore rapidly, with a tattered foretopsail only in sight, and Bazin quickly took the alarm.

He started the big horn, while Alice tugged away at the fog-bell, and Spot (who had been so taught) set up a fearful barking, by way of warning. But upon the lifting of the thick mist, the vessel was discovered close in shore; and very soon she struck the fatal rock-bar, broached to, and lay a helpless wreck, upon the outer reef.

Bazin sprang into his dory, Alice seized an oar, as was her habit — for she had long been inured to this exercise — Spot jumped up on the bow, standing with his eyes glistening seaward, eagerly looking out for what might turn up next, and in a few minutes this earnest trio were within hail of the crippled craft — over the side of which, upon a rudely-made raft of spars, eight or nine men and women were hurrying into the foamy sea, from the sinking bark.

The flood-tide was setting strongly in, shoreward. The vessel's boats had been stove, her main-mast was split, and more than half the crew had previously been washed overboard, by the heavy seas she had shipped during the storm. And now the Captain, his wife, the stewardess, and half a dozen sailors were fleeing upon this raft; hoping to reach the land, which they had no idea, until the vessel struck, was so near them.

Bazin discovered the raft, a moment after it was set free with its human freight, and he at once fell in its wake, though the sea ran very high. But he doubted if it would hold together, to the shore. On a sudden, a sweeping wave struck it, turned it almost over, and washed the nine men and women into the riotous waters. The dog saw all this, and in an instant *he* was overboard, battling with the plunging waves.

Bazin and Alice pulled away sharply, and picked up the Captain and second officer — one of whom seized Alice's oar, and relieved her — when two other men were caught, and saved in the boat.

Of the other five, Spot had the dress of one of the women in his stout teeth, tugging shoreward, while Alice,

EARLY HARVESTING — THE TOILERS IN THE HAY FIELD.

from the boat's prow, grasped the other female's skirt, and she was drawn in; while the remaining three men were lost sight of.

The dog struggled on, supporting the Captain's wife until he got her into shoal water, and the rolling breakers that combed in along the cove threw woman and dog up to the shore. But Spot hung firmly to his half-drowned prize, and never let go his hold, until he had her safe on dry land, out of danger.

Then, away he went again! For he had seen the three men struggling for their lives. And mounting the great wave-crests as if his ample skin had been inflated, he floundered outward, bound to afford the jeopardized sailors help, if he could. In these exciting scenes, Spot seemed to take the keenest delight, and he shortly had the satisfaction of finding another subject for his prowess; for the body of a child was being hove about in the sea, there. And seizing the loose jacket of this boy, the dog soon had *his* head out of the water.

It was the Captain's only son, five years old. Spot put away landward, once more, and clung to the lad's shoulder until they landed, in safety — though the boy knew nothing of his preserver's achievement, until five hours after he was thus saved from drowning.

Both the Captain's wife and this boy remained unconscious, a long time after their fearful drenching and fright. Spot smelt at their faces, licked their hands, set up a howl of alarm, and then rushed away to the old Lighthouse —

where the boat had already landed, with the other rescued persons.

The dog quickly made old Bazin and Alice understand that there were others yet to be looked after, and the Captain — who was in great distress at the supposed loss of wife and son — at once joined the Lightkeeper and his daughter, who followed the dog's lead to the shore, where the agonized husband and father found his wife and boy in season to restore them to life, after the trying scene through which he and they had just passed.

The two unconscious sufferers were taken to the hospitable dwelling of Bazin, and thus seven of the nine wrecked unfortunates were in this case saved from death.

Farmer Blount had business one day which called him over to Cape Ann, and he visited the Lighthouse, while he was there, out of curiosity. He encountered Spot at the door of the Light, and while he was being shown about the isolated premises by the Keeper, he noticed this handsome animal and took a fancy to him.

Miss Alice told Blount the dog's history, and the farmer at once made the old Lightkeeper a liberal offer for the animal. The man was poor, and a hundred dollars to him — all at once — looked like a great pile of money.

"I can't afford to keep no hunder'd-dollar dog 'ere," said the light-keeper, frankly. "The government pays me forty-five dollars a month, for doin' my duty 'ere. An' with three mouths to feed, an' the clo'es we wear out in a twel'-month, this don't leave us much, fer Chris'mas gifts, at the e'end o' the year, sir. I hate to part wi' Spot, that's a fact. But if he's wuth any hunder'd dollars to yeu, he ain't to me. An' yeu ken take him sir, an' very much obleeg'd to yer, fer yer offer."

The Lightkeeper took Spot over to the rail-station, old Blount paid him down a hundred dollars, and the dog was taken safely to Sunnyside — where he became an immense favorite, in after years.

"He's a good dog," said Morris, after hearing this record. "Spot and I have been excellent friends from our first acquaintance."

"So he is, indeed," insisted Miss Eunice. "And we think the world of him. There is no animal upon this farm that father Blount, or any of us, would not sooner part with, than beautiful, gentle, intelligent 'Spot.'"

CHAPTER XVI.

MORRIS AND DAVID MAKE A MUTUAL GOOD TRADE.

AFTER David Morehead returned home with his sixteen hundred dollars, which he had rather unexpectedly received for his pair of ponies, he went forward easily and steadily. He made his money occasionally by a fortunate horse-trade, in this way, but more largely by raising good cattle and sheep in numbers.

The grocer who had lighted upon the young tramp in the sugar-hogshead, (see chapter xxv.) obtained for little Jerry Burt a situation with a farmer not far from Blount's place, and the boy had gone to work there some months previously, under promising auspices.

Before David had been upon the worn-out Grimes farm five years he had brought it under good tilth, and had a stock of Shorthorns and Ayrshires that were equal to the best in the State; while his Cotswold and Merino sheep multiplied generously on his hands, and he sold them at highly remunerative prices.

The six-year-old gelding which he had mentioned to Morris, he had known from the week it was foaled. Old

Winkham valued this horse at a round figure, for that country, and those days, but David had kept his eye on him — and soon after he returned home, he bought him.

THE PLOUGHBOY MOUNTED THE FENCE.

The ploughboy Jerry, whom the grocer had sent out here, proved a steady lad, but he was a little 'homesick' and uneasy for a time, in his new quarters.

One morning he espied the letter-carrier trotting down the road toward Sunnyside farm, and mounting the fence beside the field where he had been set at work, he hailed him.

"I say, postman!"

"Well — what is it, Jerry?"

"Got any letters?"

"Yes — a lot of 'em."

"For me?"

"You? No, lad. Who should send you letters, pray?"

"It mought be, though."

"From whom?"

"Maister Mowland. He got me a good place, here, you know. And he said he'd write to me."

"Well, I've nought for you — but two for Morris Deans."

"He's over at Blount's."

"I know it."

And away went the Brandville mail-carrier, with the letters for Morris Deans. One was from David, informing him that he would soon be at Sunnyside with the Winkham colt. The other was from Frank Meyers, at New York.

The postman halted shortly at the farm-gate, and selecting the two envelopes for young Deans, delivered them a moment afterwards, upon seeing Morris coming down the driveway on his road to the hay-fields.

The little fellow watched the carrier, as he turned away, and then resumed his hoeing.

"They don't write to us poor lads," he murmured, discontentedly. "An' if Maister Mowland did, who'd read it for me? *I* can't, anyway. But he don't know that, p'raps. He didn't arx me could I read, or write. But he said he would send me a letter. Maybe he will."

Then humming an old song he had caught up among his former strolling companions, he went at his toil again, cheerfully, for he was pleasantly situated now, and had enough to eat, daily — which was quite a novelty in his young experience!

The fame of Morris Deans as a stock fancier became noted in the course of three or four years after he took to farming so kindly; and his opinion was consulted and quoted by the neighbors, far and near, upon points of excellence in live stock.

Farmer Slow — who lived half a mile above Sunnyside (on the wrong side of the River,) had plodded along in the time-worn furrows of his ancestors all his life. But he went so far out of the old ruts, on one occasion, as to venture upon procuring a sample of improved Berkshire swine, to cross upon his previously bred long-shanked wiry-haired native pigs.

In the fall of the year, his new black pigs grew so obese, and their appearance to his eye became so extraordinary, in comparison with what he had hitherto known in this class of animal, that he made up his mind the new breed he had ventured with, upon Morris' recommendation, must be dropsical. He sent for Deans to come over and examine his pens, and advise him what to do for the "pursy creturs." He showed the new and the old breeds together, and said —

"It's a dre'dful thing, Mr. Morris. That 'ere hog is a wonder. I never seen the like of him. But I reck'n he's an unfort'nate beast, arter all. It's jess my luck! Now I paid three times the price fer 'im, as yeu know, 'at I ever did afore fer a shote in my life, an' he turns out nought but a bladder o' bloat."

Morris smiled at the old-style farmer's earnestness, and alarm.

"An' yeu recommended this new-fangled stock too, Morris. He's gone up ter that 'ere figger jess like a balloon. That pig has widen'd, an' widen'd, an' he hain't hed harf the feed o' t'others. I darsen't let him eat. But, do my best, he's got so fat 'at I think he'll bu'st afore killin' time — sartin. Wot's the matter with the poor crittur?" he asked.

And Farmer Slow pointed at the two swine in his sty, as they stood side by side — the substance and the shadow! The Berkshire and the native — for the fate of the former of which he had latterly become seriously alarmed, since he had never before in his experience witnessed so extraordinary a result, and had not been educated to appreciate this improvement upon the old races.

"I should say," observed Morris, with a smile, "there is a difference in the breed of these hogs, Mr. Slow."

"An' you don't think the black' un is onhealthy, then?"

"No," returned Morris. "He is rather corpulent, to be sure. But I don't find this a serious complaint, in swine — Mr. Slow. The *other* beast you have here, is in a galloping consumption, evidently!"

Farmer Slow scratched his head — looked curiously into the face of his young friend — and concluded to discard the old farm swine he had so many years fed to little profit, and eventually vastly improved his stock of pigs, which became famous subsequently for their " remarkable obesity " at killing time.

David Morehead purchased the fast colt of Mr. Winkham, intending it for Morris.

"And you say the gelding can foot a mile in two-thirty-five?" asked David, when he paid old Winkham nine hundred dollars cash down for the pony.

"An' better, David."

"Better than 2.35?"

"Any day in the week. He's as sound as a roach, too — gets up well afore an' behind, has a clean *trot*, no hop-skip, or jump, an' he's as 'onnest as a cooper's cow at it. Yer can't break him outen his nat'ral gait, wi' no fair treatment, David. Square on his pins, every time; an' wi' proper trainin', that ere colt'll do his mile away down n the twenties, sure's yer live, boy, afore he's a year older. Now I tell it jest as it is. And don't yer fergit it," concluded old Winkham, rolling up his nine hundred dollars; which was three times the price he had ever before been paid for a Morgan colt — and he had raised a hundred, first and last.

"Nine hunder'd dollars is an orlmitey price for a six-year-old colt, though, Winkham," muttered David, "at fust hands."

"It's enough, I allow. But *yeu* don't put nary nine hunder'd dollars out, 'nless yeu know jest what yer goin' to do with yer animail, David! We all know *yeu*, hereabouts," returned the keen old fellow, with a chuckle.

THE NEW HAMPSHIRE COLT.

"If I git a thousan', or twelve hunder'd dollars for him, Winkham, I'll be satisfied," suggested David, indifferently.

"No yeu won't, David Morehead. Yeu won't arsk less'n fifteen hunder'd for him, now — will you?"

"I'll do the best I can, o' course."

"Got a customer?"

"I hope so. *I* don't want him."

"I reck'n yeu hev, then, anyhow. Wal, good luck to yer. Le'm me know what comes of him, will you?"

"Perhaps," said David — turning away with his splendid new trotter.

Within ten days, he found his way down to Brandville again — where he called on Morris, and showed him his new purchase.

"How do the ponies get on?" asked David.

"Which ones?" returned Morris.

"The black pair o' colts."

"Oh, yes. Gone — a week ago."

"Sold 'em?"

"Yes. A man came up from Worcester 'at wanted a pair o' nice carriage-horses, and he took them away."

"How much?"

"Never you mind. What have you got here now?"

"This? That's the Winkham colt — comin' six year old; an' as good a bit of hoss flesh as they make 'em, up our way, Morris."

"He's a good looker, 't all events."

"You're right, there, Morris. An' he ken *travel*, too, he ken."

"What's his speed, now?"

"Here. Get in, an' we'll take a turn down the road," said David, pleasantly — "an' you shall see."

After a half hour's exercise, Morris made up his mind that he had never gone over the ground so fast before in his life, as he had behind that beast. And this with two men in the wagon!

"What does Winkham ask for him?" inquired Morris.

"Nothing, now," returned David.

"Looking for a customer, eh?"

"No. He don't own him."

"No? Who, then?"

"He's mine. I bought him."

"What is *your* figure, then?"

"I want two thousand dollars for him, but I dassent ask it," said David. "I'm a goin' to look 'round a little. I'm told 'at *fast* 'uns are bringin' big prices down 'n York; an' I donno but I may kinder get down there with this 'un, an' see what he'll fetch among the knowin' ones."

Morris had sold his two colts, which he purchased of David for sixteen hundred two months previously, at three thousand dollars. He had determined, already, that he would own this Winkham colt before night.

"What is the bottom dollar you'll take for this fellow, now, David?" he asked insinuatingly.

"*You* don't want to giv' two thousand dollars for a hoss, I s'pose, Morris?"

"No! You're right, David, the first time. I don't."

"Then you don't want *this* 'un."

"Yes. I'll buy him — at a decent figure."

"You'll git a heap more'n that for him, Morris. *I* know. You can't fool me."

"But I have got to find my customer, you know, David."

"True. Well, I'll sell this colt, Morris, here — now — sharp's the word, an' go home — for jest eighteen hunder'd dollars."

"I'll give you fifteen hundred for him."

"No —— you won't."

"Well," said Morris, looking the superb animal all over — "I'll make it sixteen hundred."

"No, Morris."

"Let's trade, David," suggested Deans.

"I want to, Morris."

"And we'll split the difference. Come! Seventeen hundred — and it's done."

"If I hadn't a' named eighteen hunder'd, I wouldn't budge at less'n two thousand, Morris. Now you jess say *no*, at eighteen hunder'd, an' I'll give yer twenty-five dollars for doin' so. Here."

And David drew his wallet, holding out the money.

Morris opened the big farm-gate, again — at these words.

"Drive him in, David," he said. "He's mine. You're a tough fellow to bargain with, that's a fact. Now, how much do you make on him?" queried Morris, a few minutes later, as he counted out the eighteen hundred dollars.

."Never you mind, Morris," returned David, repeating the other's words. "*You'll* do well enough with him; for I tell you he's a good 'un, sure as preachin'."

So he was, to be sure.

David went home to Polly, with his clean nine hundred dollars profit made on the Winkham colt — and within the succeeding month Morris Deans concluded to take this fine gelding down to New York — to show him to some of the live horse-fanciers, and get a record for him, as to his speed, upon the Union mile-course there.

The old Boston companions had kept up a friendly correspondence in the years since they had been separated, and Morris had latterly informed Frank Meyers of his intention to make him a visit in New York city; where the latter had been flourishing so signally for a few years, as we have seen.

When he got ready to leave Sunnyside, on his contemplated trip to Manhattan, Aunt Chloé came in to bid him "good-by Mass'r Mor's;" for the good old negress had become very much attached to Deans — like the rest of Farmer Blount's household — and pretty Eunice, now past four-and-twenty, also entered the keeping-room, to give her friend good-speed on his intended journey.

"You won't be long away, Morris?" ventured Eunice, kindly.

"Only a week or two, at farthest, Euny," returned the young man. "I've got a splendid colt, in the Winkham horse, and he is too valuable to keep here. Down at York, so my old friend Meyers writes me, such animals bring great prices. And I am bound to get what he is worth, out of some one of the fancy buyers of such stock there."

Eunice Blount and Morris Deans had got to be very good friends, since the now matured young man had come from Boston to Sunnyside, a moneyless but handsome lad. And she parted with him, reluctantly.

He had never been away from his later home over twenty four hours at a time, since he came — and old Blount and his pleasant wife had come to look upon Morris as an adopted son, almost — so well had he comported himself, and so faithful had he proved in his devotion to the rich farmer's interests.

He had had a comparatively easy time of it, on the farm. He had latterly carried things pretty much in his own way, and he enjoyed his leisure of late more than when he first came to Sunnyside.

Young Deans was a good angler, and the western Massachusetts brooks were at that period alive with sparkling trout. Morris was fond of this pastime, and Miss Eunice in her floral searchings sometimes joined her friend in his fishing bouts. But the contented twain never talked of love during these very pleasant woodland excursions — so enjoyable to both.

Now, Morris had possessed himself of the Winkham trotter, which he appreciated, fully. And upon going to New York, he carefully bestowed this really valuable colt at a private stable recommended by Meyers.

He was delighted to find Ely Hawes there, who was actively at work in introducing his Bank-safe locks, at this time; and to learn also that Reuben Downer, whom he remembered as the former poor printer-lad, was on the high road to fortune, in his prospering weekly "New York Leader" establishment.

The friends cordially greeted each other, and turned back in their memories to the old days, when neither one of these four young men had a shilling in his pocket, beyond what his current demands for food and clothing absorbed.

"Those were hard times, to be sure," said Morris.

"Yes," returned Frank, gayly, "but we were among the lads who were not afraid, eh?"

"I confess that I had *my* fears," observed Ely, "at times."

"But still you were quite as hopeful as any of us, and have proved yourself more resolutely determined, in adversity's face, than the rest."

"Well, boys," interrupted Reuben, "we are surely all doing well enough, now."

"*You* may say so, Reuben, with emphasis," returned Frank.

"And you, my dear Meyers?"

"Ah, well. You know I never complained."

"Nor I," added Morris.

"Nor I, egad," continued Ely. "It has been a little rough, sometimes, but daylight broke upon *my* prospects two years ago; and every thing is now as promising as I could wish. I'll have my hundred thousand, now."

"Good! And you, Morris," continued Reuben Downer, "I hear you are making your fortune, too, upon a farm?"

"I have done very well — so far."

"What is it Meyers tells me about your live stock operations? You have brought a good piece of horse-flesh here with you, eh?"

"A *very* good one, Reuben."

"What is it?"

"A bay gelding."

"Blooded?"

"Morgan," said Morris.

"A trotter?"

"Yes — and as clean a one as you ever saw."

"How fast?"

"I really don't know that, yet. But, lively — I promise you."

"I am the owner of two or three good 'uns, Morris. You shall ride behind one of them, if you like, to-morrow."

"Thank you. I have heard that you, and other gentlemen in York — Jerome, Vanderbilt, and Lorrillard, have paid high figures for some of your nags."

"Yes. That is so. But some of us here have got flyers — Morris."

"In speed, you mean?"

"Yes."

"What do you call a 'flyer,' Reuben?"

"Oh — anywhere well down in the twenties."

"Yes. That must be fast."

"It is. A young horse bought down in Maine not long since, owned by a friend of mine, has shown a speed upon the track, this month, of 'twenty-four."

"Twenty-four? What is that?"

"A mile — around the track — in two minutes and twenty-four seconds."

"What is such an animal worth, Reuben?"

"If he can beat that time, and is sound and right — there are half a dozen men in New York to-day, Morris, who will check out five and twenty thousand dollars for such a colt — willingly."

"Twenty-five *thousand!* Or, twenty-five hundred, Reuben?"

"Thousand, I said, my boy."

The heart of young Morris leaped into his throat at this off-hand announcement of Reuben — who he had been informed had paid some heavy prices for his favorite horses. But the Connecticut River "countryman" was *not* prepared for this!

"I had no idea that even good horses brought such prices," he said.

"Oh, yes. And there is sharp competition, too, among those who want the best. *I* will give thirty thousand dollars cash, for a good sound colt, not over six or seven years old, that can do his mile, in two minutes and twenty seconds," said Downer, squarely.

"And what for one that can trot a mile in 2.28, or '30?"

"That is good. But I don't want that kind of a nag, now. I can beat all that sort of time, with what I've got, Morris."

"Yes, I s'pose so. I don't know what my colt can do. But I propose to ascertain," said Morris, after a moment's thought.

"I would like to see him trot, Morris."

"You shall, of course."

"It *may* be you've got a good 'un."

"I have, Reuben."

"If he can go down to twenty-three —"

"He has never been trained, at all."

"Ah, well. Noble can tell you."

"Noble?"

"Yes. He is a professional whip. He can judge, and so can I, upon seeing him perform. My way is to 'hold the ticker,' myself. If you've got any such colt as I have indicated, you can get his full value, here in York, I assure you, any day."

"To-morrow, we will see, then."

"Yes. I will take you out in my phaeton. You shall see what we have got here, now, and we will see what you have brought us. There's money in a right good 'un, though, Morris."

Young Deans thought his prospects promising, now!

He left his friends, and went to examine his new purchase. "Two-thirty-five, and two-twenty-five," he said to himself. "There's a difference, there. I thought this colt was a stunner. But he can't touch *that!*"

However — he would be able to get a handsome advance upon the price he had paid for his animal, anyway, he concluded.

And *if* he showed any thing like the speed they had been talking of, he would really make a small fortune on his venture.

Ely was now getting ready for the approaching Institute Fair that would soon come off in New York, where he intended to exhibit his Safe Locks, in competition for the Association's Medal. And he was busy.

Frank Meyers appointed a meeting with Reuben Downer and Morris, for the following afternoon — when they were all to learn something about the speed of the lauded colt young Morris had brought to New York.

"I don't know much about these 'flyers' they have here" murmured young Deans, "but I do know that this Winkham colt is a hard one to beat, for his years. We shall see what he can do, to-morrow."

And with this he went hopefully to his lodgings, confident that he possessed a rare young animal in this promising trotter.

CHAPTER XVII.

HOW MR. TWEEDLE MADE, AND LOST IT.

"—— a hundred years ago,
If men were knaves, why, people called them so.
The Ten Commandments had a meaning then,
Felt in their bones by least considerate men.
Now — since to steal by law is grown an art —
Whom " rogues " the sires, their milder sons call " smart! "
J. R. LOWELL.

As a contrast to the *rightful* mode of " making money," we set down just here a brief record of the course pursued by noted Mr. Tweedle, of Gotham — who made a goodly fortune, and lost it — with his ill-gained reputation.

The fate of this bad man was but one of many, on a lesser scale. And a sketch of his career may possibly serve as a healthful warning to those who incline inadvertently, blindly, or wilfully to be tempted by the base advice of those like the miserable votary of avarice whose dying injunction to his hopeful heir, was " Get money, my son — honestly, if you *can;* but get money ! "

Tweedle, from his boyhood, was both heartless and avaricious — "a captive fettered to the oar of gain." As he grew to manhood, he became more grasping, more determined in his will to obtain gold unlawfully, more ambitious of the possession of a hoard of wealth, and more reckless as to the means through which it might be attained.

Though he did not openly announce the fact perhaps, yet his erratic life demonstrated that it was of no consequence, in his opinion, *how* riches are obtained, so that the desired end be reached, successfully. Thus he went on, unscrupulously, and conquered fortune marvellously, until he found himself the master of millions, first — and then became an inmate of a loathsome prison; where he may scarcely live long enough to atone for the hideous wrongdoing that characterized his worthless life, for years and years before he was brought to account for his folly and misdeeds.

The brute is happier than such a human beast can ever be! The stupid jackass is thought to be miserable. Yet his evils are not brought on by himself, or through his own fault; *he* feels only those which nature has inflicted. But this 'poor creetur' Tweedle, in addition to the necessary ills that human flesh is naturally heir to, drew down upon his head a multitude of others — and paid the penalty at last, in part, for his wilful wickedness.

Charles Mildmay thinks that the disposition to do a bad deed is the most terrible punishment of the deed it performs. And it should never be forgotten that it is a man's own dishonesty, his crimes, his shortcomings, and his barefaced assurance that takes from him natural soundness of mind, and 'leaves but a wreck behind,' however fortunate or successful he may be in a pecuniary view, temporarily, through a course of unprincipled conduct or false dealing with his fellow-men.

(BEFORE.) MR. TWEEDLE "ON HIS MAKE."

A man is made great or little by his own will and intent. "Every man stamps his true value on himself," says Schiller. The price we challenge for ourselves is given us. There does not exist the sane man — be his station what it may — who may not be the carver of his own fortune, be it good or indifferent, in the main — under given circumstances. There is the wrong, as there is the right way, however. And Mr. Tweedle chose to travel upon the former road.

Long prior to the days of which we now write, the huge political power of New York city centred in what was then familiarly known as the "Tammany ring." In the later times, (though the nature of this fraternal combination has been little changed,) the older hard-heads connected with this colossal association have passed away; and those who inaugurated this institution have left the scene, forever — to the fostering care of men of lesser calibre, but similar in purpose and natural conformation.

Of this formidable later ring, Mr. Tweedle was an active member, for several years, and finally became recognized as one of its leading Sachems. The small fry dubbed this arch intriguer "boss," by way of compliment. And, though he was not a man of talent, he possessed a genius for "management," and passed for a good "organizer," in his palmy days.

But genius crops out of different kinds — in different individuals. It sometimes needs the spur, but quite as frequently it requires the curb. Good genius finds its first and last requirements in a love of probity, truth and honor. Bad genius eternally haunts its possessor, while it torments and harasses the community in which he lives. It again and again perils the position and fortunes of its holder, too. And lucky he is, indeed, if it do not sooner or later wreck his estate, and blast his name, irrevocably!

All politicians are not thieves, or unprincipled men — by any means. Yet, however disagreeable may be the assertion, there is unfortunately too much of these bad qualities existing among the parties in this country, of any political denomination.

Genius is called the instinct of enterprise. A lad one day approached the musical composer, Mozart, desiring to write a piece of music, and inquiring the way to begin. "Wait," said the great master. "Time enough."

"*You* composed earlier than at my age," urged the boy. "But I asked nothing about it," returned the musician, curtly.

Mr. Tweedle possessed a modicum of genius of the objectionable kind. He was not talented, but intuitively illiterate, and vulgar in his ideas and aims. He was everlastingly a prey to unruly sordid passions. He possessed small refinement in taste, little culture, less truthfulness, and no spark of moral honesty, in his *outré* composition. And *his* genius was of the character that challenges only pity; for, as Holmes has it, it " stood a good chance of dying in a hospital, or a jail — in hopeless debt, and bad repute."

Mr. Tweedle did not ask questions, either. He went forward with a recklessness and show of enterprise full worthy of a better cause — upon this wrong road — all unmindful of the truthful apothegm that he who commits wrong will himself inevitably "see the writing upon the wall," sooner or later.

But Tweedle was a politician — in his way — and he came to be a leader among modern Tammany-ites. He wormed himself into office, obtained power within the ring, robbed everybody publicly or privately, whom when and wherever he could find opportunity — and in a few years became enormously rich.

The celerity with which his great fortune was acquired, astonished even those who were associated with him, covertly.

"How do you do it, Tweedle?" asked the quid nuncs and the ambitious younger men who surrounded him, or followed in his wake.

"Never you mind, boys. It's all right," says Tweedle. "And there's more of it, in the same hopper — enough for you and for me, and for our children, and their children. There's millions in it — yet. We have only begun, boys!"

When Tweedle had five hundred thousand dollars in his hands, which he had filched indirectly from the city treasury by means of swindling, false entries, bogus certified accounts, long bills, made-up vouchers, and bare-faced unrighteous claims — he went from bad to worse with a flowing sail, of a truth.

"A mere bagatelle!" he said, contemptuously, when some one in the ring suggested to Tweedle that "he must be worth a million."

"A mere drop in the bucket," he exclaimed.

"What is your mark, then?"

"Five millions at the least," returned the bold knave, unblushingly. "And five millions more, on the top of that."

"A huge amount, this, Tweedle!"

"Nothing like doing your work thoroughly, while you're about it," suggested Tweedle, stroking his fat stomach, complacently. "A man used to be reckoned well off with fifty to a hundred thousand dollars to his name. But, bless your innocence, what would that paltry sum do, nowadays? Nothing!"

"It isn't bad to take, though, Tweedle — nevertheless."

"What?"

"A cool hundred thousand dollars."

"Pooh! Five times that sum is requisite, in *our* trade, to keep a man outside the gates of the State Prison!" ejaculated the monstrous overgrown thief, carelessly.

The months and years sped by. Tweedle rolled up his ill-gotten gains, by millions, in the mean time. He led the van in the political ring of which he had long been an active ardent member. Scores of his fraternal associates in Tammany were following diligently in his footsteps. They gathered riches, too — but he claimed and seized the lion's share.

"How much is Tweedle worth, to-day?" asked an outsider.

"Millions — at the least."

"How many?"

"No one knows."

"Where does he get it, thus rapidly. He was a poor laborer but a few years since."

"I know it."

"Now — a nabob!"

"Yes. A modern Crœsus."

"He is not a speculator?"

"No."

"A stock-jobber?"

"No."

"A merchant?"

"No."

"A banker, haply?"

"No."

"What then?"

"A fat office-holder."

"Ah. Yes — I see. But where does he get his money?"

"Steals it."

"Tweedle!"

"Yes. That is the plain English of the thing. *Convey*, I think is the word used, commonly. But this other is the way honest men pronounce the term."

"Convey?"

"Ay — 'appropriate,' if you like the word better. He's a big thief, that is all."

"Why don't they stop him, in this plundering?"

" Who ? "

" Anybody ! The government."

" *He* is the government, here, man."

" I know he is " high in the senate," politically, but it's a grievous *wrong* — all this."

" So it is. Let us see you right it ! "

" Who, me ? "

" You, or anybody else."

" I have no power — "

" He has."

" And more's the pity ! "

Other years went by. Tweedle was reputed worth ten millions of dollars, at length. This might have been over the mark. But he had enough — of other people's money. And one day Mr. Tweedle suddenly found himself arrested by the municipal authorities, charged with the commission of the grossest and heaviest fraud and peculation ever alleged against any individual upon the American continent!

He was said to have purloined from and cheated the city treasury out of millions of dollars; and his name became thenceforth a by-word and a reproach.

" How much ? " asked Tweedle, with a sickly attempt at a smile, when the almost fabulous amount that he had robbed the people of was announced in the twelve formidable indictments preferred against him by the grand jury.

" Over eleven millions in the aggregate, that we have

thus far discovered," responded the District Attorney, severely. It proved over thirty millions — all told — in the end!

"Those who joy in wealth, alone, says a good man, grow avaricious; those who joy only in their friends, often sacrifice nobleness of spirit; those who joy in surroundings, sink dignity of character; but those who joy in true liberty — which is simply that all should act upon the golden rule, and do as they would be done by — possess the happiest of joys. This is a joy that no one can barter away. But very few possess it."

From the nature of things, it is certain that the wealth of a majority of people in this world must be limited. The product of labor throughout the world, if equally divided, would not make the share of each individual large. It is impossible that every one should be what is called rich. But it is by no means impossible to be independent. And what is the way to compass this "glorious privilege"? The method is very simple. It consists in one rule. *Limit your wants.* Make them few and inexpensive. To do this would interfere but little with your real enjoyment. It is mostly a matter of habit. You require more, or you are satisfied with less, just as you have accustomed yourself to one or the other. Limit your wants, estimate their cost, and never exceed it, taking pains to keep it always inside of your income. Thus you will secure a lasting independence. Young men should think of this. A great deal of the happiness of their lives depends upon it. After having made your money, spend it as you choose, honestly; but be sure you make it, *before* you spend it.

But as avarice increases with the increasing pile of wealth obtained in haste at others' cost, so Tweedle's grasping disposition had driven him on to the assumption of greater risks, and more inordinate measures through which to add to his rapidly augmenting riches, wrongfully obtained, until he suddenly went to the wall — and hopelessly.

It is but a question of time. At the terminus of this wrong road, stand destruction, and death! The wicked may flourish for a season, but " they shall not always prosper," saith the Book of books.

The community had been so outraged and utterly scandalized by Tweedle's bold villany and the wrong-doing of his aiders and abettors, after a term, that farther endurance of this evil ceased to be deemed a virtue, in the metropolis where this big offender had gone on so long in his successful infamy. And one fine morning, while he defied his critics and bade his opponents do their worst, the over-confident and unscrupulous Mr. Tweedle went up.

Still, he had flourished until the Devil got him well 'down in the depths' — and left him to get out of his dilemma, as best he could.

"And what do you style this principle, Mr. Tweedle, which you say is the governing element in your association?" asked an anxious inquirer, one day.

"Dimocracy, they call it," said Tweedle, as he rubbed his ponderous fat paunch, contentedly.

"A very good name, Mr. Tweedle."

"Euphonious," said Tweedle, with a leer.

"But you consider this mere gammon, eh?"

"That is another word for it, yes."

"It evidently pays?" suggested his interlocutor.

"Well — that depends," replied Tweedle. "Ekal rights is a fine thing, in the abstrack. We go fer the greatest good o' the greatest number, allers."

"And what is that?"

"Why — number one —— ain't it?"

"Ah, I see."

"It's a great blessin'," continued Tweedle, "this bringin' all men on a ekality with each other."

"So it is," returned his friend.

"A big thing," replied Tweedle, in his undaunted style of impudence and self-assurance.

It was a big thing, to be sure! A crime of crimes — considered in all its bearings — under the peculiar circumstances of this man's case.

And what resulted?

"He escaped punishment, of course," suggests the casual observer. "They always do. These big thieves are rarely convicted. It is the poor deserted hungry lad who takes a loaf of bread from the rich man's door-step in the winter's morning to save him from starvation, who is caught and sent to prison. No such offenders as Mr. Tweedle can be reached, ordinarily."

True. But wait a moment.

" Ah, I can see! Tweedle defied them. He had too much money for them. Able attorneys, and plenty of them, stood ready to defend the wealthy thief, and Court, lawyers, jurors, officials could be bought — with ready gold! All of them have their price, he claimed. And in Tweedle's case, there was money enough to purchase a regiment of these people."

Wait — gentle reader.

Let us see.

The best legal talent in the land was employed by Tweedle to defend him against the vast charges of " irregularities " in which he at last became involved.

From month to month — for many months — the case was put off, postponed, deferred, delayed. Mr. Tweedle, meantime, found himself called on to furnish responsible sureties for bail in the trifling sum of a million of dollars — to begin with!

This was readily furnished, the rich villain being able absolutely to secure his friends — as he did — by transferring to them double this amount of unencumbered real estate, for the favor desired by Tweedle.

" Then he was tried — at last — and acquitted ? "

Not much!

Mr. Tweedle travelled 'around the circle,' for months, thereafter. Now in England, now in Canada, now in Havana, now West, now South, now East. But when time was called, eventually — he put on his boldest front, snapped his fingers contemptuously in the face of accusers, court, jury, and the public — and appeared for trial.

Meantime, his guilty partners in the monstrous robbery of the people's chest had decamped — and, like the rats that leave the sinking ship, they made themselves scarce — upon Tweedle's instigation, and at Tweedle's cost, in the principal instances.

But justice was upon Tweedle's heels, in earnest. It is a long lane that has no turn in it, however bright and promising the path may seem, for the nonce. Tweedle had now actually come within sight of the turn in that wrong road, upon which he had for years been travelling unmolested, and so thrivingly.

The trial was prolonged, and his well-paid counsel did their utmost legally, technically, sympathetically, and earnestly to show that Mr. Tweedle was as white as milk, as pure as snow, and had been foully calumniated, in the allegations made against him.

The judge charged clearly and forcibly. The Jury retired for but brief conference — for a long deliberation was unnecessary. They could not be bought, or bribed, or scared. And they came into court with a decided verdict — to which all the people cried *amen*, — GUILTY, on *all* the twelve indictments!

Tweedle's under jaw fell, sensibly, at this crushing announcement. *One* count might possibly have been sustained, by the overwhelming array of testimony that had been introduced against the hitherto lively politician.

But twelve of them — guilty upon *all* — and no exceptions permitted!

What next, for heaven's sake?

The Penitentiary — of course!

The sentence of his Honor followed quickly; and so scathing and severe a line of remarks preceding this finality, in Tweedle's case, never before or since fell from the lips of an honorable minded upright judge upon the American bench.

Vigorous efforts were now made to save the wretch from his just doom. Tweedle was sentenced to twelve years' incarceration in the State Prison. And all Tammany stood aghast at this result in the famous Tweedle trial.

" It carn't be!"

" It arn't so!"

" What? Tweedle sent to the penitensherry!"

These were the fierce ejaculations that burst from the lips of the faithful, when the news came that " Tweedle had gone up, at last."

" A big gun spiked, there!"

" A bully Tammany boy provided for, now!" suggested others.

Tweedle wriggled — fought — objected — appealed — argued — swore — fretted — threatened — begged —— but all to no purpose.

He had sinned. Justice had overtaken him. He was fairly tried, convicted, and 'put away,' at length, as he richly deserved.

We may see Tweedle, drawn to the life, as he was in the days of his wicked prosperity, a jolly fat Tammany leader — at the commencement of this chapter.

Here is another photograph of this same personage,

(AFTER.) TWEEDLE AMID HIS REFLECTIONS.

above, in his subsequent prison-quarters — where he was serving out his sentence of a dozen years for gaining his pile through robbery of the public chest; a mode of 'making it' which can never become popular, and which in all ways or manner is heartless, dishonest, and despicable to the very last degree.

We note these facts simply by way of caution; and turn from this disagreeable contrast, to follow out the more creditable modes adopted by those in whom we take the greater interest — and in whom our readers will find far more agreeable illustrations, either for study or emulation — no doubt.

CHAPTER XVIII.

"TWO-TWENTY-TWO" FOR THE MORRIS DEANS COLT!

When Meyers, Downer, and Morris Deans met the next day after Morris came down to New York, they examined the bay Morgan gelding he brought with him, critically, and Downer pronounced him 'a good 'un to look at.'

"And he's a good 'un to go," observed Morris, confidently.

"No doubt of it," returned Downer, warming up, as he scrutinized the fine points of this extraordinary young horse.

The muscular shoulder, broad chest, long deep hip, full loins, prominent withers, short pastern, small clean foot, even lined back, and ample fore-arm struck the connoisseur in horse-flesh as highly promising.

"But," taking up his fore-leg, "what have you got upon his feet?" he asked.

"Shoes," replied Morris; "what else should he have there?"

"Do you call these things *shoes?*" asked Downer, with a smile.

"Yes. I had him fresh-shod just before I left Brandville," continued Morris.

"Marcus!" said Downer, hailing the private stable groom, with whom he was acquainted.

"Yes, sir."

"Take this colt over to Weber's, and tell him, with my compliments, to put a set of Downer's style of shoes upon his feet."

"Yes sir."

"We know how to *shoe* a horse in New York, Morris — any way. And now, while your colt is absent, step over to the stable and we'll take a look at my nags."

The three friends examined Downer's fast horses in their stalls, and Reuben ordered his best trotter into a light wagon. Meyers remained behind, (he had been there, previously,) and Morris with Downer took a turn upon the Bloomingdale Road; where young Deans went over the ground as rapidly, for a two-mile spurt and back, as he cared to ride, in this world — so he declared — behind his friend Downer's favorite trotting mare.

An hour or two afterwards, the gentlemen went to the course, Morris driving his new bay colt over, and Meyers taking a seat beside Downer in his wagon.

It had been arranged by Downer that an experienced driver, accustomed to the track, should hold the ribbons over Morris' horse, and that Downer, Meyers, Deans and the track-keeper should occupy the judge's stand, where they could have a favorable chance to view the colt's performance, in which all felt a deep interest.

The animal was in very good spirits, and for his heavy lumpy country shoes a neat thin trotting shoe having been substituted, the horse evidently felt much easier on his pins and more free in his footing than his owner had ever seen him, before.

Downer held his stop-watch in his hand, to time the colt — and gave the word to 'go!' after his driver had moved him up and down the track smartly, a few minutes, by way of exercise. He went round the mile track, and crossed the line at the close in 2.31.

"That is very well," observed Downer, "for a first attempt. He's a trotter."

"Try him again," said Morris, eagerly.

"Let him breathe a little," suggested Downer.

"O, he's as fresh as a newly caught blue-fish," observed Morris. "And he can beat all that sort o' gait. *I* can drive him five seconds better, myself."

"Go!" shouted Downer, as the colt came up sharply, a moment afterwards.

And he went. And returning, he passed the score in 2.27, with apparent ease.

"Better! He's a good 'un, Morris," cried Downer.

"Put the Buckskin horse beside him," suggested Downer, "at the next trial. *He* can show a 2.28 gait, ordinarily. Let's see how badly the colt can beat him."

David jogged down the road, and came spinning back again, past the Blount farm, at a tearing gait — and away to the Brandville tavern-stables — saying quietly to himself, "I've found a customer for the Morgan colts." [CHAP. xiv. page 213.

After ten minutes' rest, and walking exercise, old Buckskin was brought out from the course-stable, and away went the two horses, for an exhibition of their best speed ; the three friends being greatly exercised at the prospect of this improvised trotting-match.

Downer watched the young animal with his experienced eye as he went, and announced his time — "first quarter-post, 36 seconds, half mile 1.12, third quarter 1.49, at score in 2.26!" leading Buckskin nearly two lengths, and never making a skip in the entire mile.

"Bravo! he *is* a good 'un," exclaimed Downer, enthusiastically.

"I told you so," said Morris, intensely gratified at this splendid performance.

Then the handsome beast was carefully groomed, and the friends returned leisurely to the private city stable, where Morris bestowed his horse once more.

"Well," observed Deans, "what do you say to that, Downer, for a six-year-old?"

"I say this, Morris. And you will appreciate my disinterestedness, I think. If you will put that colt into Noble's hands, for training, I believe that within three months he will show a clean record of 2.22 or '23."

"What would he be worth, in such an event?"

"All you can get for him, my dear fellow. *I* may want to buy him," returned Downer.

"What will you give for him?"

"I won't take any advantage of you, by an offer, now.

Wait. Let him show us what he can do — and there are enough to bid for him. I will buy him, if no one will offer more than I am then disposed to give."

"Thank you, my friend. I will take your advice," responded Morris. "I will return to Brandville in a few days — and leave the pony behind, in care of the party you have recommended. At the end of three months, I will come down to New York, again — see what the colt can then do — and act accordingly. I think he is cut out for a winner, Reuben — and you may make a pile with him, if you manage rightly."

"If I purchase your colt," said Downer, "he will never 'win' any money for me."

"Why not, then?"

"That is not my style, Morris. I never wagered a copper upon the speed of a horse, or upon any other object. And I never intend to."

"No? But you go in to beat 'em all, I notice."

"For the pleasure and the satisfaction of the thing — yes. I mean to own the fastest trotters in the world. This is my hobby, if you so please to term it. But I will never bet a dollar, or trot a horse for a shilling at stake, under any circumstances whatever. Upon the road, I dislike to 'take the dust' of those who ride for pleasure, as I do — and I manage to avoid *this* inconvenience, as a rule. But that is all. Never for pecuniary gain. I have no occasion to enter into this sort of competition, thank fortune."

And Reuben Downer adhered to this — upon principle — in his future; though he did own the fastest trotting stud in America, as everybody knew.

Morris remained in the city a week, during which time he was constantly in the society of Meyers and Ely, riding about with Downer, or looking after his colt, occasionally.

Then he went back to Sunnyside, where the Blount family received him right cordially — Miss Eunice being foremost in congratulating her enterprising friend upon his safe return to the farm again.

"It has been *so* lonesome, Morris," she said, naively, "since you left us! I wouldn't have believed we could have missed any one thus, from our always happy household."

"I had a right good time, Euny, among old friends of my youth, there, I assure you," replied Morris. "And I am to go down there again."

"Soon?" queried Eunice.

"In three months."

"Did you accomplish your object, Morris?"

"No. But I laid the train for this, towards a result beyond my most sanguine anticipations, I assure you."

Then he explained his recent experience in New York city — and old Blount entered, to join in the conversation.

"Seems to me," observed the farmer, "that's an awful price for a man to pay for a single horse, Morris. Did you say twenty *thousand* dollars?"

"I agree with you, sir. But I am correct. Ten to

twenty thousand dollars have been paid, I know — in some instances, and I hear, in exceptional cases, even more than this."

"What in the world do they find in a horse to command any such figures, I wonder?"

"Speed, sir."

"Speed?"

"Yes, sir — and bottom."

"Well, upon my word, it will pay to raise good colts, at that price. And you say you didn't sell yours?"

"No sir. Not yet."

"Why not? I thought he was a very superior beast."

"So he is, sir. But he is quite undeveloped, I think. And his trainer — in whose care I have left him — says he is 'too soft,' and too fleshy, to do his best at present. I leave him in New York therefore, three months — in this expert's care, and then I will go down there to look to him. My friend Downer, who knows the men and the market there, and is himself a right good horse-fancier, thinks I may then obtain a round price for the colt, if he comes up as we are constrained to believe he will, from what he has performed already."

"I'm glad to hear of your success, Morris. But, really, I don't believe I could put on the face to take ten or fifteen thousand dollars for one horse! I couldn't — that's a fact."

"You remember what you paid for your best short-horn bull, "*Arack*," sir?" asked Morris, referring to Blount's purchase of a fine stock animal he had imported, at a cost of six hundred guineas — over $3,000.

"Ah, well — yes. That was a superior blooded animal, and of great service to a man's stock, towards improving his grade blood."

"But this is a fine Morgan colt of mine, sir; and those which I have referred to, that command such wondrous prices, are also pedigreed stock, or imported bloods."

"Well, there's some difference between three thousand and twenty thousand, Morris! Either is bad enough."

"Will you sell your *young* Arack, sir — (out of your imported animal, now three years old) for three thousand dollars?"

"No, no! Of course not —"

"I thought you wouldn't. But why not, sir?"

"He's not for sale," said Blount.

"No — I know it. And you wouldn't take five thousand for him! I can get it, if you will part with him, sir."

"No. No —"

"Then if I can find a man who wants my young horse on account of any particular virtue or extraordinary capacity he possesses, at a figure say five and twenty thousand dollars above what I gave for him, you would not have me reject such a proposal, would you, sir?"

"No, no!" responded Blount. "That is right. At the same time, it is an extravagant price for a horse, I say. *I* wouldn't give twenty-five thousand dollars for twenty-five of the best horses on earth — for my own use, Morris."

And with this the old farmer left the room, as Eunice said —

"You will make a fortune out of your purchase, Morris, at this rate."

Matters went along smoothly for three months afterwards, and Morris proceeded to New York again. He found his friends once more and learned that the horse had continued to improve, wonderfully.

They went out to the track, once more — Morris, Meyers and Downer. The day was fine and cool, and Noble brought the colt out to give him a final trial, before Morris offered him for sale.

He was in splendid condition, and after two or three circuits around the course, the word was given him, and Noble drove him a measured mile, from score to score, in the unlooked-for time — 2.22! without a break in his trot, from the word 'go!'

Morris Deans left New York the next day for Brandville and Sunnyside, in very good spirits.

Reuben Downer had purchased his fast colt, and paid him cash for it, five and twenty thousand dollars!

That horse could not have been bought of Downer, one month subsequently, for fifty thousand dollars.

But Morris was content with this trade.

"I did very well with the colt, sir," he said on his return to Sunnyside.

"Yes, you did," admitted Blount.

"The man who bought him can afford the luxury, too."

"I hope so."

"He is rich, sir."

"He ought to be!"

"Ten years ago, he wasn't worth five dollars, sir."

"2.22, MARKED TIME," FOR THE MORRIS DEANS COLT.

"Who is it, Morris?"

"Reuben Downer, sir."

"Ah, yes. I've heard of him. The "*Leader*" man?"

"Yes, and an old friend of mine. He knows what a good paper ought to be, sir."

"That is so. And he knows what a good horse is, too, I presume," concluded Farmer Blount.

CHAPTER XIX.

HOW A SECRET GOVERNMENT "INFORMER" MADE IT.

WHATEVER may be "done at *any* time," is never done at all. We must begin right at the beginning — and keep on doing, in this life — to gain our lawful ends. This world is fortunately a grand work-shop, where there is plenty to do, and the tools are at hand, if we but choose to take them up and use them.

Men did not make this world, but they may mend it. He who keeps his eyes open, by daylight, will find that this same world, though a precious good one, mostly, contains a great many fools who are too dull to be employed by anybody, and many a knave, as well, who is too sharp to be! But it is the compound of this twain that we oftenest meet, and with whom we may have, perhaps — in the long run — the most to do, directly or indirectly.

Mose Topley — christened Moses — for example, was a first-class intriguer. He had passed fully twenty years of his early life in "laying round" upon his poor relations, whenever he was not supported through shiftless dependance upon his victims — and he had contrived to wheedle and over-match all who harbored or trusted him, from as far back in his history as any one who knew any thing at all about him could remember.

Mose Topley was a very extraordinary being. Never ill-tempered, never out of sorts with the world, or any mortal in it — but eternally pre-disposed to dodge, or shy responsibility, and to put off till to-morrow, or next week, or next year, what might and should have been entered upon to-day.

Indolent, uncertain, and shiftless as he was, he was a keen fellow in small trickery, and regularly up in all sorts of "sharp practice," in his way. But his way indeed was a very poor way.

For years and years he never had a dime that he fairly earned. He could never find the implements that lie about in this great working world, ready to be lifted and applied to good uses, by the industriously and honestly inclined. And no living mortal could tell, for the life of him, how Mose Topley lived, where he lived, whither he came from, or where he went to, from week to week, and year after year, for upwards of thirty years.

Mose travelled, nevertheless.

That is to say — he absented himself from Boston, (where he nominally hailed from, for a long period), and he turned up in Springfield, New York, Philadelphia, Washington, Richmond, Canada — California — everywhere, anywhere, at times when apparently the least expected.

He was frequently stumbled on, without warning, in the corridors of the public buildings, at the Capitol, and his smiling face and stealthy form mousing around would confront you at any unlooked-for turn, emerging from beneath the arches, or from behind the pillars, as he groped about with velvet foot, apparently busy, but never engaged in any actual pursuit or object that any official or clerk in the Departments at Washington had any knowledge of.

MOUSING MOSE TOPLEY.

Yet he was always ready with an explanation, if needful, and constantly on his ever smooth tongue he had some plausible inquiry to offer, to ward off suspicion that he was up to mischief; though in justice to this curious being, it should be said that he was as indolent and as harmless as a lizard, and apparently about as aimless.

But he never had any ostensible business. He journeyed without luggage — and came and went, none knew or learned whence, or whither. He never paid tavern or hotel fare — coach or railway transportation. Everybody seemed to know Mose Topley, but no man could tell you who he was, what he was employed about, or how he subsisted.

He run up bills at the hotels, but never thought of paying a landlord a dollar, any more than if he had never seen him! If he were asked for money, he would immediately disappear, and try another house in the same place — or elsewhere.

Pay? Mose Topley *pay* anybody any thing? He never dreamed of such vulgar nonsense!

At one time, in his later experience, Moses was said to be employed by an Express Company, in some sort of capacity that was never understood. But, through some gerrymandering process or other, he got upon the blind side of one of the leading Directors of this Company, and he played the amateur Detective, in their service, for a term — as one of his make-shifts.

He was a perambulating human mystery. He went up and down from Boston and New York to Washington, and South, or West. But what he did, how much he accomplished, or who he interfered with for ten years (in this last mentioned capacity), was never discovered.

"What do you pay Mose, for this service?" asked a creditor of his one day, of one of the Express Company principals.

"Nothing," said the proprietor.

"Does he work for nothing?"

"He doesn't work!"

"He is in your employ?"

"Is he?"

"I hear so, sir."

"Who told you that?"

"I don't remember."

"If he is, *I* don't know it."

"But he travels for you?"

"Not that I know of."

"He represents you — en route."

"Does he?"

"Yes, sir."

"What does he say?"

"That he — that he belongs —"

"Well, to *what?*"

"I declare I can't say."

"Nor I!"

"He's a very queer fellow."

"So he is."

"Owes me thirty dollars."

"How long?"

"Over a year!"

"Loaned?"

"Yes, sir."

"I wish you may get it."

"And you don't owe him any thing?"

"Not a dime. Never did."

"It is a strange case."

"Very," said the Express man.

This was all that the anxious money-lender who had accommodated Moses could learn about his status, in that concern.

And still Mose went, and came.

Amongst the politicians, Moses somehow made himself a marked favorite. *Why*, no man could say. He never cast a vote in his life, he never paid a poll-tax anywhere, and he had no more 'influence' among his race than a house cat.

Yet everybody liked Mose, especially in Washington. He was intimate in the Departments. Went in and out without question or challenge at Committee-rooms, at the Capitol, through the public buildings, the White House — anywhere — as freely as he did at the hotels, the restaurants and the railway stations.

Moses never spoke an unkind word to anybody, and no man ever uttered an offensive word to him. He could eat anybody's bread, drink anybody's wine, or smoke anybody else's cigars — save his own.

For that matter, he never had any thing of his own. And he did not carry with him, in all his tens of thousands of miles of journeying, first or last — even a carpet-bag.

"A queer fellow is Mose Topley," observed a Congressman one day in our hearing, in Washington. "What does he do?"

"Do? Surely you ought to know."

"But I don't! I've known him here and elsewhere, now, a dozen years. But I never knew what he employed himself about."

"He doesn't do any thing, I reckon."

"What supports him?"

"I don't know."

" Got any money ? "

" I never saw him with a shilling in his possession, in my life."

" Singular."

" Very."

" We all tolerate him, here."

" What for ? "

" I don't know, I'm sure."

" Did he ever do any thing for you ? "

" O, no. Mose doesn't hail from my State."

" What State does he hail from ? "

" 'Gad! I don't know that. But I know he's a very clever fellow — from down east, I hear."

" How is he clever ? "

" Well, 'pon my word, I can't say, to tell the truth."

" Then you don't know any thing about him ? "

" No — that's so. But I return your query. Do you ? "

" Not a syllable."

" Nor any one else, I fancy. He is a very mysterious personage."

" About what ? "

" I don't know that, either."

" Do you know any one who does know ? "

" Not a soul."

" Did you ever hear of anybody who ever heard any one else say they knew Mose Topley ? "

" Never ! "

"That will do. I think he must be the great (or small) 'Unknown'!"

This was precisely what resulted, upon inquiring who this strange being was, of anybody — anywhere.

Moses had an impressive style of imparting information (in his way) to those who were curious to learn what his

"IT'S A BIG THING, I TELL YOU."

occupation might be, or what were his mysterious intentions, from time to time. But he never accorded any one the slightest clew to his actual business, his purpose, or his designs — although he appeared ready always to answer questions, and pretended in the most off-hand style, to be very willing to "tell you all about it."

"It's all right," Mose would insist, ambiguously, but good-naturedly. "If it isn't, we'll make it right in the morning. Somethin's up. *I* can guess. It'll come round, after a little. I know what I know. I'm satisfied. It's a long lane 'at has no turn in it. Never you mind. It's a big thing, I tell you, but I can swing it. You'll see —" and this was the extent of all that could be gathered from this queer biped, regarding himself or his business objects in life.

Still, Moses travelled — ate and drank, in Washington — hob-nob'd with Senators and House Members — knew every man worth knowing, from the Aroostook to San Francisco, or Oregon — and always went and came with a smiling countenance and a full stomach.

And did he keep his secret — whatever it was?

Well, he did!

That is to say, for years.

But finally it came about that a Congressional investigation was inaugurated in Washington, over some foggy peculation that was turned up by an inquisitive M. C. who "didn't know Mose Topley," (so he said) "from four-and-ninepence."

And Moses' name was found upon the secret pay-roll, as one who had for years been tugging at the government teat with an earnestness that proved absolutely astounding!

A *mittimus* was issued for the arrest of poor Mose Topley. He was summoned before the august Committee, to testify who he was — where he belonged — what he had been about — who employed him — how much Government money had been paid him — what he did with his plunder — who shared it with him — and what his mysterious connections were, or had been, with all the honorable gentlemen with whose names and acts *his* name thus came to be so singularly associated. And all these several items Moses alone could explain, it was asserted.

"We shall have a good witness in Mose Topley," suggested a zealous honorable member, who had half unearthed the supposed fraud they were looking into. "*He* will tell us all about this abuse. And thus we shall 'kill two birds with one stone;' Mose and his accomplices here."

Did the authorities find him?

Not for the time being.

For weeks and weeks, Mose Topley had business in another direction. He didn't go to Washington, now! The party intrusted with the legal service of the writ "searched for a needle in the hay-mow."

Moses could not be found.

He knew they were after him!

How did he know this?

Ah — well. Mose had his friend at court.

But finally they collared him. And Mose went demurely to the capital, and then before the Investigating Committee, in his innocent style.

It was alleged that Moses Topley had been paid over

two hundred thousand dollars, first and last, out of the Treasury till. And there were those among the House members (who had *not* shared with Moses any of this colossal " secret gain ") who were so impertinently inquisitive as to be desirous to know something in detail officially about this trifling affair.

So they openly went for Moses, (though, *sub rosa*, they were after a very different sort of man!) — And this is what they gleaned from this reliable witness, as the " official report " of the examination set forth. Moses was placed upon the stand.

" What is your name, witness ? "

" Moses."

" Topley ? "

" Yes, sir. Moses Topley."

" What is your business ? "

" I'm a traveller."

" Traveller. Commercial ? "

" No, sir."

" What then ? "

" General."

" Brigadier ? " asked the M. C.

" No sir. General traveller."

" Ah, yes. Who employs you ? "

" Nobody, sir."

" *How* do you travel, then ? "

" By rail, mostly, sir."

" Of course. I mean who pays your expenses ? "

"I do, sir."

"Now, witness — you are before the honorable House Committee; and you must answer my questions, or you will be held in contempt by this Committee."

"Well — don't scare me, Sir! I will answer — every time."

"So you have, in your way."

"I can't answer in your way, Sir."

"Why not?"

"Because I don't know what it is!"

"Now then, Moses — Mr. Topley —"

"Yes, sir."

"Are you not employed by the Government?"

"No, sir."

(Moses had taken care, under advice of his friend at court, to *resign* his place, two weeks previously.)

"You are *not* thus employed?"

"No, sir."

"This, on your oath?"

"Yes, sir."

"Has not your name been carried as an employé upon the books of the Treasury, for several years?"

"I cannot swear, sir."

"Why not?"

"I never saw the Treasury books."

"Has not the Treasury Department paid you, in the last five years, some two hundred and thirty thousand dollars, in cash, Mr. Topley?"

"No, *sir!*"

"Two hundred and twenty thousand?"

"No, sir."

"Not upwards of two hundred thousand dollars?"

"Not *one* dollar, sir!"

"What do you mean, by this?"

"Just what I say, sir."

"Have you had no business with the United States Treasury, in all those years?"

"O, yes sir."

"Ah. Well — what was it?"

"Secret, sir."

"Secret, there. But not *here*, sir."

"Everywhere, sir."

"I insist upon an answer, witness."

"I have replied that I *have* had business there."

"Now — they paid you many thousands of dollars?"

"No, sir — never."

"What then?"

"I paid *them* thousands."

"How?"

"In cash, sir."

"Where did you get it?"

"I cannot tell. It would be impossible, sir."

"Why so?"

"Because I keep no books, and can't remember."

"What source, or sources, did this large amount of money come from?"

"I cannot inform you, sir."

"Why not?"

"Because I say I don't know."

"What was the aggregate?"

"I do not remember."

"What is an approximation to the amount?"

"I don't recollect."

"How near two hundred thousand dollars?"

"I couldn't say, sir."

"*Less* than that sum?"

"I can't swear."

"*More* than that, Mr. Topley?"

"I couldn't tell."

"Was it one hundred thousand?"

"I don't know, sir."

"Was it fifty thousand?"

"I am unable to state."

"Yet it was *some* thousands?"

"It might be, sir."

"Not hundreds?"

"I am not positive."

"Now, Mr. Topley —"

"Yes, sir."

"Who *else* did you pay money to?"

"What money, sir?"

"This money we have inquired about?"

"To nobody."

"You paid nobody but the Treasury Department?"

"Not of *that* money."

"I ask you if you paid no one else but the Treasury, during that time?"

"And I answer, of that money, *no* sir."

"Of *any* money, sir?"

"Oh — yes. I paid out other money. My own money — of course — in all that time."

"Exactly. Now, sir — to whom?"

"I can only speak from recollection, sir. I keep no books."

"Well, from your best recollection, to whom?"

"My board bill, to Mr. Jones —"

"No trifling, Mr. Topley."

"My washerwoman —"

"Stop, sir! To whom did you pay two-and-twenty thousand dollars, in cash, at Boston or New York, on a certain day in July?"

"Nobody, sir!"

"Eighteen thousand, then?"

"No one, sir."

"Did you pay *no* one such a sum, or **about that sum?**"

"Not that I remember."

"Or fifteen thousand?"

"I can't recall it, sir."

"Or twelve thousand?"

"I wouldn't swear, sir."

"Why *not*, Mr. Topley?" thundered the enraged Committee man, bringing his fist down with a crash upon the table.

"Because I don't recollect, sir," said Moses, with a complacent smile, that strangely contrasted with the irate Congressman's show of choler.

"Now, Mr. Topley, you are evading the object of this investigation, evidently."

"I do not intend this, sir."

"You know why you are before this Committee, of course, Mr. Topley?"

"O yes, sir. I think I do," replied Moses, with a very sly wink at another member of this Committee, with whom he was familiarly acquainted.

"Well, sir — what do you think we sit here for?"

"I don't wish to be considered in contempt, sir — in my answer, if you please — but I think it is for about ten or twelve dollars a day, and mileage."

A slight titter might have been noticed, at this juncture, among all the honorable Committee, with the exception of the burly gentleman who conducted the examination. But Moses was clearly "one too many" for *him!*

"You say you know why you are summoned here, Mr. Topley?" continued the M. C., changing his tactics.

"Yes, sir."

"Have you given us all the information upon the subject-matter under consideration now before the House Committee, that is in your possession?"

"I have answered all your questions, to the best of my recollection, sir. You might ask me more — if you like — " said Moses, demurely.

"That will do, Mr. Topley. You can step down," said the baffled M. C.

Moses stepped down, and out, accordingly. And by the very first train that left the capital afterwards, he quit Washington, *and* the Congressional Investigating Committee; who, as it will be seen, did not extort the first syllable out of this witness, implicating any one!

Moses hastened vigorously to the Dépôt. The last train for the day was just about to leave for the north, and Topley was desirous to avail himself of his opportunity. He

"UNCLE SAM" GOES FOR MOSE TOPLEY.

had not chanced to see the dog during his present brief visit to the Capitol, but the brute saw him rushing down the street towards the station in hot haste, and "Uncle Sam" went for Moses, upon general principles.

Mr. Topley increased his speed to the uttermost, for he heard the last bell clanging in the station, where the cars were just about to start. He made a short cut and very good time — as he went. And the dog followed him as closely as his short stout legs would permit.

Moses saw "Uncle Sam" at his heels, suddenly, and he

did his level best to leave him in the rear. It was "nip an' tuck," but Mr. Topley won. He dashed away with "Uncle Sam" sharply upon his coat-tails.

With one bound he vaulted over the high picket-railing near the Dépôt — and saved the train, as it was moving out of the station, for Baltimore; the dog having missed him in this final spurt, about three feet, as the fleeing

MOSES GOES FOR THE LAST TRAIN — AND SAVES IT!

object of his aversion went heels over head beyond the reach of the excited beast's open jaws.

Now the simple fact in Mose Topley's case, on this occasion, was that under the old law he had quietly collected two hundred thousand dollars in 'moieties,' and he had paid one half this sum into the Treasury. The other half "went to the informer" under the law of 1799, giving to these political bummers the lion's share of all they could beat the merchants and manufacturers of this country out of, who chanced to have committed any 'little irregularities' in dodging their revenue obligations.

Thus Moses Topley made *his* hundred thousand dollars in gold — in a very few short years.

But he never worked an hour in his life for it. There is little need to caution the reader against attempting *this* mode to make a fortune, since the law has been repealed, and there is no likelihood that a similar opportunity will occur, in this country, to heap up money.

At all events, there are no Mose Topleys about, just now, that we wot of. If there be any such, that we have not met with — we advise them in all candor to seek out some honest employment, and turn their attention to work, and reform, without procrastination.

For, as a good author has it, "if you ask me what is the hereditary sin of human nature, I answer *not* pride, ambition, or egotism — but indolence." He who will conquer indolence, may conquer all the rest. Get work! And be sure this is better than all you work to get.

In the past score of years, there have been several Mose Topleys thus employed by the Government, secretly — all of whom have realized fortunes, at the expense of careless American merchants in high standing, who have been fearfully mulcted, or blackmailed, by these over-indulged secret agents of the Treasury — as the official records show, conclusively.

Congress repealed the old moities law, at a late session.

and the lucrative but indolent occupation of these gentry was supposed to have gone up. The original operators resigned, and the work of smuggling and defrauding the national revenue goes on, again.

There *ought* to be a cure for this public wrong and plundering. But our wise men have not yet concluded if the old or the new mode of checking this grievous offending is best. Who can suggest a rightful, just, and efficacious remedy for this glaring evil?

We have thus given a partial history of certain representative characters within our acquaintance who commenced their careers without ready capital; who in the main, as far as portrayed, got upon the right road to fortune. We will now show what became of these diligent followers of the true course of action towards success.

Mose Topley whom we have mentioned by way of contrast to these examples, was the exception to our proposed rule; and *his* success simply verifies the assertion that it occasionally falls to the lot of the indolent and unworthy to become suddenly rich — through covert and disreputable means.

Mose may still be living, and his gains are supposed to have been duly "salted down." But, as no one ever yet knew when he had a dollar, so none will ever know hereafter where his plunder is located, how much or how little he really gathered, or who helped him to stow it away! And here we leave Moses to his "mysterious" reflections.

CHAPTER XX.

TWO CLEAR HEADS SOMETIMES BETTER THAN ONE.

In our preceding chapters, we have detailed the events that followed each other in the lives of our heroes, during a series of years when they were actively employed in working out their several destinies through a course of aptly chosen and well-directed effort in the right direction, each, to compass a fortune.

And by way of comparison, we have described the career of one or two other representative characters, whose fate has been recorded as a warning against a dishonorable pursuit of riches.

We now continue our narrative towards the record of subsequent particulars occurring in the history of the parties in whom we are more directly interested, and whose aims continued laudably towards realizing a fortune in an honorable manner, as their efforts had constantly been directed, from the outset — as we have already explained.

Six years had passed, since Fred Fordham, Fannie's husband had visited his "uncle Isaacs" hopefully one morning, with the wedding-jewelry of his young wife in his hands, which amidst the panic of '37 he was compelled to dispose of for a third of its cost, to obtain temporary relief from pressing want.

In that half a dozen years, Fred, like his other companions in penury, had gone to work again, at a reduced salary at first; but he had toiled early and late at his profession of bookkeeper, since then, for a sustenance for himself and his little family, and had latterly done satisfactorily well.

Fannie had not been idle, in the mean time. She had two babies to care for, and her household duties for a time, were quite sufficient for one pair of hands, in all conscience! But she was more ambitious than many young women similarly conditioned, and she insisted upon helping Fred out, in his strait — though he realized how she taxed her energies, and would gladly have had things otherwise.

But Fannie was too willing, too stout of heart, and too strong in bodily health fortunately — either to give way to despondency, or to halt in her good intentions to share in making the fortune that Fred had always promised himself — sooner or later.

"Bless you, Fred," the hard-working wife would say, when the kindly-disposed husband besought her to favor herself, "I never am so happy in my life, as when I find full occupation for my time."

"I know it, Fannie. But if you toil so hard, and stick to it so incessantly, you'll break down, deary."

"Break down," exclaimed Fannie, cheerily, "Not a bit

of it, Fred. I am stronger than ever I was. And I get along splendidly."

"Your earnings don't accumulate very rapidly, my dear, nevertheless!"

"What do you know about that, Fred?" asked his wife, with a knowing smile.

"I know very well that the pay you receive for your work can't reach a very formidable sum, in the aggregate — at the best. And you've now been at it five years — day and night — most of the time, that is certain. With my present income and prospects, I don't want you to labor in this way. And there is no need of it, Fannie."

"Well. Go on with your 'prospects,' Fred. You are doing well enough, now, — and so am I. We shall conquer fortune, in time. While we both have health, strength, youth, and good heart, is the time to make the most of our opportunity."

"That is true. I shall do my part, Fannie — "

"And I will do mine, too. Now, Fred, how much money have I saved out of my own earnings, do you think, since I obtained the regular work sent to the house and taken away so unostentatiously by Messrs. Godfrey & Co.?" asked the wife, cheerfully.

"Well, it can't be much, at all events," responded Fred. "And you've been hard at it, off and on, almost half a dozen years, Fannie."

"Yes. So I have. Now, how much cash do you think I've got in Bank, and at interest?"

Fred laughed a merry laugh, at this query, and exclaimed —

"Upon my word, I don't know, Fannie. But —"

"Guess, now, Fred."

"Five years — at embroidering and crocheting. Well, two or three hundred dollars, may be. They have paid

HOW FANNIE FORDHAM DID IT.

good prices, I know. And you have given them some nice work, too."

Then Fannie laughed, in turn.

"In the last three years you know Fred, I've kept help. You have accorded me a generous allowance for house expenses, and we have lived very economically, remember."

"Yes. But it was your *earnings* we were speaking of, Fannie."

"I know. Yet a penny saved, is twopence earned, you will allow."

"Well — savings and earnings?"

"Yes. How much?"

"You may have more than three hundred, then, deary. At least I hope so," returned Fred, kindly.

"Six times three hundred, Fred!"

"Eighteen hundred dollars!" exclaimed Fred, surprised, though he was aware that Fannie had been very economical, and knew she had her private account in two good Savings Banks, at least.

"Over two thousand dollars, Fred of my own," exclaimed Fannie, triumphantly.

"That really astonishes me, my dear."

"Much of it I have *saved*, Fred, in housekeeping. But, half of it I have earned with these fingers, my love."

"You have been busy, I am well aware. Now, if you are so rich, you *must* take a rest. I insist."

"Not yet, Fred. By and by, when you come to be a partner with Messrs. Dowell, Brothers — as you say they have promised you you shall be — then I will 'play lady' on a moderate scale; for this will be a grand opening for you."

Fannie went right along, and so did Fred. Twelve months afterwards, he became a member of the firm he had served faithfully for seven long years. And in a few

Morris Deans was a good angler, and fond of this pastime. Miss Eunice sometimes accompanied her friend — but the contented twain never talked of love, during these pleasant woodland excursions — so enjoyable to both. [CHAP. xvi. page 239.

years more, he had a snug fortune of his own, as it eventuated. But it had been up-hill work, in his case — though he accomplished his aim at last, honorably and satisfactorily.

Frank Meyers had saved most of his ample salary, which was eight thousand dollars per annum, at last.— And what with the rent of his four brick houses in New York, and the interest upon his subsequently carefully invested and well-secured money-loans, he too had gone onward and upward rapidly in fortune, in the later years.

Reuben Downer, the once pennyless printer, had carried the regular issues of his popular weekly " Leader " up to an immense circulation; and his current wholesale cash receipts from the news-agents who took his heavy editions off his hands as fast as issued (in addition to a generous mail-subscription list,) gave him a splendid and certain income in ready money.

He was able to purchase more fancy horses, which was one of his enjoyable hobbies, and he paid enormous prices for them, when he 'lighted upon those that could make better trotting time than those he had. To-day, Mr. Downer's less than a dozen choice animals have cost him over two hundred thousand dollars, in cash! And they are the fastest in the world.

During these six years, Morris Deans, the former Boston broker's lad, had been steadily progressing at 'Sunnyside,' where the advantages afforded him by Farmer Blount in the later half of this term, enabled him to lay by several thousand dollars; since, as Mr. Blount grew more advanced in life, after he made himself acquainted with Morris's rare good qualities, the old man gave up the financial management of the great stock farm, almost exclusively to his young friend's discretion.

With the prudent and skilful manipulation of Blount's affairs upon the farm by Deans, the proprietor made money far more rapidly — though still legitimately — than he had ever begun to do, himself.

Morris was active, earnest, ambitious, and deeply devoted to his work there; and at length becoming personally interested in the results, he wrought assiduously for his employer's benefit, while he shared in the gains individually, upon his own account. So that while he made money for Blount, he amassed it for himself, also; and both were amply content with this arrangement.

When Morris received his five-and-twenty thousand dollars in ready cash from Downer, for the splendid Morgan trotter he sold him in New York, this set the lad up fairly.

He had already accumulated some fifteen thousand dollars, during his term in Blount's service previously, and his surplus was duly invested at paying interest; which increased in good time, advantageously, while he continued on in his farm-stock operations, in the customary profitable and sure way.

David Morehead also moved along upon the old place he came into possession of from the long since dead

Grimes, and still the keen New Hampshire live stock seller continued to coin money.

Polly proved a faithful good wife to David, and she never had cause for regret that she accepted the bluff offer of her good-hearted drover-husband and married him, at such brief notice. The worn-out farm was brought up into good condition, and David lived a happy contented prosperous life with his chosen Polly White.

And Ely Hawes, the studious inventor, was now permanently in New York, engaged in furthering his interests with his finally patented Bank-Safe lock, aided by the counsel and suggestions and ready means, (whenever these were needed,) of his early friend Frank Meyers.

Through the advice of the latter, and the freely accorded assistance of Reuben Downer, subsequently, Ely had left New England and settled in New York city — where he went to work in earnest to put his invention upon the market.

He found the competition in this particular branch of mechanical trade very lively, in Gotham! The famous Hobbs' Lock, the Eastman Lock, Hall's Combination Lock, and others held the market — and very deservedly — at that period.

Ely's invention was an innovation. All these men had passed through the same ordeal which Hawes had latterly and previously experienced, in his efforts to get before the public. They were not disturbed by any professed novelty that came up, in their line, and took little heed of the squibs that found their way from time to time into the columns of the daily papers, through Reuben Downer's management, in his friend Ely's behalf.

Reuben thoroughly understood the value of printer's ink. He "had been there," and knew how to do *this* kind of thing, as well as any man living.

"I've got a good thing here, Reuben," so Ely insisted.

"I know you have, my dear fellow," responded Downer, when they were discussing the merits of the poor inventor's lock. "But what is the use of having a 'good thing' of this sort, which you want everybody to know something of, if you keep it all to yourself? You must advertise it, my boy. Tell the public what you've got, and keep telling them of it. Insist upon it, in the daily papers. Talk it right out, briefly, sharply, to the point, judiciously and honestly. And the 'children will cry for it,' you see, long before you have a supply commensurate with the demand that will ensue for this admirable invention."

"I reckon you're about right, Reuben."

"I know I'm right, Ely. I can't do much for you in the *Leader*, because I don't advertise for anybody, in my own paper. But I can fix it for you, in other channels, where it will do you good."

"Thank you, Reuben. When you can do so, remember me. You're rich. I *shall* be so, one o' these days."

Within a week, a half column advertisement appeared one day in the daily Tribune, Herald and Sun, in these words — repeated over and over, forty times — in a single line, each —

   "Get Hawes' new Bank-safe Lock!"
   "*Get Hawes' new Bank-safe Lock!!*"
   "Get Hawes' new Bank-safe Lock!!!"

  "This is the only Impenetrable Safe Lock!"
  "*This is the only Impenetrable Safe Lock!!*"
  "This is the only Impenetrable Safe Lock!!!"

"Absolutely Burglar Proof — is Hawes' new Lock!"
"*Absolutely Burglar Proof — is Hawes' new Lock!!*"
"Absolutely Burglar Proof — is Hawes' new Lock!!!"

Ely was vastly surprised at this announcement. He did not know where it originated, at first. Frank Meyers explained it to him. The public were on the qui vive, directly.

The merchants, bankers, railroad directors, factors, store-keepers, everybody who read the three great daily New York papers, were at once set agog at meeting with this advertisement.

"Who is Hawes?"

"What is this new invention?"

"Let us see the Impenetrable Safe lock!" ejaculated hundreds of people, at once.

Letters of inquiry poured in upon Ely by the dozen, within ten days. Orders came by scores — with the proviso "*if* it is what you represent it to be, Mr. Hawes."

The old safe-lock inventors were now the most excited and anxious. "This fellow Hawes is either a charlatan, or else he knows his biz' — " they said.

And Ely went right *on*, from that day, forward.

The manufacturers of Safes went after Mr. Ely Hawes. They examined his new patent Lock, as Frank Meyers had done. And all united, with universal accord, to admit that it was a rare thing.

"You did me a lively good turn, Reuben, that's a fact," said Ely, gratefully, when he met Downer a week or two after this queer advertisement appeared in the dailies.

"That's what I intended to do, my boy," responded Reuben. "How are you making it?"

"Splendidly. Got more orders than I know what to do with, Reuben."

"Go ahead. You're on the right road, Ely."

"Thanks to you and to Frank Meyers —"

"No! Thanks to your own talents, skill, industry, and perseverance, my good fellow," insisted Downer. "This other is but collateral. You *have* got a grand thing here. I know it. All you needed to do, was to let the people know what you and I know about it. Go ahead, then, and make your hundred thousand dollars, now — off hand, Ely."

"I will, Reuben. But the first thing I make, will be the best vault-safe that iron, steel and my ingenuity can compass — to be secured with my Patent Impenetrable Lock — for *your* use. And if you don't accept it as a free gift, Reuben, to remember grateful Ely Hawes by — don't you ever call me your friend again," returned Ely, thankfully.

"All right, my boy. But, safe or no safe, I will do you good every time, whenever it comes in my way — be sure of it. I was a poor hard-working lad once, myself," concluded Reuben.

This safe was ordered directly by Ely, of a leading manufacturer who had been latterly negotiating with Hawes for placing some of his new locks upon them, after he had thoroughly examined the ingenious device of the youthful inventor, whose prospects now began to look highly promising.

The Institute Fair was to come off in a few days, and Ely had four safes ready, with his new patent lock attached to them, for competitive exhibition during the continuance of the show.

All the old inventors had samples of their locks entered at this exhibition, also. And there was a deal of lively speculation as to who would probably win the Association's first Gold Medal there.

We will learn in detail what the character of this interesting competition was to be, in the next chapter.

CHAPTER XXI.

EVERY MAN THE ARCHITECT OF HIS OWN FORTUNE.

INVENTION, says Sir Joshua Reynolds, is, strictly speaking, " little more than a new combination of those images which have been previously gathered and deposited in the memory. Nothing can be made of *nothing*." And so he who has laid up no material in his brain, can produce no combinations.

It is also truly said that all originality is but undiscovered plagiarism. Still, modern invention is activity of the mind, as fire is air in motion; a sharpening of the spiritual or intellectual sight, to discern hidden aptitudes.

This was what Ely Hawes had accomplished. He had had his intellect sharpened through study, application and determination to realize a certain object, which had been the purpose of his life.

And he had produced what — if it were not an originality in invention, or combination — was at least a cunning device that was entirely novel; and the plagiarism (if it were such) had never yet been discovered by any other modern mechanic.

The complete design of Ely Hawes consisted of his lock itself, his mode of attaching it to the Safe, his peculiar manner of locking it, and the application of the secret spring for the self-closing outer casing.

It was in no wise complicated. Its very simplicity was its chief recommendation. And yet it was varied in its arrangement, upon each individual safe.

Thus, no two door-safes opened through the self-acting spring being placed in the same position. One would have this attachment affixed underneath the bottom of the safe; another at the back; a third on one or other side; a fourth in either corner; a fifth half way up, on either side, or back — and otherwise.

By this mode, no man owning one Safe could know where or how this secret spring was attached upon another man's safe; and it was thus not easily found, by a stranger to the particular safe not in his own possession.

The casing was entirely plain, and all four sides were exactly alike; a simple square iron box, to look at — when closed. No indication was in view that pointed to the spot which must be known, and manipulated, to cause this *outer* casing to open, when in position. Upon a proper movement, at the end of this secretly-placed spring, the outer *door* of the safe gently slided open of itself.

But even *this* device was varied in construction, differently upon each safe. It was thus acted on by a concealed lever, by a strong spiral or curved spring, by a simple pressure upon the point, or otherwise. And this particular form of operation, or concealment, **was made** known only to the party who purchased a particular safe.

When this outer door opened, the safe itself was seen within this casing; upon the inside of the door of which *interior* portion, the Impenetrable Lock **was** attached. All that was now to be seen here, different from the plain *outside* formation, was a stout polished steel protuberance, having the appearance of a common door-knob; which, upon handling, turned round freely, in its closely fitted socket — during which rotary-motion, a slight click-click could be heard, like the ticking of a large clock.

This was all that was visible.

Within, however — this easily turned knob acted upon the machinery of the lock in a secret way; which when shut, it was simply impossible to unlock, without the secret *key* to its closing.

This outer knob acted upon the lock through its stout steel shaft, **but its** position outside **was** no indication pointing to the exact spot inside where the lock itself was attached. It was above, or below, or directly back of this spot, on different safes.

There was no seam or cavity to be found, (so nicely were all the parts put together) into which the finest grains of powder could be pricked, or thrust. And thus it was proof against being blown open, by the evil-disposed.

This, briefly, was Ely's invention. And he claimed that it was just what he had christened his safe-lock, "impenetrable," without *his* key to it.

When the friendly advertisement of Downer appeared in the New York dailies, the inventors and manufacturers of *former* styles of bank and safe locks — and there were two or three popular ones, which had for some years been in use — became seriously exercised.

Some scouted the idea which this novel announcement conveyed. Others declared it to be a sham. And others claimed that *their* locks " advertised themselves " — which was far better than resorting to the aid of the newspapers — which they did not find occasion to do.

But all these gentlemen were desirous to know what this suddenly announced " wonderful discovery " might be; and each one found himself an anxious investigator into the mystery that was all at once thus but partially promulgated.

Hundreds of visitors now crowded Ely's apartments, day after day — where he had a dozen safes set up, upon which his Patent Impenetrable Lock was ingeniously affixed.

Nobody could open a safe without his aid. When opened from the outside, none could 'penetrate' the inside. He showed them all 'how to do it,' as he had shown Frank Meyers. But not a man could open one of his safes, by himself.

And why?

Simply because *he kept the key for sale.* And he did not furnish this secret, except with a safe, and then only to **actual buyers.**

All sorts of criticisms were uttered — reasonable, and unreasonable, frivolous and ingenious, fallacious and probable, querulous and derogatory — regarding this wonderful lock, on the part of experts.

But none of them could open one of them, blow it out, get into it, or destroy it, except through actually cutting it in pieces with the cold chisel; and this last process Ely would not permit — at present.

When this idea was suggested to him, he simply said 'well gentlemen, it will require more than one long night of constant work upon it, to do even that; and it could not be thus destroyed, without a very considerable amount of noise; which would cause alarm that would frustrate the plan of a burglar who might attempt to burst it in that way, surely."

But the great State Exhibition was shortly coming on. And Ely had a little scheme in his head for the Institute Fair, whereby he proposed to test his invention, thoroughly, in open daylight — and establish, or break its reputation, thenceforth, forever.

During Morris Dean's last visit to New York city, when he went from Brandville farm to dispose of his valuable Morgan colt (which Reuben Downer purchased at such a magnificent figure) the four friends met — Hawes, Meyers, Downer and Morris — and the young inventor informed them of his contemplated plan for the Institute Fair.

" I will exhibit four safes," he said, " manufactured by Hart & Co. expressly for this occasion, upon each of which I will affix one of my patent locks.

"Two of them will be closed, and the other two will be left open — one showing the clear interior, and the other with the outer door only open.

"In one of the two closed safes, I will deposit a thousand dollars in gold. And I propose to notify the public that the inventor of the new "Impenetrable Safe Lock" will award to the party who can open those safes, the money thus deposited within one or both — provided any one can get into either of them, in twelve hours — by unlocking it, picking the lock, or destroying it within that period; provided also, that any other safe-lock competitor will offer a similar proposal; to be open to all comers — inventors, experts, professional burglars, or otherwise. And I will enter the arena myself as a contestant for the thousand dollars to be so deposited in any safe secured by any *other* inventor's lock.

"This will form an attractive feature in the mechanical department of the Exhibition, it will advertise my lock, splendidly, (as Reuben suggests) and I believe I will win the society's great Gold Medal; and can thus establish the reputation of my invention immeasurably, silence all cavil on the part of other inventors, convince American safe-manufacturers who really has the best lock, earn a thousand or two dollars pretty easily, by finding my way into the safes of one or more of my old-fogy competitors, and show the merchants and bankers of this city that Ely Hawes *has* got a good thing, in his Impenetrable Safe Lock — eh, lads?"

"Bravo!" shouted Frank Meyers, delighted with this little plot.

"A capital scheme," said Reuben, who had listened to the animated utterances in which Ely had explained his contemplated proposition.

"It's a mighty good idea, that," added Morris. "And if you succeed, it will be a big feather in your cap, Ely — that's a fact."

"Succeed? Of course I shall!"

"You *have* succeeded, thus far, that cannot be denied. But how will you get into the other man's safe?"

"Ah, well. I don't know about that. I have a general idea of all this sort of lock-machinery, of course. I give, and take. I will employ the same means to attack *their* inventions, that I permit them, or any of them, to use upon mine, and none other. This is fair, isn't it?"

"Yes, if they agree to it," returned Morris — "of course."

"It is to be a friendly contest of skill — brain against brain," said Ely. "*I* say they can't penetrate my new patent lock. If they can, they can beat me, and take my thousand dollars, which they are welcome to. I think I can get into any of their safes, locked with any present known invention, (except mine) if they will allow me the same time that I will grant them for trial — say twelve hours.

"And this is long enough to test the question fairly; because no burglar has much more than half this time in one night, ordinarily, to peck away at a safe he aims to force, before daylight overtakes him, you see."

"That's so," says Frank. "Your plan's a good one. I take only one exception to it, Ely."

"And what is that, Frank?"

"While you're about it, make it an object, my dear fellow, for these chaps to work in good earnest. Make the forfeit-money five thousand dollars, Ely, instead of one thousand. Why not?"

"I can't, Frank."

"Why not, then?"

"I haven't got the money."

"That's no reason. I have."

"No — it is too much to risk, my boy."

"Then one thousand is too much, old fellow! Don't you play at this sort of game, except to win, Ely."

"No! That's it," said Morris. "That's good advice, any way."

"If you haven't sufficient confidence in your own invention, to believe that your lock is really what you claim it to be," suggested Reuben, seriously, "don't you risk any thousand dollars in your safe, Ely. You may thus lose your money, your reputation and your future prospects, all at once!"

"O, look here, you rich nabobs, who don't mind spending twenty or thirty thousand dollars for a trotting horse, or lending a man five or ten thousand dollars upon call, at a moment's notice. It's all very easy for you to moralize, and talk thus glibly about a big pile of money."

"Then you're *not afraid*, Ely? That isn't your trouble?"

"Afraid o' what?"

"That they will **get into your safe**?"

"It is impossible, I tell you — unless they absolutely smash it to pieces, with sledge-hammer and cold-chisel. This *I* won't do, or allow them to do, of course."

"All right, then," added Frank. "Put *five* thousand dollars in gold into it. If they get it — *I* will lose it. You sha'n't, anyhow. And I will furnish the money. This will make the thing 'respectable,' my boy," concluded Meyers, enthusiastically.

Thus the proposition was settled, as the friends were about to separate.

"When the trial comes off, Ely, I will come down and witness it, sure," said Morris, at the close of this pleasant conference. "I shall be delighted to see you triumph, Ely, and it will be the making of your fortune. If you don't slip up in this, *you* can count upon the 'hundred thousand dollars in gold' you marked out as the sum of your ambition, years ago — when we were all poorer than Job's cat, I remember."

"Thank you, Morris. I can't *lose* any thing, by this little experiment. I may not be able to get into their safes — but I *know* they cannot penetrate mine."

"It will be a very interesting scene to witness, Ely. And besides, Eunice desires to come down to the Fair," continued Morris, "and I will bring her with me."

"Hallo!" cried Frank. "Who was that you spoke of, Morris?"

"When?"

"Just now — 'Eunice.' Who is Eunice, Morris?"

"Beg pardon. Haven't I mentioned it before? That's a friend of mine, at Brandville, Frank. Mr. Blount's daughter. The prettiest and best girl in the village — or out of it, my boy."

"O-ho? That's what's the matter, eh, Morris? Sly dog! The old farmer's daughter, eh?"

"Yes. And about my own age. A nice young lady, I assure you. I'll bring her down, and introduce her to you, and Ely, and Reuben. She's a good catch, for any man, Frank. You're a bachelor, now — rich, growing richer every day — and you ought to get married, my friend."

"Hear him!" shouted Frank. "Wouldn't you say, now, that butter wouldn't melt in this rogue's mouth, boys?"

"Well. You shall see Miss Eunice, when the safe-lock-bursting comes off at the Fair," concluded Morris. "And you shall tell me then if she isn't a buxom nice girl. So —— by, by, lads. We'll meet again in a few weeks. And I have no doubt that Ely will not only be richer by five thousand dollars in cash after this trial, but that this happy experiment of his will prove the means of establishing his invention, beyond doubt, as the best of its kind in the world, to-day. Good-by!"

They parted — to meet at the Institute Exhibition, one month from that bright pleasant day.

CHAPTER XXII.

WHAT HAPPENED AT THE GREAT INSTITUTE FAIR.

CONSCIENTIOUS rivalry is a noble passion, and just, withal. It limits a man within the terms of honor, and makes the contest for reputation fair and generous. True emulation consists in striving to excel in any thing that is commendable; and the competitor thus raises himself fairly, through his own merits, and not by depressing others.

Bishop Hall asserts that while worldly ambition is usually founded on pride, or envy, true emulation — or laudable ambition — is actually founded in humility; for it evidently implies that we have a modest opinion of our own present attainments, and deem it necessary to be advanced.

This characteristic is signally exhibited even among the brute creation. Observe the tremor and zeal of the thorough-bred horse, at the starting of the race. And note the lumbering dray-horse; the latter does not tremble — but he does not emulate!

Laudable ambition " is a germ from which all growth of

nobleness proceeds," affirms English. And "there is a kind of grandeur and respect which the poorest and most insignificant portion of mankind endeavor to procure, in the circle of their friends and acquaintances."

The humblest mechanic draws around him his set of admirers, and delights in that superiority which he enjoys over those who may, in some respects, be beneath him. This ambition, which is but natural to the soul of man, may receive a happy turn, if it be but rightly directed, and contribute largely to an individual's advantage, at the same time.

But, where this emulation can be so happily adapted as to cover its contemplated enterprises, even to the person himself, under the mantle of principle, it is the most commendable as well as inflexible of all human passions — and is truthfully described as a grand spur toward the attainment of the higher virtues.

Ely Hawes had proceeded from his earliest start in life upon true principle, in all his aims and ambitions. He had genuine talent naturally implanted in his composition, and he made himself morally sure of his ground, as he went along, before he attempted to push his way farther.

He was now convinced, in his own mind, that he had consummated what would prove a grand thing for the commercial world. And he felt pretty certain that his fortunate invention — upon which he had spent years and years of ardent study — would turn out not only a benefit to others, through its positive value and security for its intended good purpose, but he thought his own reward was now close at hand — at last.

He made his proposition for competition openly, and some of his competitors accepted his manly challenge at the coming Industrial Fair. One of them only ventured to make a deposit as he did of five thousand dollars in a safe secured with his own lock, however; and this was a prominent inventor, who had hitherto carried away all the leading prizes at previous Exhibitions, and who did not hesitate to meet the young mechanic, very confident of vanquishing him, upon his own offered terms.

He entertained no thought that Ely could get into his safe, (where he had deposited the requisite five thousand dollars,) while he fancied that his superior knowledge and experience as a first-class lock-maker would enable him, after a while, to force an entrance into Hawes' safe.

He would thus gain the five thousand dollars at issue, and enhance his own already very creditable reputation; while he would by this means effectually dispose of one more competitor, as he had for years vanquished others, who had aimed to rival or excel him.

With the best feelings towards all concerned, Ely Hawes entered the Exhibition, at last, where the four safes with his patent lock affixed upon each, had already preceded him.

The money was deposited duly in the competing safes, and the terms were clearly understood upon which the test of mechanical skill was to be attempted. The day was fixed for this extra exhibition — and at the appointed time the operators were promptly on hand.

Morris Deans came down to New York the day previous to the trial, accompanied by pretty Eunice Blount, whom he presented to his friends at the Fair, all of whom thought the "Sunnyside" girl a very comely and interesting young person, greatly to the gratification of her friend Morris, who was very fond of her, to be sure.

The proposed novel trial of the leading safe-lock men against the new comer in this field, caused a large gathering of interested and curious spectators to press around the ticket offices of the Institute exhibition rooms, on the bright morning upon which this event was to come off.

The newspapers had previously announced the affair, and Reuben Downer had taken care that the public should be thoroughly posted, beforehand, regarding the claimed merits of his friend Ely's invention. On the morning of the anxiously looked-for day, the following announcement was *Herald-ed* and *Tribune-'d* and *Sun'd*, in advance of the opening of the exhibition: —

$5,000 GIVEN TO THE BEST SAFE LOCK, TO-DAY, AT THE FAIR!
$5,000 *given to the best Safe lock, to-day, at the Fair!!*
$5,000 given to the best Safe lock, to-day, at the Fair!!!

WHO WILL FIND THE $5,000 IN THE SAFE, TO-DAY, AT THE FAIR?
Who will find the $5,000 in the Safe, to-day, at the Fair??
Who will find the $5,000 in the Safe, to-day, at the Fair???

WHO WINS THE $5,000 TO-DAY, AT THE FAIR, FOR BEST SAFE LOCK?
Who wins the $5,000 to-day, at the Fair, for best Safe lock??
Who wins the $5,000 to-day, at the Fair, for best Safe lock???

This was 'puffy,' so many averred. Others thought it a tip-top advertising dodge for the safe and lock-makers, generally. And everybody who could get into the great building, was there, before eleven o'clock A.M.

The operators upon the safes commenced at eight o'clock in the morning — to enable them to avail themselves of the entire long summer's day in their experiments, before the exhibition closed, at eight P.M.

Frank Meyers was on hand, early — and so were Reuben Downer, and Morris Deans, with pretty Miss Eunice Blount upon his arm. Ely Hawes did not come in till after ten o'clock. Then he was greeted with a hearty round of welcome, by those who knew him.

"What brings you so late?" inquired all his friends anxiously, who had been looking for him, three hours, at the least.

"Time enough," said Ely. "We drew lots for the chance to begin, and I lost. I shall do nothing until to-morrow, you see. The others have all day to-day to peck away at *my* safes and lock. And to-morrow comes my turn to try my hand upon *theirs*. This is the arrangement."

Then edging his way through the crowd, he asked "how do they get on, Frank?"

"Who?" returned Meyers.

"The safe-lock pickers?"

"Oh! Yes. Nothing yet has transpired."

"And it is three hours nearly since they began, eh?"

"Yes. They haven't got the outside open, yet!"

"I will assist them," suggested Ely. "This outside arrangement is no part of the *lock*."

And gliding up to his *safes*, he exchanged a pleasant word or two with the expert who was pegging away to open his outer safe-door. Then, moving behind the safe, he applied his stout thumb in the right spot, and the safe-door glided open of itself, apparently — and the operator thought he had 'made a point,' on a sudden, he hardly knew how.

"Now you'll do it!" said Ely.

"I reckon I shall, my young friend," returned his lively competitor. "That is what I'm here for."

"Go ahead," said Ely.

"I have given you the key to *my* safe-lock," said the old inventor, with an air of triumph — "and if you can thus open my lock, without my aid, you win. Now, where is your key?"

"It is directly before you," said Ely. "You have only to apply it, and open the inner safe."

"I do not see it, sir."

"It is there, nevertheless."

"Where?"

"Here," said Ely, modestly. And he placed his hand upon the bright steel revolving knob.

"I said *key*, sir. This is the door-handle. I see that."

"That is both handle and key, if you will. But that is all the key there is to my lock, sir," insisted Ely Hawes.

And the crowd applauded the young inventor's coolness and manly address.

The old mechanic turned the knob forward and backward, pulled at it, strove to push it inward, and back again — but made no headway whatever.

The multitude looked on and smiled, and nudged each other, and watched the toiler with increased interest as the moments, or hours, went by at last — and they saw no progress made.

At three o'clock the inventor asked Ely if *he* could open that lock, in the presence of the spectators, without any other key or implement than what he had provided his competitor with?

"O yes, sir," said Ely, blandly. "Of course I can. But I must open it with that key you now have your hand upon. It cannot be opened in any other way."

"*Will* you do this, sir?"

"With pleasure," said Ely, advancing. "I will show you how to do it — then I will re-lock it, and you can try it again. You have nearly five hours yet, in which to open it; and surely you can do this after being shown *how*, before eight o'clock to-night?"

"Yes — yes," responded his rival.

The crowd were in good spirits, as Ely went to the front of his open safe — turned the steel-shafted handle round and round a moment — precisely as the old inventor *seemed* to have done — and drawing gently upon the knob, the door came open, without any exertion; exposing the inside of the safe and the new lock — *and* the $5,000, in shining gold, that was deposited there for the benefit of the stranger who could open it from the outside.

Another round of applause rang out, at this performance — when Ely closed the door, again, turned the knob slowly, and said to his competitor —

"Now, sir — you have seen how *I* did it. Proceed."

The rival went at the lock in earnest, now!

He had four hours and a half to do his work in, yet — before the expiration of the twelve hours allotted him for the trial. But he turned, and twisted, and tugged at this steel knob, in vain. And at half past four, he took up his cold-chisel to remove this *knob*. This out of his way, he "could see into the thing," he fancied.

No objection was made by Ely to this performance. His lock might be ruined; but he knew the old man could not thus open the safe — whatever resulted. And *this* was what he had to do, to earn the enclosed $5,000.

The shaft that run from this knob into the lock, was nearly an inch and a half in diameter, and it was of the finest Bessamer chilled steel. It was not an easy or a brief job to cut this stout bar off. There was no chance to work at it, the shoulder fitted so closely to the orifice through which it passed, inward.

But at it he went, fiercely. And at half past five, he had cut the knob away. But he was no better off then, than at the beginning! Then he cut, and hammered, and slashed, and pried, and wrenched, and chiselled — but seven and a half o'clock arrived, and the "Impenetrable Lock" of Ely Hawes was still intact.

The expert could not get into it — he could not pick it — he could not force it — and he had not cut the steel-fronted door through, when "time!" was called. Eight o'clock had come round — and *he* had failed in his attempt to penetrate his young rival's new lock!

A shout went up from the assembled throng. Ely Hawes gracefully raised his hat in acknowledgment of the intended compliment, and received the warm congratulations of his intimate personal friends, who crowded around him, as he advanced and quietly closed the *outer* door of his safe again; while the tired old inventor remarked "that *is* a good safe-lock, certain; I say it — and I know," as he disappeared among his own associates.

Next day, at eight o'clock A.M., the young inventor's turn would come, to try *his* hand upon his rival's lock. $5,000 in gold were deposited in this man's safe, also. And Ely said he would get at it, if he could.

The excitement attendant upon an exhibition of this character, where the contestants were really so unequal, was naturally intense. The old inventor was the owner of a most excellent lock, which had been improved upon from year to year by him, until it had taken its deserved position at the head of this class of device, and had at that period no real competitor, in fact.

The young mechanic had made a remarkable discovery, during his long ingenious practice and tireless study; but he was almost entirely unknown, and he relied solely upon the merits of his invention for any success that might in this contest attend him.

His opponent had established his own fame, years previously. Ely had just "opened the ball" in his experience. But he was self-reliant, and believed in the value of his enterprise. He was confident that his lock was the best yet constructed, and he had entered the lists, on this occasion, determined to prove what he had latterly publicly and privately assumed.

When the crowd separated at the Fair that evening, it was agreed on all hands that so far as the Hawes invention was concerned, it was a very good one. His chief rival could not get into Ely's safe. So much had been gained.

On the morrow, they would learn whether the hitherto favorite lock would stand a similar test, at the hands of the skilful young machinist.

CHAPTER XXIII.

FIVE THOUSAND DOLLARS AND THE GOLD MEDAL.

ELY HAWES was in earnest, now — as might naturally have been anticipated, in this undertaking.

"It is neck or nothing," he said, pleasantly, when he left the Fair rooms, for his lodgings, in company with his faithful friends Meyers and Downer.

"I have seen one point carried," he added, with honest enthusiasm, "and I am not surprised that the old man did not succeed. But I must beat him, at his own game — if possible."

"You have shown very clearly that you have not assumed more for your own invention than has been verified to-day, Ely," observed Frank. "Now, if you can do with your rival's lock what he has satisfied himself he can't do with yours, you will accomplish a complete triumph."

"I will *try*," returned Ely, hopefully.

The throng of visitors was in no wise lessened upon the second day of this entertaining trial, when it was made known that the noted and experienced inventor had failed to penetrate Ely's lauded lock, in a twelve hours' bout at the young man's novel contrivance. And all the personal friends of Hawes were promptly on hand to encourage him in his forthcoming experiment.

"You'll win, Ely," said Frank Meyers, when they met at the Fair the next morning. "You can do it, my boy. I feel it in my bones."

"I don't know that, Frank," returned Ely, modestly. "It isn't an easy thing to perform. This man has got a grand good lock, I can tell you — that has stood the test, bravely, hitherto, as is well known. I may not be able to get into his safe, in the twelve hours allowed by the terms of our mutual agreement. But one thing is certain; he didn't get into *mine*. And so your five thousand dollars are safe. We sha'n't *lose* any thing by my offer. This is a satisfaction to me, I assure you."

"And the reputation of *your* lock is assured, too, beyond question," observed Reuben, delighted with the result, thus far.

"Dear me, what a crowd!" exclaimed Eunice, clinging to the arm of Morris. "I never saw so many people, I believe, in all my life before!"

"I shall have to put you temporarily in charge of my good friend Meyers, Euny," remarked Morris. "By and by, when Ely gets at his work, I want to be near him. And the crush yonder is so great, that you will be uncomfortable there."

"Where are you going?" asked Miss Eunice.

"I want to be a witness to Ely's performance upon his rival's safe-lock, Euny. But the throng is so eager that *you* would be crushed yonder."

"And Mr. Meyers may perhaps be of the same mind, Morris."

"No, he says he will show you the Institute attractions, with pleasure."

"All right, then. I hope your friend Mr. Hawes will succeed in his object. But this throng of people seem a deal more interested in the details of this matter than I do."

Frank Meyers came up, at this moment, and soon afterwards he offered Miss Eunice his arm, and they moved away slowly together, to examine the numerous contributions that were displayed elsewhere in the great Institute Exhibition.

At half past eight A.M., Ely threw off his coat, turned up his shirt-sleeves, and sat down in front of the rival safe, which was locked with the best device then known in America.

And it was really a good one.

He had a general knowledge of this lock, as he had of others. But he did not know how to pick it.

He worked at it steadily three long hours. The key was of no use in his hands, since there was but one way to use this implement, successfully, upon the lock; and this secret was like his own — communicated only by the patentee to the party who bought his differently construct-

"Now, young jackanapes!" shouted the burly grocer, whip in hand, as the homeless lad came out of the upturned hogshead, "what are you doin' here?" — "A sleepin', sir," cried the boy. "Don't hit me. I ain't done no harm, sir!" [CHAP. XXV. page 349.

ed keys and locks; though all were upon the same general principle, in their formation, it was known.

The old inventor opened this safe (as Ely had opened his, the day before,) to show the spectators that it could be done; and the other glistening five thousand dollars were exposed fairly to the public gaze. Then it was re-locked, and Ely went at it again.

He adopted his own tactics, and labored assiduously until high noon, without making any impression upon the rival lock.

The multitude wavered in opinion, as they watched the young mechanic's arduous efforts to win a triumph, in this attempt. But it was evident that his success was doubtful, until at three o'clock, he commenced systematically to pick it. He could not open it, from the outside, with the key — though he manipulated it over five hours, diligently, and tried half a dozen different skeleton-keys, besides.

"It has never been forced, by a stranger *yet*," remarked the inventor. "And I don't believe this sharp fellow can accomplish it, if he is given twenty-four instead of twelve hours, to try his experiments upon it."

But Ely went on, without talk, or halting to notice what was said about the probabilities. There were five thousand good hard dollars in gold, in that safe. And he wanted to earn this sum, if he could. "It is good round pay," he said, "for twelve hours of toil and study."

He had around him a variety of ingeniously constructed tools — files, probes, chisels, skeleton-keys, worms, springs, gouges, awls, hooks, pliers, clamps, hammers, and whatnots — and finally at a little past four o'clock he hit upon a device that gave him a fresh idea.

He contrived soon afterwards to catch up one of the inner tumblers of the lock and displace it. He followed up this 'vantage, and secured a second one. After half an hour's digging, and twisting and probing, he threw up the main lever that shot the chief bolt across the centre of the lock — and forcing this aside, he got a clamp-purchase upon the under bolt.

At ten minutes past five o'clock, the ratchets were broken, and the lock was forced. At half past five he had disengaged both catches, above and below; and, with his bar and cold-chisel, and twenty minutes more 'sharp practice' — Ely stove the sockets out, released the heavy steel bolts, and pried the door open, with the crippled lock in ruins, inside its hardened steel casings!

The multitude yelled out their note of acclamation, upon this triumph for the youthful inventor. And Ely's friends crowded around him with their earnest plaudits and congratulations.

He won his honors fairly. He gained the five thousand dollars he had competed for. And at the close of the Fair, the grand gold medal of the Institute was awarded — in this department — to the Patent "Impenetrable Bank-safe Lock" invented by Ely Hawes, as the BEST lock contributed to the Exhibition.

This was glory enough for poor Ely — for the present!

And he made the most of his opportunity, as we shall shortly discover.

The old inventor came forward at the close of Ely's labors, and himself withdrew the five thousand dollars in gold from his safe.

"You have won, my friend," he said, good-naturedly. "But a man who can construct a lock like yours, can beat *me*. Where will you have this money placed? It is yours. I can afford it. I have no reason to complain at my success, heretofore. What shall we do with this gold? You have broken my lock to pieces, and it is no longer safe *here*," continued the old man, smiling.

"Put it into my safe, then," replied Ely, going towards one of his that had remained unassailed, and which he opened at once.

"It will remain undisturbed *there*," said Ely.

"Yes. You have got a big thing in your lock, assuredly," returned his rival. "I congratulate you, young man. Your fortune is no longer a question of doubt, sir."

From that hour, Ely Hawes went upward steadily in his course. All sorts of offers were made him for associations, co-partnerships, and sharers in his future promising enterprise. But Downer and Meyers watched him.

"Keep it, yourself, Ely — " said Frank, earnestly. "Don't give it, sell it, or part with it to anybody. You have worked for it like a Trojan, and you've got money enough to carry on your business, amply. If not, call on *me*, whenever you need aid. Don't allow any of these 'anxious mourners' to get into your secret, or your pockets, at present."

"I won't, Frank — be sure of it."

"And, whatever you do, Ely," continued Reuben, advisedly, "don't touch any partnership, in an undertaking of this character. It is *yours* — the work of your own brain, your own toil, and your long years. Keep it, and make the most of it. Partnership in a thing of this kind, you'd find the worst ship you ever sailed in, my lad!"

Ely needed no such urging. He had clung to his invention from the outset, with remarkable pertinacity; and he had nursed his bantling for years, when he hadn't money enough to pay his board-bill from month to month. Now he resolved to see the end of his success, alone.

And within the succeeding three or four years, *he* had his 'hundred thousand dollars gold' laid up safely, outside of his then increased and constantly increasing profitable business.

CHAPTER XXIV.

FRANK MEYERS GETS STRANGELY BEFOGGED.

MORRIS DEANS had placed his lady friend Eunice Blount in charge of gallant Frank Meyers at the Fair, while he, having become so warmly interested in Ely's operations, crowded his way up beside the busy young mechanic, to watch his progress — and forgot all about the young lady, for the time being.

He knew she was in good hands however, and he enjoyed the scene where Ely was toiling at his rival's safe so intensely, that several hours passed before he remembered that Eunice had been left with Frank in a distant part of the great Exhibition rooms.

Now there had never yet passed between Morris and Eunice the first word expressive of over-affectionate consideration towards each other, and Morris had never yet mentioned to Eunice the fact that he was especially devoted to her.

They had dwelt under the same roof together for several years. Morris had come into her father's family a spruce city lad, who ventured upon the experiment of turning his hand to farming and stock-raising because he could find nothing better at that time to do, through which to support himself.

He had succeeded in this field beyond his most sanguine expectations. And he continued to adhere to it, because he found there was money in it, if well followed. He had gone on, from a very moderate beginning, until he had accumulated over fifty thousand dollars. And his prospect was never so good as it now was, shortly to realize the utmost acme of his hopes.

"I will have *my* 'hundred thousand dollars in gold,' yet!" he said quietly to himself, in these later days, when he remembered that for a long period he had been quite willing to compromise with Fortune for the possession of ten, or, at the outside, twenty thousand.

But Morris Deans had never spoken to Eunice Blount of love. He was very much attached to her. He had become strongly attracted to the rich farmer's daughter, through being constantly in her companionship in Blount's household. On her part, she had conceived a warm regard for him, at an early period.

But Morris was a very sensible youth, and he had entered this kind old man's employ to do his duty as a workman. And he had no leisure to talk soft nonsense to Euny, nor did he consider it manly or honorable to make any pretensions to the pretty country girl which possibly might not be agreeable to either her father or her mother — and, so far as he knew, even to the young lady herself.

Still, they had always been good friends. There was no need of urging matters, as there was no one in Morris's way, had he entertained any feeling towards Eunice beyond that of respectful admiration. He was constantly with her, when not occupied out of the house, and nobody interfered to interrupt the pleasant tête-a-têtes these unconscious young lovers indulged in.

But they had never been "romantic." And while Eunice was always to be seen, and from the very beginning of their acquaintance had clearly favored Morris, so he went quietly along, enjoying her society in a rational way, and never had given her an intimation that he entertained any disposition towards her save that of earnest good friendship.

He had taken Eunice down to the great Institute Fair because he was bound to be there himself, and because she desired to witness the exhibition. Morris had intrusted her to Frank's charge because he desired to be a near witness of his friend Ely's labors, while Meyers deemed the job which Hawes had undertaken very monotoous work.

Frank found himself highly pleased with Miss Eunice Blount, as it eventuated. He knew nothing about the relations that existed between Morris and this lady, but he made up his mind he would ascertain how these two young people stood affected towards each other.

To say truth, it was rather a delicate undertaking to venture on, this attempt to sound the young woman about whom he knew so little, and who he really supposed must long since have been betrothed to his friend.

There was a bare possibility only — in his estimation — that this might *not* be the case ; and so he resolved to satisfy himself of the facts, in the politest possible manner.

Miss Eunice was a charming girl, he thought. He was vastly delighted with her naive innocence, and ripe beauty.

They sauntered through the aisles of the Institute rooms, and passed several hours in examining the various articles exposed for exhibition and competition, the character of which Frank Meyers explained to Eunice, who was very curious, very talkative, very pleasant, and very companionable, as Frank discovered.

They got very well acquainted with each other, during that long interesting meeting, and the friendly conference they enjoyed. And Frank Meyers absolutely made up his mind to " see about this affair ! "

" And Morris tells me," observed Eunice, as they loitered along leisurely, " that you and he are old companions ? "

" Intimate friends from boyhood," returned Frank, enthusiastically.

" A very nice young man he has proved, within our acquaintance, at Brandville," said Eunice, complimentarily.

" I am glad to know that my old chum has succeeded so well, at farming, as I hear he has," continued Frank. " But Morris is a driving fellow, and a very worthy young man."

"He has shown himself both ambitious and skilful, since he came to Sunnyside," responded Eunice, "and father Blount has good cause to value him for his talent and usefulness, both."

After a while, Miss Eunice invited Meyers to visit 'Sunnyside,' at a future opportunity.

"We shall be delighted to meet you there, Mr. Meyers,' she urged, pleasantly.

"*Who*— Miss?" asked Frank, looking straight into the beautiful girl's face.

"Me, and Morris, and father Blount — all of us," returned Eunice, cordially and innocently.

"Morris? Well — perhaps he wouldn't care to meet intruders there," rejoined Frank; a suggestion which Eunice did not at the moment appreciate clearly, it was evident.

"Intruders? No. He would not," she remarked. "But *you* are his friend. You would not be considered an intruder, surely."

"Well, Miss Eunice — that depends — " continued Meyers, in a softened tone.

"Upon what?" asked the young lady, inquiringly.

"Well. I should say upon what your relations to Morris may be, Miss Blount."

"My relations?"

"Yes. Morris is very fond of you, I think."

"Well, I know that," said Eunice, archly, "and I am very fond of him, too."

"So I supposed, Miss Eunice. And therefore I say he might not care to have visitors at Sunnyside, such as I am."

"Why not, pray?"

"He might be jealous, you see."

"Of what?"

"Of you — or me, perhaps. And I am *really* his friend. Now — tell me, Miss Eunice. Come! You are a very good frank spoken girl, as I can see. You love Morris, and he loves you, I do not doubt. Are you under any obligations to each other?"

"Obligations? As how?"

"Beyond those of friendship?"

"No. Isn't that quite sufficient — if we are true friends?"

"But are you not pledged — engaged?"

"Engaged in what?"

"Why, Miss Eunice, you surely comprehend me, now?" persisted Meyers.

"Surely I don't, then, Mr. Frank," insisted the girl.

"Morris has promised to marry you, of course," ventured Frank, squarely, at this juncture.

At which the Sunnyside beauty halted, withdrew her arm from that of Meyers, and laughed right heartily in his face, to the latter's astonishment.

"Why, Mr. Meyers!" she exclaimed, "what ever put that idea into your head?"

"I supposed so, Miss Eunice, naturally — upon my word I did. Isn't it so?"

"Not a thought of it — I assure you, Mr. Frank."

"No? And has he never proposed to you?" asked Frank, eagerly.

"Proposed?"

"Yes. Has he not offered you marriage?"

"He never once spoke to me upon that subject, I pledge you my word — nor gave me a hint akin to such an idea — in his life!"

Mr. Frank Meyers was really quite surprised at the young lady's frankness and assurance. Then he asked —

"And if he had done so, Miss Eunice?"

"O, I should then know how to reply to him. But I assure you again he never did."

"Yet you have a tacit understanding between you, of course?"

"About what?"

"Upon this very interesting subject, Miss."

"Have we?" queried Eunice.

"You say you like *him*, vastly?"

"Yes — I do. That is so."

"And I know he is quite attached to *you*."

"Does he say this?"

"No! But you have just now told me that you like him."

"So I do, indeed."

"But you are not pledged to him?"

"Not at all."

"Nor to any other gentleman?"

"No. Never."

"Then I will accept your invitation, Miss Eunice, with great pleasure," added Frank, unhesitatingly.

"And what was that?"

"To visit Sunnyside, Miss Eunice."

"But Morris may be jealous — you suggest?" said Eunice, shrewdly.

"No. I am mistaken. I thought you were engaged to be married to each other, really."

"Oh, no!"

"I will come to Sunnyside, then, Miss — at an early opportunity."

"We shall all be happy to see the friend of Morris Deans there, be sure of it," returned Eunice.

"I am told it is a nice place — that 'Sunnyside.'"

"*We* think so."

"Well, Eunice — I am rich."

"I'm glad of that. And so am I, they tell me — or shall be, one day, probably."

"And Morris?"

"O, Morris Deans is very well-to-do, I assure you, Mr. Frank. He has made money, in the last five years — so father Blount tells me."

"And your father is fond of him?"

"Devotedly. Father Blount thinks every thing of Morris. So does mother. And so do I, too. He's a great favorite in our family, and always has been," continued Eunice, enthusiastically. "But *what* a notion was that of your recent suggestion! He never thought of this, I really do not believe, Mr. Frank."

"Well, Miss Eunice, you ought to be best informed upon this point, assuredly."

"For why?" continued the fair girl, innocently.

"Morris Deans has been in your family several years?"

"Yes. But the busiest of busy workers upon the place."

"True. Yet it seems to me that he would inevitably have found time to declare himself, nevertheless."

"What about?"

Frank Meyers glanced into the open handsome face of his interlocutor, to learn if she were not toying with him. But he discovered no evidence of deceit in the clear eye and innocent expression of the rustic beauty's countenance. Then he continued, pleasantly —

"I am out in my reckoning, I see, Miss. Still, I thought — from this long association, his position, your father's admiration of him, your own attractions, Miss Eunice — all taken together — that such an earnest young fellow as Morris Deans has always been, would be likely to have fallen quite in love with such a nice young woman, in the midst of such rare opportunities as he must have enjoyed at Sunnyside."

"Perhaps he has, then," replied the young lady.

"But I say you ought to know this, surely, if it were so."

"Well — I s'pose I had. But we never have talked about this matter, at all."

" That is strange, then."

" Is it ? How ? "

" Why, that two such young people should in this peculiar manner be thrown in association, at your ages, and continue so long thus without becoming intimate."

" Why, we are intimate."

" Yes. But you have never exchanged a loving word between you ! "

" O, yes. Morris is always very kind and affectionate. But he is not demonstrative, you know," ventured Eunice.

" No. I should say not ! " concluded Frank, who had seen more of the world than either Morris or Eunice had ever dreamed about, at quiet Sunnyside.

" Here he is, now," exclaimed Eunice, as Morris, who had been hunting for them, approached and relieved the smitten city lover of his temporary charge.

" Ah, here you are ! " said Morris, offering Eunice his arm, politely.

" And where have you been loitering, all these long hours ? " asked Eunice.

" I trust you have been pleasantly occupied, Euny," returned her friend.

" Oh, very. Mr. Meyers has been very attentive, and has managed to amuse me wondrously, I assure you, ' observed the young lady, without explaining *how!*

" Well. The contest is over, and Ely Hawes has won," exclaimed Morris, delightedly.

" I knew he would," added Meyers.

And a few moments afterwards, the friends got together and left the Institute Hall in the best possible spirits; though Frank Meyers had become completely befogged by the interesting conference he had enjoyed in the society of the belle of Brandville!

"To the man who is uncorrupt," murmured Frank, that night, "and who is properly constituted, a lovely woman remains ever something of a mystery, as well as a romance. It is difficult to interpret her, quite literally. She, on her part, is constantly striving to remain a poem, and rarely becomes weary in the work of bringing out new editions of herself in novel bindings!

"This rustic beauty is a paradox — indeed. But if I have not misinterpreted her, fair Eunice Blount may be honorably won. And I will not miss my opportunity, on this promising occasion."

CHAPTER XXV.

THE TRAMP'S STORY, AND BLOUNT'S OPINIONS.

The village of Brandville, not far distant from Sunnyside farm, had its periodical visitors in the shape of tramps, who wandered up and down the country in all directions — idling away their lives and loafing about from spot to spot, picking up their precarious living.

Too indolent to work — though they always pretended they were in search of employment — they roamed over the State to obtain what they could through charity, or petty theft, and were unknown by name to any one. Still, they were sharp and shrewd in their way, and managed to subsist. But one half this world know little as to how the other half live — that is certain!

This assertion may be appreciated by the reader who will consult the illustration on page 331, where a phase of life among the lowly is admirably delineated. From this class of impoverished city boys, these country tramps are originally largely made up.

Born in poverty, brought up loosely amid indolence, want, penury, and petty vice, they approach to manhood without trade, calling, or education — and wander away oftentimes into the interior in clans, to join the crowd of older idlers who thus roam over the state, and beg or filch their living from the charity, the fears, or the indifference of the public.

In older countries, they pass for "gypsies." In this country, they are simply itinerant beggars. Our picture shows one of these forsaken boys, who has trespassed upon the premises of a well-to-do store-keeper, who has been annoyed by the pilfering and mischief of lads of a larger growth, and he has been on the watch latterly to ascertain who may be the petty offenders that have inconvenienced him so frequently.

Turning out at an early hour in the morning, he fancies he has discovered the cause of his annoyance — and he valiantly goes for his intended victim.

"Now, young jackanapes! What are you doin' here?" demands the burly grocer, as he stands whip in hand over the hogshead, from which one terrified youngster emerges in hot haste, replying as he springs out from his late humble lodging-place — "sleepin', sir. Don't hit me! I hain't done no harm there."

"A sleeping? Wot do yer mean by that, you rogue?"

"I been asleep there, las' night, sir. That's all."

"Asleep? In that hogshe'd?"

"Yis, sir."

"Wot for?"

"'Cos I hadn't no other place, sir."

"Why didn't you go home?"

"I hain't got none."

"Got no home?"

"No, sir."

"Where do you live?"

"On the w'arves, sir."

"On the wharves! Why — God bless us — is that the way you manage?" continued the big grocer, astonished and not a little softened, as he gazed at the trembling lad before him, incredulously, and then assumed a disposition more sympathetic.

"That's where we sleep w'en we can't do no better, sir," continued the lad.

"Come wi' me, then," decided the shop-keeper, "an' we'll see. An' you hain't had no breakfast?"

"No sir. Ner supper — ner dinner eyther, yisterday."

"Aren't you hungry, boy?"

"Awful, sir."

"Who's your mate, yonder — inside?" he asked — pointing to the hogshead.

"My brother."

"Call him."

"You won't beat us, sir?"

"No! Bring him along. We'll give you something to eat. And then we'll see what can be done."

The two boys followed the mollified grocer up the lonely street, and within an hour he had provided them both with a hearty meal.

He learned the true story of these two poor deserted lads, and subsequently procured them both good places out at service in the country, where they fortunately grew up to be good men, years afterwards.

But they never forgot the fright that came over them that hot morning, when the portly shop-keeper hailed them so unceremoniously after their free night's lodging together in the empty down-turned sugar hogshead, upon the town wharf, near his grocery.

Of such as these, in infancy, are made a majority of the wretched itinerants who circulate over the country roads of New England in their later years of life in warm weather, and who fill our alms-houses, station-houses, or jails, in winter time!

The older tramps who came to Brandville, were enjoying their 'nooning,' one warm bright day, and the best talker among them told the following story to his homely unkempt mates, as they sat around him and listened to his narrative, which vastly interested his idle companions. (See next page.)

"She's a purty cretur," said the itinerant, "an' she's grow'd up wi' mitey good stock — this same ole farmer Bl'unt's darter. I've know'd her, now, fust an' last, more'n fourteen year. She wus an orflin."

"A orflin?" queried one of his hearers. "Wot's that?"

"O, I carn't 'splain — ef yer don't know, Bob."

"A orflin," observed another of the clan, "w'y that's as

THE TRAMP'S STORY.

"That's what's the matter over at Sunnyside farm, lads."

plain as a mile-post. *We* are all orflins. It's a boy or gal 'at hain't got no father ner muther, lads."

"Jess so, Spook. Yer right," said the first speaker. And then he continued his romance, as follows.

"Well, this gal Euniss, wot ole Bl'unt *calls* his darter, wus a orflin. She aren't his own chile, though her mother was a Blount. He never had no child'en. *I* know. But this gal 'at's grow'd up to be sech a rite out-an'-out beauty, wus leff to old Bl'unt's keer by a distant poor relation, w'en she wus a baby. She don't know whar' she come from, an' she never know'd no parients but ole Bl'unt an' his wife. An' they think the world of 'er, to be sure. So it's jest as well.

"An' she's a nice gurl, that's a fact. *She* never turns none ov us away empty-handed, w'en we goes to Sunnyside, eyther hungered or lackin' a cast-off jacket or shirt, yer know."

"That's so," interrupted the ugliest looking loafer of the clan. "But I mind the big dog, thar, o' late — nevertheless. *He* don't like us, much!"

"Ah, well. Spot's a good dog. He won't hurt nobuddy 'at don't go to filch any thin' off the place, lads. An' don't yer ferget this now.

"Well — as I wus a sayin' — one bright arternoon, a'most twenty year ago, this gal (then a little baby) was brought to Sunnyside by a play'd-out poor relation of Bl'unt's, an' left thar. They took it in, an' done for it, an' got to lovin' it, 's if it war the'r own. An' now they'r so fond ov' 'er, 'at the old farmer 'ud part wi' his whole place sooner'n he'd part with *her*, I can tell you.

"An' the old man's richer 'an mud, now. Thirty year ago, farmer Bl'unt wusn't wuth rats! But he wus a hard worker allers, an' he was a lucky dog. Every thin' he put his hand to, turned into cash. Au' he piled it up, arter a w'ile."

"I'd like jess sech a chance," muttered Spook, lazily.

"*You?* W'y, ef a siller spoon wus put inter yeur mouth, Spook, you'd drop it out quicker'n scat!"

"I mought, yas."

"Yeur too lazy to make a dollar, ef yer hed never so good a chance.

"Well, I've told you how this young 'ooman come to old Bl'unt's, an' how they've made a lady ov 'er. Now — jess see wot follers. The ole farmer goes down ter Boston a few year ago, an' he runs afoul ov a lad 'at wus in a bank thar, an' he takes a likin' to *him*, too. He fetches this boy, twenty year old, up ter the place, an' sets him to work. The ole man larfed w'en he did it, an' said 'it's no go! This boy wus never made ter do nothin' but lay roun' loose among other people's money-bags; an' he ain't wuth shucks on a farm, surely.'

"But the lad come ter time, right off. An' he turned out the best hand ole Bl'unt ever had — by a heap. Ther' wus nothin' he couldn't do, better'n any of 'em he'd ever hired. An' he's gone on — a makin' money fer ole Bl'unt, an' some fer hisself, 'ntil he's well-to-do, w'ile the ole man's better off, by thousan's, than he ever wus, through this boy's help.

"An' wot follers all that, as a consekence — eh?" queried the tramp, looking into the stolid faces of his companions.

"I dunno," returned one.

"Ner I," added another.

"W'ot?" asked Spook.

"Wal — the gurl falls in love wi' this city lad, an' he don't go back on 'er — o' coorse."

"An' wot o' that?"

"He'll marry 'er — won't he, stoopid?"

"I dunno."

"No. Yer don't! An' it's mitey little yer do know, any way," retaliated the leading tramp. "But *I* know. I've heer'd all about it, up t' the village. An' they're goin' to be married — this orflin gal an' this city boy that wus. An' it'll be a nice soft thing fer him, to be sure. She'll be old Bl'unt's heir — an' he'll be rotten rich, by the means. *That's* wot's the matter up 't Sunnyside farm, lads.

"An' it's a right lively match, too. She's as 'ansome as a pictur, an' Morris Deans's smarter'n litnin'. Ef yeu don't b'lieve wot I tell, you try him on some day, in a trade — ef yer can come to it, an' see. He knows more 'bout hosses, an' cattil, an' sech like, 'an all the farmers in this Valley — young as he is. But he 'tends to his biz', ev'ry time now, sure's yer alive. An' he knows wot's wot.

Ole Bl'unt's wuth more'n a hunder'd thousan' dollers, terday. An' Morris Deans 'll be wuth as much as that 'n less'n ten year, mind wot I tell yer."

The tramps had smoked their clay pipes out, by this time — but they had been unusually interested in their leader's tale.

"It's a good yarn, ef it's true," suggested Spook, rising and knocking the ashes out of his exhausted dudeen, in his habitual leisurely manner.

"That's just wot's the history o' the Bl'unt crowd, then," insisted the tramp. "They begun from nuth'n, an' they've got a pile o' money 'mongst 'em, terday — sure's preechin.' The orflin gal's the purtiest in the County, the city lad's the smartest young farmer'n this part o' the State, an' the Bl'unts ar' as good a pair as ever grow'd on the C'netticut River."

The five tramps rose to their feet, looked about them, and exchanging the customary signs, at separating, they went their way, in different directions, upon the forlorn hunt for their suppers and the coming night's lodgings.

They had no aim, they possessed no spark of ambition to be anybody, or to do any lawful thing for a decent livelihood — save tramp, tramp, **tramp**.

And yet they lived.

They went and came, and were poorly fed and clad, through the charity of those who either pitied them or gave of their surplus to get rid of the offensive presence around them of these poor creatures, who are tolerated in society's midst all over the interior of our country — and who multiply astonishingly in all directions, unfortunately, in the later years among us!

In the year 1875, while we write these lines, this miserable race of indigent and listless beings have come to be a crying nuisance indeed, in all quarters — notably in the interior of Massachusetts.

While the majority of the common tramps have been hitherto comparatively harmless, amidst their wanderings — in the later days there have cropped out among these cliques bad men, who have been guilty of robbery, assault, and criminal acts of a graver character, in numerous instances.

The press throughout New England have taken this subject in hand, vigorously, and some of the State Legislatures have adopted new and stringent statutes in reference to these marauding pests; though, up to this writing, without much effect, unfortunately.

They are devoid of all active principles, and exist only from hand to mouth; and yet in the sunshiny days of summer these miserable tramps seem to take things very philosophically, and quietly, as if it were all right with them, and there was no higher plane to move up to.

On page 352 we give an illustration of samples of these public dead-beats, in a picture where the leading tramp is telling what he knows about the Blount family.

In the main, the narrative was true. Miss Eunice *was* an orphan. But Farmer Blount and his good wife loved and cherished her as if she had been of their own flesh and blood.

She never knew the love of father or mother other than that of those whom she had dutifully called by those endearing titles, from babyhood. And she had no need to think of other relatives — near of kin, or distant; for, all that parents could be to a child, old farmer Blount and his wife had been to pretty Eunice, from her infancy.

Farmer Simon Slow came over to Sunnyside to chat with farmer Blount, not infrequently, when the latter had come to be the portly well-to-do leisurely country gentleman, at last.

Old Blount was always gracious, pleasant and talkative, but he had a mind of his own and he never hesitated to argue his convictions for the edification of those who sought his opinions — whoever they might be, or whatever the subject under consideration.

The village postmaster was a warm appreciative friend of Blount's, and like Jack Bunsby, he was disposed to maintain that the old farmer's assumption was " an opinion as *was* an opinion," upon all occasions when he chanced to be present during a discussion.

"He carries his p'ints," insisted the postmaster, "every time. And you can't dodge 'em."

Farmer Slow happened to meet this petty officer at Sunnyside one afternoon, when the old-style yeoman got into a debate with Blount.

Morris Deans was near by, too, and he always took an

earnest delight in seeing Blount vanquish his contestants, especially when his own favorite theories concerning modern farming or live stock-raising were in question.

"There's plenty o' room up on top," said farmer Blount. "You must mount, Simon. Go *up* — and onward. They'll crowd you, down below — always. But if you get up, on the outer surface, you will find ample working and breathing space there. Quit the old ruts. Go forward. And, be sure of it, you can only triumph by advancing. No matter how carefully you do this. But never go backwards, and never halt. Thus you may win."

Old Blount then gave his slow neighbor some useful hints in managing his stock and his farm, which Simon dutifully but dubiously listened to.

"We are all too prone I know, Simon," advisedly continued farmer Blount, "to embark in enterprises that seem to have thousands in them; and many of us look for perennial crops, or unreasonably big returns, in our new undertakings.

"Fancy chicken-raising is a mania, but a vast improvement is already made upon our old-time barnyard fowls, with the later foreign bloods. Our horses and cattle and sheep are two, three, five hundred per cent better, and far more profitable legitimately, than the breeds you and I raised twenty years ago. But the hens that lay two eggs a day are not found yet; and the cow that gives her twenty-four quarts o' milk a day even in clover-time, is very rare, to be sure.

"Some of us attempt to improve the garden-sass, and a neighbor is turning out what he calls mushrooms, for the city hotels, o' late. *He* has done this to profit. But a dozen others will attempt it, who don't know a real mushroom from a toadstool, or a hole in the ground. *They* will fail, through ignorance in management.

"And yet all these things are very simple, when you know how to accomplish what you undertake. It took me six years to find out how to put yender meadow in good tilth. But you remember the old swamp there, Simon, ten year ago, eh?

"We aren't born with hereditary experience, mind you. We live to learn. And we must study, work, experiment judiciously, and acquire a knowledge of our business, to win in the end. We should feel our way, and look before we jump — o' course. But we must go *on*, all the time, in this age of progress; or we shall be run down or over-slaughed. I say it's all simple — but it must be attended to.

"The merest boy with his bean-shooter — if he buckles right down to it — can make all Brandville respect his ideas, and prefer his friendship, Simon. And this pithy assertion of Mr. Billings is very truthful — that a single lively determined wasp, upon the rampage, will break up a camp-meeting, easy.

"You and I have been worried in past years with the potato-bug, and the apple-borer. Now study, among the diligent scientific men, has latterly discovered an insect that will destroy the potato-bug."

"Sho! Yer don't say so?" exclaimed Simon — for *this* hint was especially interesting to him.

"Yes. They have found this worm. But they have found too that he eats his way into the potato, first, and lays in wait there for the other pest. But while he waits, he *eats* — and the bulb suffers. What we must do next, is, to discover the bug that will be satisfied to eat only the bug that kills the original bug, after he has performed this good office, you see. Then we'll have reached the right thing, in *that* direction. But it all takes time, I know. Yet we must keep at it — and live and study, and practise, to learn and appreciate."

"He's makin' p'ints, now," said the elated postmaster, eagerly watching Blount's arguments, and noticing their effect upon his immediate listener.

Then taking up a spade close at hand, with a bit of chalk the village official commenced to mark them down; while Morris Deans, as deeply interested as the other friend, pointed in triumph to the record, as Blount clinched his opinions, and the Brandville postmaster duly noted the "points," in tally — as portrayed in the illustration on page 367.

CHAPTER XXVI.

THE FRIENDS ALL MEET AT 'SUNNYSIDE.'

MORRIS and Eunice tarried in New York but a day or two after the close of the Exhibition.

The young farmer asked no questions, and the innocent girl vouchsafed no details to Deans, regarding what had transpired between herself and Frank at the Institute rooms.

She was thoughtful, nevertheless, and Morris did not fail to notice this, upon their return to Blount's residence.

Perhaps the unanticipated hints which Meyers had made aroused certain speculative thoughts in the fair maiden's heart, and not unlikely was it that Morris awoke — subsequently — and "took in the situation," at length, as events soon afterwards indicated. But his friend Mr. Frank Meyers was an upright trusty young man, in all respects, and did not know how to go about committing a dishonorable act.

Still, he could not divest himself of the conviction, since Miss Eunice Blount was fairly 'in the market,' (according to her own frank admissions,) that he had the right to make an effort to win this country beauty. And he essayed this little undertaking, with a will.

"Morris Deans is a privileged member of the household at Sunnyside, evidently," he said to himself on reflection, the night after the Fair. "He has been resident there boy and man six or seven years. This artless ingenuous young lady has grown up with Morris, in her father's house, and very likely — although they may be fond of each other, as Miss Eunice states — it is merely a commonplace fraternal feeling that animates them, and there is probably no love existing between them.

"Now, though this is a remarkable instance, it is certainly strange that Morris has not made some declaration, under the circumstances. And *I* fancied they were engaged, as a matter of course.

"But she says no. And furthermore, she declares that not the slightest intimation has ever been suggested by Morris, in reference to any contemplated serious intentions he may have entertained towards this nice young lady.

"Possibly he has no such intent, or purpose. Very likely, this is so — on farther thought. Morris Deans was never much of a lady's man, any way," continued Frank Meyers, as he looked over the prospect, and indulged his quiet speculations regarding the Sunnyside people.

"I'll go up there, at all events," concluded Frank. "No harm in that. She's altogether a charming girl, to be sure — is Miss Eunice. She invited me to visit her. What for? Morris has made no approaches, it seems.

He don't want to get married. He isn't a marrying man, I suppose. I am rich, I shall shortly be at my leisure, and I've no doubt Eunice favors me. Though, what a simple-hearted beauty she is, indeed! Frank, open, and unaffected as a child — and yet she must be five and twenty, at the least.

"I wouldn't mind getting married, and I should be glad to settle down somewhere in comfort and ease," continued Meyers. "This young lady would make me a good wife, no doubt. I will go to Sunnyside, and learn just what the situation is. Morris Deans — if he doesn't want to marry Eunice himself — can of course have no objection to his friend's making himself agreeable to the beautiful country girl. I'll try it on. I *think* Miss Eunice was pleased with me, at the Fair. I reckon it will all come around right. The boys are going up, in response to Morris's invitation, and I will go at the same time. We shall see."

Frank Meyers was really very hopeful. He was an honorable young gentleman, worthy of pretty Miss Eunice, or any equally admirable young lady. He was rich, of good habits, and was fairly smitten with the Sunnyside charmer's attractive manners and simplicity of character. So artless and comely a girl, in town or country, it had never been the good fortune of handsome stylish Frank Meyers yet to encounter. And he was quite ready to acknowledge this to Miss Eunice herself.

But he was prudent, as well as impulsive. And he deemed it but just to Morris first to ascertain what *his* position actually was in the premises, and whether he made or had any prior claims upon farmer Blount's handsome daughter. If the coast were clear (and he hoped and believed it was,) Frank resolved to win fair Eunice Blount, and marry her, at an early day.

This was his present plan, and when the friends went up to the Blount farm together, a few weeks afterwards, both Downer and Hawes observed that their companion Frank was in exuberant spirits at the prospective pleasure they were about to enjoy, in this trip. But he took care to enter into no explanation of the motive that actuated him, in this demonstration, and no one suspected the nature of his real thoughts and hopes.

"We shall have an elegant time, lads, at Sunnyside," he said, happily, at the start. "This old man Blount is wealthy, and he has accumulated his property by hard work and settled application to one chosen pursuit, which he has adhered to faithfully, from boyhood."

"His family must be a very interesting household," rejoined Ely. "The lady Blount is said to be a charming person, and the proprietor of Sunnyside is described as a most worthy good gentleman of the old school. They will no doubt give the former companions of their favorite, Morris Deans, a hearty welcome."

"And then there's the pretty daughter, too," suggested Reuben. "She's a marvellously fine specimen of the true woman, I judge — though she seems simplicity itself, in her manners. Morris is very sweet on her, and he will secure a jewel, in that girl, I predict, when he makes her his wife — as I presume he will, from appearances."

"Nothing of the kind has as yet been suggested, in that direction," returned Meyers, confidently. "Not a bit of it. It looked that way, certainly. But I happen to know that never a word has been exchanged between those two young people, on this interesting subject."

"That is singular, then," said Downer, thoughtfully. "I supposed they were engaged to be married, long ago."

"No. They are simply good friends," insisted Frank. "They have been in constant familiar contact, for years; but neither of them ever expressed a syllable that pointed to any feeling or disposition other than that of ordinary friendly admiration."

"There's a good chance there, then, for some enterprising young man," added Ely. "Miss Eunice is certainly a very lovable young lady, as far as I am a judge of such matters."

Meyers, Downer, and Hawes reached Brandville together, and Morris Deans received them with heartfelt cordiality. Old Blount and his wife were exceedingly affable and attentive to the New York friends of Morris; and Miss Eunice was delighted to meet the three gentlemen, whom she welcomed to Sunnyside, right earnestly and cheerfully.

They found the Blount estate at this time a splendid country place. The broad acres of the farm were in high

"Now he's makin' p'ints," said the village postmaster. And taking up a spade, he marked them down with a bit of chalk, as Deans pointed Simon Slow to the record triumphantly. [CHAP. xxv page 361.

tilth, and the neat stock, horses, and sheep were in fine condition. Mrs. Blount was exceedingly gracious and pleasant, and the city residents were vastly gratified with their reception and generous treatment during this agreeable visit.

When the four friends sat down together, at length, to chat over past days and present prospects — "it seems like the old times, boys," began Morris, "to get all together, once more. I am very happy to meet you here, I assure you. And while you tarry, make yourselves at home. *I* am quite at home here, I assure you."

"So it appears," responded Downer. "And you've made the most of your opportunity here, Morris, as I knew you would. I congratulate you on your success, hitherto, and upon your promising prospects still ahead. You have done well, Morris. And you have deserved your good fortune, I am glad to know."

"The times are changed, to-day, lads," observed Ely, "from what they were in the years ago, when we four pennyless young men began, and were struggling with Fortune, eh?"

"That's so!" added Morris. "I am content. My means have accumulated far beyond the mark I had set for a competency. While the rest — you, Downer, Frank, and Ely — have all compassed more than your originally coveted hundred thousand dollars in gold, I am happy to hear."

"And Fred Fordham is piling up money also, I am

informed," said Meyers. "His firm are very prosperous now, and they are all getting rich. I wish he were with us here. He would enjoy this, vastly, and it would complete the circle, Morris. Why didn't you think to invite Fred up, and Fannie and the babies? It would have been very agreeable to meet them here."

"I did not forget it, Frank. They were all to have been here last night — for a visit of two weeks. They will be up to-day, probably."

And so it eventuated. On the second evening after the arrival of the New York guests, Fred and his family came from Boston — and a right cheery greeting was enjoyed, when the friends got together at beautiful Sunnyside farm, after years of separation.

Morris cordially received all his old companions with open palm. And each could now fortunately exclaim to his chum of former time —

> "Your hand, old boy! The days are past
> When we, tried friends, were all so poor.
> And Fortune brings us here, at last —
> Together — hopeful as of yore.
> But months have flown, and years have sped,
> Since nought but woes *we* brooded o'er;
> And now those early fears are dead.
> The days are gone, when we were poor!"

There was ample room for the convenience and comfort of them all at the Blount mansion; and what with the rides and drives, and walks and country parties, the good cheer and the pleasant companionship of these happy folk, all round, a highly enjoyable week was passed at this fine old place; where farmer Blount and his household exerted themselves untiringly to render everybody happy and at their ease, when under this hospitable roof.

The conservatory was in its most attractive condition, and the garden flower-beds had been set out but a week prior to the coming of the visitors. The weather was warm, but not hot yet. It was late in May, and the season was most delightful.

Morris had a dozen nice young horses in the stables. Downer and Ely rode over the country, up and down the river's margin, to and about the pretty neighboring villages, or went fishing and roving in the woods and over the fields, continually.

Morris and Fred were out about the farm, admiring the choice live stock. And Frank paid quiet court to Eunice, upon every possible opportunity, during his visit — growing more and more interested in this charming girl, as he became better acquainted with her; and really indulging at last in "great expectations" regarding his future, in connection with the fate of sweet Eunice Blount.

On her part — strange as it was that she had never given Morris the opportunity to declare himself, up to the time they went down to the New York Fair together — it was stranger still that she did not appreciate the ardent attentions and fine speech that Frank Meyers had latterly addressed to her. She never once suspected his designs, or his inclinations towards her!

But he had come up from the metropolis mainly to satisfy himself "how the land lay," between Morris and Eunice. So he exerted himself during his entire stay at Sunnyside to make a favorable impression upon Miss Eunice and her father's family. And Frank succeeded in this, to admiration.

But — when he came at last to the day before they were all to quit Sunnyside, on their return to New York — and Frank ventured to make an open declaration of love to Eunice, the gentle girl woke up, and quickly disenchanted her anxious city lover — greatly to his surprise!

They were in the Conservatory together — Eunice and Meyers. And Frank had not up to this time had the opportunity he desired to 'speak his mind' clearly. Now he thought his chance presented itself, favorably. They were alone — and he spoke of the prospective parting, that would ensue on the following day.

"And you are wearied with Sunnyside, I suppose," suggested Eunice, pleasantly. "There are few attractions here for you city gentlemen, I know."

"I never passed a happier week in my life, Miss Eunice, than that which has just ended, here, and I assure you that we all leave Sunnyside reluctantly. For myself, I have something more than this to say, though, Eunice. Will you listen to me?"

"Am I not always attentive to what you say, Mr. Frank?"

"O, yes. But now I am about to leave you, Miss

Eunice. I have become very much attached to you. And since you assured me, when in New York, that my friend Morris or no other gentleman had ever made proposals for your hand, in marriage, *I* venture to lay my fortune and my heart at your feet, Miss Eunice. I am not unworthy of your favor, I trust — and I should be proud to make the fair daughter of Mr. Blount my wife."

"Why — Mr. Meyers!" exclaimed Eunice, halting in the great avenue among the flowers, and extending her right hand kindly towards him, with unaffected surprise, but no emotion — "how *could* you bring yourself to make such a mistake as this, pray?"

"Mistake — Eunice?"

"Most certainly, Mr. Frank."

"As how, then?" returned Frank, straightening himself up, and returning her gaze of astonishment with a look of firm earnestness. "How have I erred, Miss Eunice?"

"You have entirely misapprehended *me*, my dear Mr. Frank — while I had never suspected *you*, in our late pleasant intercourse. That is all," said Eunice, kindly.

"Misapprehend you?" ejaculated Meyers, "in what way? You have been very candid with me, I am sure. And I thought I could understand plain English, Miss Eunice."

"But surely, Mr. Frank, you will do me the justice to admit that I have not encouraged you to make this proposal to me, in earnest!" said Eunice, courteously.

"You informed me that no such proposition had ever yet been made you, Eunice; and I thought I thus had the right to make you the honorable offer I have now ventured to suggest," replied Meyers, affably.

"When I was in New York," said Eunice, "I did make this statement, I remember. And it was true. Up to that time, I had never heard a word upon such a subject."

"Yes. That was what you said."

"When we returned to Sunnyside, Mr. Frank, my dear old friend Morris Deans took an opportunity, within a week, to do just what *you* now have done!"

"He offered himself, formally?"

"He did. And I accepted his kindly proffer, with all my heart; for you know I was very fond of him, long years agone. And we are now engaged to be married, Mr. Frank. This is a sufficient answer to your proposal — is it not?"

"Quite sufficient, Miss Eunice," returned Meyers, a little chap-fallen, and really disappointed at his non-success with the country beauty.

"Still, I congratulate you, Eunice, and I will congratulate my friend Morris. I would have been a happy man, indeed, had the way been open for you to have accepted my offer. But not at *his* cost, believe me. You could not have made a better choice, Miss Eunice. But I still think my young friend has shown himself very tardy in his declaration. However, I give you joy, in advance. Now — you and I will forget this mistake, which I have blundered into; but you will none the less allow me to assure you of my continuous friendship. When does the happy event come off, Eunice?" asked Frank, pleasantly.

"O, by and by. Three months, or six months hence. There is no hurry. We are constantly in each other's society, and both father and mother are delighted with our prospective plan, Mr. Frank."

"When you are married, Eunice, I bespeak the post of groomsman beside my friend Morris."

"That will be splendid, Frank! And you shall be notified in good time, be sure of it."

"Thanks, Eunice."

"Now we comprehend each other?" queried the girl, with a pleasant turn to the conversation.

And Frank said 'yes'—as they left the conservatory together, on the approach of the other friends, who had just returned from a long jaunt over the fields.

Next day, Morris formally announced to his visitors this news, and extended a cordial invitation to them all to come to Sunnyside again, on the occasion of the wedding, in the fall of that same year.

After eight days of delightful experience at the Blount farm, the New York friends departed, as they came; and a week subsequently Fred, Fannie, and the two babies left, for Boston.

Their joint visit to Sunnyside was long remembered as one of the happiest social events in their lives; and all the friends mutually promised to return, on the occasion of the wedding, which was to take place between Morris and Eunice early in the succeeding fall.

CHAPTER XXVII.

WHY SHOULD WE NOT HAVE "PANICS"?

We have thus far given the brighter side, and detailed honorable modes through which to make money in this thriving busy land of ours.

The incidents described in the foregoing chapters of our present story occurred at and during the years which immediately succeeded the memorable panic of 1837, as we have shown. The country afterwards resumed its wonted prosperity, for a period. The dark cloud of adversity passed away. Trade and commerce revived. And labor received its remunerative reward, once more — for a term. But there is another side to the picture; for "history repeats itself" alike in this as in other respects.

Twenty years afterwards, the monetary crash of 1857 came; and thousands of business-men, master-mechanics, bankers, merchants, and brokers live to-day — not yet recovered in their financial condition from the terrible effects of *that* periodical visitation.

Then succeeded the money wreck in 1861, and following this we had the fratricidal rebellion — which tore the nation asunder, and swallowed up the fortunes and the lives of a million of our citizens, ere the difficulties involved and the horrors this wretched imbroglio entailed were brought to a climax!

Half a dozen years later, we experienced the fearful panic of 1873. In view of all that had transpired previously in this country, and noting the recorded startling facts embodied in this chapter — which are patent to the American nation, and which may be verified, almost tenfold, by any one who will examine the files of our daily city journals for any single given year within the last decade — the observer of events is led to ask why *shouldn't* we have " panics ? "

In the earlier times of our national history, it was not thus. Things were then called by their right names. But nowadays, as a New England poet recently has put it —

> " With generous curve, we draw the moral line;
> *Our* swindlers are permitted to " resign "!
> Their guilt is wrapped in deferential names,
> And twenty sympathize for one that blames.
> Steal but *enough*, the world is unsevere, —
> Tweed is a statesman, Fisk a financier;
> Invent a mine, and be — the Lord knows what —
> Secure, at any rate, with what you've got.
> The public servant who has stolen or lied,
> If called on, may resign with honest pride:
> As unjust favor put him in, why doubt
> Disfavor as unjust has turned him out?
> Whitewashed, he quits the politician's strife
> At ease in mind, with pockets filled for life."

We deem this topic pertinent, since it is no longer a secret among the people of this country that corruption in upper society (and too often among the lowly) is general. The public records show that legislative bodies have latterly grown venal, in more than one of the States, and that even in the national councils there has been disclosed a modicum of taint, in recent years.

Lobbyists, great and small — the most unprincipled, grasping, worthless and unscrupulous of cormorants and political rascals that ever disgraced any country on earth — influence or control public legislation largely, backed and fostered as they are or have been by moneyed men (and the government itself in some instances) in all directions. As in the days of the Roman Republic, so in ours, alas! "Judges and Senates have been bought for gold," and the former have not infrequently been shown to have been guilty of accepting bribes for a favorable ruling or decision in behalf of wealthy rogues who have fallen under the ban of the law — in instances that might be veritably enumerated.

Capital and corporations rule the "wise men in council" who convene to make laws for the government of the people, at the national Capitol and in various of our commonwealths. Of a truth has it been latterly demonstrated that "great wealth covers infamy, and success knows no shame;" while the triumphant scoundrel assumes an unblushing front high above the head of his neighbor who chances to be unfortunate — though honest, honorable, and virtuous. Why, then, shouldn't we have an occasional panic?

Colossal estates, lucrative offices, and remunerative positions have been derived through subtle cunning and downright knavery, while honors were obtained but rarely through the merit of the wearers. Corruption in high places has " boiled and bubbled till it o'errun the stew," and bold-faced bribery has purchased the active support of scores and hundreds of " influential " political hucksters, at paltry figures, where the universe would not be rich enough to buy the vote of a poor but *honest* man! Why shouldn't there occur among us a periodical crisis?

Public opinion is too unsound at the core; and there exists little sentiment of contempt for wealth acquired — no matter *how*, so that it be got possession of — among thousands of the leading operators, speculators, and commercial gamblers frequently classed as " enterprising business men," in this country. There is no need of mentioning names, no call to point at individuals, in this sweeping assertion. *The records of our day* verify all this, and more, unfortunately. Why shouldn't we experience a crash, now and then?

The besetting sin of our age, wrote Sir John Herschel, " is the temptation to squander and dilute, in a thousand different ways." The American people have speculated and gambled in stocks, in food, in clothing, in paper money, in every thing. They have " squandered " their swiftly-acquired riches with a profligacy and shiftlessness unparalleled. They have "diluted" values (merely nominal at the outset) until their watered "fancies" have lost the semblance of reality. And they awake from the wretched lull of security into which they have deluded themselves, to find only ashes in their palms, and to realize that all "is but the baseless fabric of a dream." Why shouldn't chaos follow upon such inexcusable folly, blundering, and crime?

It is an expressive proverb of the Russians which declares that "misfortune is next door to stupidity." And yet there be those — in the midst of such crises as have thrice within the last five and thirty years been brought about in the United States through the recklessness and positive stupidity of our people — who whine about the *misfortune* of these results; all unmindful that Heaven rarely sends such calamities upon men as men bring upon themselves! Why, then, shouldn't we sometimes be called to atone for our remissness?

The leading characters whose history we have interwoven in the thread of this story were fortunately not of this class. The wealth accumulated by Blount, and Downer, Meyers, Ely Hawes, and Morris Deans was earned by honest industry and skilful application of natural talents to well-timed opportunities which they availed themselves of, and wrought out to honorable results.

But when we meet with such disastrous examples of folly and recklessness as have latterly been thrust publicly into notice — the colossal *fiascos* of a Cooke, a Duncan and

Sherman, a Jackson, a Ralston, a Collie, a Clewes, a Fisk, a Shepard, a Tweed, and a hundred others that might be cited; when we learn through the public press day after day of the infamous frauds, defalcations, wholesale robberies and disgraceful thieveries which occur — and through which dishonorable means men grow rich, but go unwhipt of justice for the crimes thus committed — we deem it but just to point at these offenders, by way of comparison, at least; though we are constrained to exclaim, while such scandalous cases of wrong-doing multiply and increase in magnitude — why should we *not* look for panics in our midst!

Let us glance at a few instances that are notorious, which have been bared to view within the last few years among us — and from which a lesson may be learned, if we but ponder well the fatal moral and social results that attend such folly and iniquity.

A single Wall Street stock operator and Railway manipulator is discovered to have appropriated to his own private use over seven millions of corporation assets, out of property belonging to a thousand individuals, rightfully, who will never become possessed of a dollar of this "missing" fund! Five millions more go "where the woodbine twineth," through the sharp practices of another noted speculator and law-scouting intriguer. Thrice both these huge sums are gobbled up by another ring of city-corporation robbers, who have squandered other millions that cannot be reached, meantime. And, when the crisis comes, at last, in one single day following closely upon the discovery of these deficits — the "shrinkage" in nominal values of stocks and fancy securities in Wall Street that have been bandied about from Peter to Paul, or from James and Daniel among the jay-hawks of the speculating ring on 'change, is found to exceed a hundred millions more! Why, in the name of all that is reasonable, *shouldn't* we come to grief, amidst bold cheatery such as this?

As these pages are being closed, the author takes up his evening daily to encounter the details of a "Grand raid on Counterfeiters." And he reads the particulars of the greatest crusade against *this* fraternity, on public record. Upwards of seventy American outlaws and their confederates in the manufacture and distribution of counterfeit National notes and U. S. currency in North Carolina are arrested. These counterfeits — to the amount of millions — have been circulated for genuine all over that State and in Tennessee, at wholesale, by jobbers and dealers — like any marketable commodity! This counterfeiting ring proves to be enormous, and their false money-transactions have been immense — while the criminals secured by the U. S. authorities actually include men in every station in life; lawyers, doctors, justices of the peace, United States Deputy Marshals, clerks of courts, and numerous merchants. Sufficient evidence as to the guilt of the parties having been obtained to justify action on the part of the Government officers, warrants for the arrest of ninety were issued by the United States District Attorneys in East Tennessee and West North Carolina, and seventy-four were sent to prison. Why *shouldn't* we hear of panics?

During a period of two years preceding this crisis of '73, which at length overwhelmed the people everywhere as we have indicated, defalcations, robberies, money-losses, United States Revenue defaulting, Customs defrauding, stock gambling, over-importing, extravagance in living, etc. without limit among the rich and powerful occurred; and the contingent evils attendant upon the flush times of this period, to wit, counterfeiting, forgery, embezzlement, thievery, cheating, and plundering among the poor and powerless, in less degree — marked that time as an era of nominal prosperity. Yet it was one that covered an extent and aggregate of crime hitherto altogether unprecedented in American annals.

Within a single twelvemonth, a noted U. S. Revenue officer in New York State (who subsequently found his way to Sing Sing) proved a defaulter to the Government to the tune of over two millions of dollars. Another, in this same service, in Missouri, made way with seven hundred thousand dollars of U. S. funds, in a few months. A third, in Pennsylvania, defrauded Uncle Sam out of upwards of a million. A fourth, in Indiana, couldn't (or wouldn't) show where six hundred thousand dollars of Treasury funds had gone, after he had collected it. A fifth, in New York State, found himself (so he stated upon resigning) *minus* three-quarters of a million. A sixth in a New England State, did not account for half a million that belonged rightfully to the Internal Revenue Bureau. A seventh, in New Jersey, couldn't produce four hundred and sixty thousand dollars that his vouchers to the people showed he had gathered, when he was suddenly called upon to pay up. Three others, all in this Department of the Government service — in Southern States — bagged, together, or squandered in stocks, speculations, and riotous living in that year, upwards of another million and a half. In New Orleans, a huge loss was similarly sustained by the Administration. In Georgia, in the Carolinas, and in Virginia, other enormous sums were, during this brief period, in the same villanous and reprehensible manner purloined by *great* thieves, from the rightful owners of the public funds. These dozen instances cited occurred in a single year, in but one Department; and reached, in all, the enormous sum of more than thirteen millions of dollars, that were stolen outright from the Government, and which "went up in a balloon," or elsewhere — never to be heard from again by those who had been thus mercilessly robbed!

These faithless public servants, in every instance, had indulged themselves in a reckless and luxurious style of living, most of them had sunk hundreds of thousands in stock and gold gambling, and all of them had accumulated wealth in a brief space of time, by taking these vast sums directly from the working and producing classes in the shape of revenue taxes, for which they never accounted to

Government, and for the squandering of which wholesale amounts their bondsmen were entirely insufficient to make up a tithe of the total loss. *Why* shouldn't we have a panic?

The whiskey-rings in the West, the corporation rings in New York and Washington, the tobacco and spirits rings in Virginia, the railway rings in almost every northern State, the political and municipal rings all over the Union, the contemptible yet powerful lobby rings, everywhere, the Custom House and Post Office rings from Maine to California and Oregon, the Credit-Mobilier ring in Congress, the stock-gambling rings in the great money centres, the cereal and Indian rings — with their outer and inner rings, combining to overreach the Government and to wring from the pockets of the people countless thousands or millions of hardly-earned dollars, to be lavished and frittered away in riotous and unrighteous living — is but another single phase in the wholesale scheme of these reckless adventurers to rob the public, and aid in compassing the ruin which prompts the query " why shouldn't we under such circumstances look for disaster, chaos and destruction?"

Within this single year just now mentioned, public *defalcation* ran fearfully riot, also. The trusted officers of city governments, of Banks, of Savings Institutions, of Treasuries, of Insurance Companies, of Banking-houses, of Railways, of Manufacturing Corporations, in Custom Houses, U. S. Sub-treasuries, Post Offices, and other public or private money-institutions, plunged into speculation wildly and furiously — involving their sureties in utter losses of millions, and robbing their employers their depositors or the Government of many millions in excess of all their bondsmen were able to meet.

In these latter named cases, the almost universal cause of the heavy losses was frankly stated by the detected culprits to be that they had dabbled in fancy stocks, or other baseless speculations, and had been overslaughed by the knowing ones. They had lived too fast and gone too far to retreat, and had added to their offence the crime of wholesale robbery of widows, orphans, and other poor men and women, who were (in the end) the unlucky victims of their excesses and their folly! Why shouldn't we hear the thunder, and see the lightning, amidst such a tempest as this?

Many of these offenders fall — at last. If they but *fell upon each other* the result would, measurably, pass by unheeded. But the catastrophe harms or crushes not these men alone, unluckily. And at the worst in their cases, as a rule it affects them but indifferently. The hard-working, honest, frugal, deserving mechanic, laborer, widow, needle-woman, "freedman," clerk, or orphan — *these*, and such as these, who have innocently and ignorantly intrusted these scoundrels with their little savings — the poor and middling classes in society, who labor from sunrise to sunset for their own sustenance and the maintenance of those dependent upon them, directly or indirectly — *they* are the mass of the ultimate sufferers, through this monstrous wrong ; and, in the main, they are the unlucky victims of this unsoundness in the upper strata of business circles. Millions of dollars have thus been disposed of wrongfully, in addition to other quoted abuses, and thousands of fresh victims have thus been added to the long procession of sufferers. Why shouldn't we have crises, and panics, and woe, and terror, and calamity — in view of these terrible evils in our midst!

Once in a score or so of years — as time flits by — such a notable " crisis " in monetary affairs occurs in this country, as witness the memorable panics of 1837, of '57, and this last great crash in commercial circles, in 1873.

These untoward events, as conceded by all, mainly result from the recklessness in speculation among a portion of the community who run riot in their baseless schemes to accumulate riches — without regard to the *modes* adopted by them to " make money ; " and with less heed to the disastrous effects so certain to follow upon their selfish and inconsiderate course.

This disaster reaches not only these men and their families, but the fearful influences sooner or later overwhelm the middle classes in society, and inevitably crush out the better hopes and prospects of myriads of hard-toiling *poor* men and women, everywhere.

This aggregation of crime and infamous wrong, operating directly in its disastrous effects upon the large portion of our people who from the very nature of things are unable, under existing circumstances, to defend or disentangle themselves from its unrighteous and crushing consequences, may well serve to occasion alarm in the community.

Philanthropists, theorists, politicians, or financiers all have their proposed antidote for this fearful bane. But no two men are found to agree upon the rightful mode that may correct the glaring evil, while the rich and the poor alike unite in their mournful denunciations of the "hard times" which have come upon us, and the prediction is freely echoed from every quarter that "the times will be harder still, before they are easier," and that the end is not yet reached!

In the brief enumeration of certain phases of criminality just now rehearsed, we have not alluded to other prominent acts of heinous wrong that, in their way, have aided to swell this bulk of infamy in our midst to enormous proportions, in later years; the commission of which offences adds fearful emphasis to the sum of human iniquity that is to-day rife in American circles, and which largely tends to account for the disastrous condition of things now current among us.

While in commercial circles, in governmental offices, in money-trust institutions, and in ring-speculations have been wrought the greater share of the evil which oppresses the nation so onerously at the present hour — the fact stares us in the face, alas! that among the foremost religious teachers of the land a laxity in morals exists that is painful verily to contemplate.

The records of the Courts within the last year or two exhibit frightful evidence in support of this assertion. In New York, in New Jersey, in the West, and at the South, prominent clergymen of various religious denominations have been indicted and tried upon charges of having committed the grossest immoralities and crime. In two or three instances, leading pastors, who for years had stood in the fore front among our most revered American citizens, and whose brilliant and exemplary careers previously had become famous throughout the world, have been arraigned and tried upon charges of the basest character — the evidence publicly adduced in confirmation of which allegations has resulted in seriously shaking the faith of tens of thousands in the constancy and truthfulness of even that long cherished and respected fraternity, whose reputation should indeed be above suspicion, and whose lives should be as spotless as new-fallen snow!

Considering all these things, and glancing at the authentic record of these examples of monstrous error and vice among the rich, the powerful, and the talented in the land — whose extravagance, wastefulness, excesses, and wilful criminality have tended chiefly to bring the country to its present calamitous condition of universal depression — *why*, pray, should we not expect such a panic as that of to-day? and wherefore, under such enormity of abuses and corruption, should we *not* count upon subsequent disaster, bankruptcy, and ruin?

It proves but a question of time. Speculation, peculation, and extravagance are thus for a while rampant in the great money centres. The nominally rich find themselves suddenly compelled to succumb — noted business firms suspend — moneyed men "fail" — merchants go under — manufacturers curtail their production — operatives are thrown out of employment — mechanics and laborers find their occupations gone — retailers lose their current trade — everybody becomes alarmed — the banks cease to afford ordinary monetary facilities — and chaos ensues.

It is the old story, retold. Yet the terrible effects are only realized, to the bitter full, by that large proportion of the American people who are compelled by the sweat of their brows and the daily labor of their hands to earn bread for themselves and those dependent upon them.

The narrative we have now penned is a record of simple unvarnished *fact*. Its details occurred as we have herein set them down. How many thousand similar histories could be written from real life, having their origin in the great cities of this highly favored land, and how many thousand such life-records could be adduced from among those who dwell beyond the cares and turmoil and bustle of the busier haunts?

No one of the creditable representative men whose history we have in previous chapters chronicled in this volume, was a politician, and neither of these successful persons ever chanced to be an office-holder under the Government. In the instances of Mr. Tweedle and Mose Topley, we have illustrations of the avaricious and unprincipled place-holder — and their fate has been recorded. Both amassed liberal fortunes — but with their ill-gotten gains they earned an infamous name, and "through the land each bears for life a stigma from the brand."

With this array of veritably existing wrong before us — thus briefly touched upon, only — another earnest query presents itself, as the unfortunate victims peruse these fearful accounts: "where is the remedy for this terrible state of things?"

To which we answer it remains with ourselves to correct these monstrous evils. We are all too prone to be deceived by appearances, and to venture upon speculations that have no real foundation. We credulously confide in wrong, forgetting that "as much of evil, so much of loss," is the real formula of human history. We make examples, and every man is bound to tolerate the act which he indulges in, himself. No large amount of good or evil is ever done that does not reproduce its like.

The everlasting passion of Americans to acquire riches largely, that they may support grand show, and indulge in shameless extravagance, is a fruitful cause for the corruption that exists among us. Yet such wanton prodigality is indeed the vice of but the weakest natures. It is a good law of fate, however, that every evil wears itself out, in time. "The greatest flood has its quickest ebb; the sorest tempest the most sudden calm; the hottest love the coldest end." Why then should we not hope that these wildest of follies among our people, may through the adversities we have more recently suffered, find their effectual quietus?

At all events, every man has it in his power to avoid encouraging this wilful waste in the community, and every individual — be he poor or rich — is able to assist in *reforming* this unhealthy state of affairs in society, if so inclined.

Preaching is of very good avail, but practice is far better. And so, with the brief record contained in this chapter — though not one-half the actual enormities are recapitulated — we will not halt to sermonize, but prefer to leave the reader to digest these "unvarnished truths," as they stand. We could add hundreds of other astounding instances of similar criminal remissness and corruption to this record — but these will suffice to show the sad reverse of the life-picture aimed to be drawn in these pages.

"*Clear and round dealing*," says Lord Bacon, "is the honor of man's nature. A mixture of falsity is like alloy in coin of gold or silver. — It may make the metal work better, but it debaseth it."

And commending this course to the reader, we pass to the conclusion of our story, without apology for what may possibly appear to some like a digression, just here; although, in our own opinion, the monstrous facts so briefly stated may well serve for notes of warning, as well as in explanation of a main cause for the existence of the "hard times" which the American people are struggling with, to-day; and the real nature of which is so indifferently comprehended by the masses in our community.

CHAPTER XXVIII.

A HUNDRED THOUSAND DOLLARS IN GOLD.

We have now demonstrated how half a dozen representative young men within our acquaintance, who began the world with nothing, succeeded in honorably accumulating the generous sum that constitutes the title to our present volume.

The agreeable result was *not* accomplished through ill-advised speculation, through "luck," or by chance. This consummation, so devoutly to be wished by all enterprising men, was effected in our quoted cases and in every instance that we have detailed in these pages, through honest toil, the true appreciation of brain-work, and by the rightful use of the talents which God gives to most persons, in greater or less degree — everywhere — to-day, as in any previous period of our history as a people.

None but the croakers or do-nothings among us will argue that the characters we have portrayed are imaginative — or, if rea. that these individuals had rare opportunities to garner wealth, which do not fall to the lot of active men generally. All this is fallacy.

The same "chances" present themselves daily to the youth of this country, in any direction. All that is needed to be done, is, to grasp these opportunities seasonably, and wisely turn them to good account.

No purpose in life can be attained without such application, and such resolve. The indolent, listless, waiting-on-Providence plan is of no avail. "Luck" is a myth. The golden opportunity may be temporarily concealed, or it may lie for a time aside beyond our reach, or observation. But it must be turned up, or arrived at through our own exertions, and availed of through our individual search.

It may be that the identical trades and professions which our several heroes herein followed to brilliant success, would not always furnish the means to precisely such an end, as in the cases quoted.

But the true *principle* involved, remains — nevertheless. And that principle we have endeavored plainly to lay before the reader, which we have faithfully illustrated in the cases of Fred Fordham, Morris Deans, Frank Meyers, Eli Hawes, Reuben Downer, Farmer Blount, David the Drover, &c.

Each of these men accumulated their handsome fortunes, as we happen to know, actually in the manner as set forth in these pages. Though the names of our chosen characters may not be familiar to the general reader, we have none of us to look beyond the limits of the states of New York, New Hampshire and Massachusetts, to learn to whom most of these histories refer.

The parties we have now described are some of them still living — and one or two are at this hour in the possession of almost a fabulous amount of solid wealth — earned and saved in the manner we have indicated in the previous chapters.

Therefore we contend that it can be done again — with the right means, and the rightful appliance of those means. And, in a single line we say then, reader, if you wish to make your fortune, proceed as these men did: *go thou, and do likewise.*

Earn it, make it, save it, enjoy it — and be happy with it; as you may do, if wise, prudent and duteous.

Five months after the visit to Brandville — to wit, in the pleasant opening of brown October — arrangements were actively entered upon for a grand wedding-fête at Sunnyside, the beautiful home of Farmer Blount.

The young friends had corresponded frequently in the interim that passed between their late temporary sojourn at the farm and the time fixed upon for the union of Morris and Eunice; and the pleasantest of anticipations were indulged in by all the parties, in view of this now early forthcoming event.

It chanced, also, that David Morehead, the fortunate drover, came down two days preceding the wedding. He brought with him another pair of fine Morgan colts he had raised, which he had for sale. When he called upon Morris, he now found his former patron busy in preparations for the happy event of the morrow.

Upon that next morning, the guests invited from abroad had all reached Brandville.

Meyers, and Hawes, and Downer had come up from New York. Fred Fordham and his good wife Fannie arrived, duly. And now the early young companions were together, once more, for a few days; which proved the last meeting of *all* these friends, on earth.

Good old farmer Blount and his wife were very jubilant, on this interesting occasion. They had never talked about this probable event much, except strictly between themselves. But their affection for Morris Deans was unbounded, and after his first year's sojourn with them, they had begun to indulge the hope that Morris would find their adopted daughter so agreeable a companion that one day he would choose her for his wife.

The end was now approaching, in accordance with their earnest wishes, and they felt confident that the future happiness of Eunice could not be intrusted to the keeping of a better husband.

Every thing was accordingly done to render the affair an agreeable one. The old mansion had been nicely remodelled, inside, during the prior two or three months, and the house was newly furnished throughout, in anticipation of the marriage of Blount's only " daughter " to the former city broker's clerk.

On their wedding-day, Frank Meyers 'stood up' with Morris, and a beautiful young lady from the village — an intimate personal friend of Eunice — officiated as bridesmaid.

Valuable marriage-gifts were duly forwarded by all the friends of Morris to his charming young bride, and the details passed off most satisfactorily to all interested in this happy event.

The visitors returned to New York and Boston, Morris and Eunice — now Mr. and Mrs. Morris Deans — departed for the White Mountains and Niagara the same evening, and the 'old folks at home' were happy.

Old Blount and his good dame were ripening in years, but the honorable course the wealthy farmer had steadily pursued in life he now contemplated with placid satisfaction; for he had aimed, to the best of his ability, to perform what he conscientiously deemed to be his whole duty towards his kindred and his fellow men. And in his quiet old age, he fully realized the happy sentiments embodied in the popular song of "the yeoman king."

> The farmer sat in his old arm-chair,
> Rosy and fair,
> Contented there.
> "Kate, I declare,"
> He said to his wife, who was knitting near,
> "We need not fear
> The hard times here,
> Though the leaf of life is yellow and sear.
>
> "I am the king, and you are the queen,
> Of this fair scene, —
> These fields of green,
> And gold between;

These cattle grazing upon the hill,
  Taking their fill;
  And sheep so still,
Like many held by a single will.

"These barnyard fowls are our subjects all:
  They heed the call,
  And, like a squall,
  On fast wings fall,
Whenever we scatter for them the grain.
  'Tis not in vain
  We live and reign
In this our happy and calm domain.

"And whether the day be dim or fine,
  In rain and shine,
  These lands of mine,
  These fields of thine,
In cloudy shade and in sunny glow,
  Will overflow
  With crops that grow,
When gold is high and when it is low.

"Unvexed with shifting of stocks and shares,
  And bulls and bears,
  Stripes and cares,
  And the affairs
Of speculation in mart and street,
  In this retreat
  Sweet peace can meet
With plenty on her rural beat."

 . . . .

Two years from that day, Frank Meyers led to the altar

a blooming girl from New York city, with whom he became acquainted soon after the wedding of Eunice and Morris. And they went to Boston to reside, subsequently.

Reuben Downer wedded a nice young lady from among his former Connecticut acquaintance — and has since resided in New York; where he has flourished wondrously with his pet enterprise, the weekly *Leader*.

Ely Hawes got married last, and not until he had more than realized his first hoped-for fortune. His Safe-lock proved a grand conception, and in the end turned out " a gold mine " indeed, in his experience.

Fred Fordham went along steadily from the time he fairly began to make money, in the house he was so long connected with as book-keeper, and in which he eventually became a partner.

His family was increased by the addition of another boy — latterly. But his circumstances were now largely improved, and he accepted this " fresh gift from Heaven " gratefully.

Fannie Fordham's third infant lay asleep, snugly ensconced in its comfortably pillowed cradle. The former " baby," (her second boy,) was a little jealous of this latest arrival. Young Fred dropped his toy, and approached the side of the basket where the new baby lay, with an anxious expression — and then inquired " wot is it, mamma?"

" That's your dear little new brother, Fred," said Fannie, smilingly.

"Wot 'ee come 'ere for, mamma?"

"To keep you company, and grow up and play with you, deary."

Fred didn't seem to see it in this light, exactly. He put his finger into his mouth, stood eying the youngster a moment, apprehensively, and then turned away.

Little Fred's nose was out of joint, plainly. *He* had been "the baby" for three years. But he had been superseded, now!

Of these little ones, and other of the 'babies' referred to in these pages, we shall write hereafter — in a companion volume to our present book. For the time being we leave them in the enjoyment of their happy innocence and infancy.

David Morehead was a guest at Morris' wedding, and succeeded in disposing of his fine Morgan horses and Durham cattle for years afterwards, upon the Grimes farm; where he is now a hale hearty brave old man — worth a handsome fortune — which he earned with his own hands and brains.

And Deacon Rounds grew richer, as the years went by, and more parsimonious than ever, as time passed, after David left him. Howard Blount grew old, but he was contented, frugal, and scrupulously honest, to the last.

The conscientious farmer approached his grave, at length, peacefully and content. He had aimed to the best of his ability through life to pursue a line of conduct that did him honor among his fellows — and death had no terrors for him. In his last moments, he spoke kindly and affectionately to the young man Deans, who had served him so faithfully, and who was now united in marriage to his adopted daughter, Eunice.

"My days on earth have nearly reached their end, Morris," he said. "I have striven in a long life to do unto others as I would have them do unto me. This method, be assured, fulfils the great injunctions of the decalogue, as well as the just requirements of the 'golden rule;' and this course continuously followed out in all the ramifications of our lives, is the right way to render our own existence happy, and at its close to suggest no heart-burnings or regrets for remissness in the past.

"The man who appreciates this world, as it is, is wiser than he who is prone to condemn, through not understanding it. To study the world, is far better than to shun it. To use the world, fairly, is always nobler than to abuse it. Our best effort to render the world better, and those around us happier and lovelier, is a wise and duteous aim in man or woman. And the chief reason why the world is not reformed and better improved is, because each of us is prone to leave this work to others to commence upon, forgetful of his own prime duty to make such beginning himself.

"You have endeared yourself to us all here, through your own meritorious conduct, my boy, and you have earned the fortune you possess through honest endeavor to follow the right, I am happy to know. Go forward, still.

There are bright prospects and many years of happiness before you, and those connected with you by filial ties — and I am sure you will appreciate me when I remind you, in these last feeble moments, that the life of the truly upright man consists in the constant enjoyment of an intercourse with the good, in seeking for good, and in the contemplation of being and doing good.

"True goodness, Morris, is the investment that never fails. The way of truth is the shortest road to our end. It carries us thither in a straight line — be sure of it. And, for the rest, remember that the pure religion of the heart scatters over the movements of our lives her constant favors, but reserves the choicest of all — her divine blessing, as a crowning solace for having acted well our part — for the final hour."

And thus the exemplary honest old farmer passed hopefully away, leaving his ample property to his gentle wife; who lived but a few years afterwards, when she bequeathed it to her adopted Eunice — and the two grandchildren that came to bless the subsequent years of Morris and his comely 'Sunnyside' wife.

These children were a girl and boy. The former took strongly after her mother — our Eunice — who was an enthusiastic botanist through her whole life; and who naturally transmitted to her first offspring a love of the beautiful in nature.

On next page, we have an illustration of this first-born of Eunice and Morris Deans, as she sits conning over the illuminated pages of her "Child's Book of Flowers," of which, like her tasteful mother before her, sweet little Daisie Deans was a most ardent admirer.

DAISIE DEANS—CONNING HER FIRST BOOK OF FLOWERS.

And on page 406 we present a picture of the boy, young Blount Deans, reclining at his leisure, with the ever faithful dog—old "Spot" beside him.

The elder parties described in these pages have all gone to their long home, now. The young men (with but one exception) are still living, to-day. They are older and wiser as well as richer than they were when we first presented them to the reader!

But each and all—through the means we have indicated — attained the wealth that these men are now enjoying. *They began right.* And all of them pursued their object with the firm conviction that permanent riches are not acquired through speculations, but always more desirably, more honestly, and more certainly, by the daily

YOUNG BLOUNT DEANS, AND HIS PET DOG "SPOT."

practice of zeal, industry, frugality, perseverance, and true economy.

Thus our representative characters gathered their gains, and thus they achieved what they started for, in life — each in his chosen way — as others may, with similar good will and application.

We are personally acquainted with the individual types whose veritable histories are herein recorded. We have known them and watched them in their progress, from poverty to wealth. We have now told how they succeeded, and shown how others — through like judicious management and skill — may make at least " A HUNDRED THOUSAND DOLLARS, in gold." And this brings our present volume to

THE END.